AMERICAN CATASTROPHE

AMERICAN CATASTROPHE

FUNDAMENTALISM, CLIMATE CHANGE, GUN RIGHTS, AND THE RHETORIC OF DONALD J. TRUMP

LUKE WINSLOW

THE OHIO STATE UNIVERSITY PRESS

COLUMBUS

Copyright © 2020 by The Ohio State University.
All rights reserved.

Library of Congress Cataloging-in-Publication Data
Names: Winslow, Luke, 1980– author.
Title: American catastrophe : fundamentalism, climate change, gun rights, and the rhetoric of Donald J. Trump / Luke Winslow.
Description: Columbus : The Ohio State University Press, [2020] | Includes bibliographical references and index. | Summary: "Explores studies of Christian fundamentalism, anti-environmentalism, gun rights messaging, and the Trump administration to understand why appeals to catastrophe are attractive. Uses rhetorical homology as a tool for understanding how people across disparate religious, ecological, cultural, and political backgrounds unite through perceived marginalization"—Provided by publisher.
Identifiers: LCCN 2019059983 | ISBN 9780814214381 (cloth) | ISBN 081421438X (cloth) | ISBN 9780814278031 (ebook) | ISBN 0814278035 (ebook)
Subjects: LCSH: Disasters—Social aspects—United States. | Fundamentalism—United States. | Anti-environmentalism—United States. | Climatic changes—United States. | Firearms—Social aspects—United States. | Marginality, Social—United States. | Rhetoric.
Classification: LCC E179 .W77 2020 | DDC 973.933—dc23
LC record available at https://lccn.loc.gov/2019059983

Cover design by Susan Zucker
Text design by Juliet Williams
Type set in Adobe Minion Pro

Dedicated to Dale and Karen Winslow

CONTENTS

Preface		ix
INTRODUCTION	Theorizing Catastrophe	1
CHAPTER 1	Christian Fundamentalism and the Catastrophic Homology	19
CHAPTER 2	Ecological Catastrophe and the Rhetoric of Anti-Environmentalism	63
CHAPTER 3	Cultural Catastrophe and the Rhetoric of Gun Rights	87
CHAPTER 4	Political Catastrophe and the Rhetoric of Donald Trump	117
CONCLUSION	Consequences and Alternatives	151
Acknowledgments		165
Notes		167
Bibliography		189
Index		211

PREFACE

THIS BOOK is about the rhetorical power of catastrophe in modern American life. It traces the decline of rational argumentation as a central governing logic and suggests that in its place a rhetoric of catastrophe has emerged to draw traditionally empowered individuals into constitutive communities bound together by the anticipation of chaos.

Three biographical experiences brought me to this project. First, I attended a private Christian university as an undergraduate when the *Left Behind* novels were popular. The novels describe the apocalyptic chaos that results after millions of people are raptured from Earth. Eighty million *Left Behind* books were sold, and when I read the first book I didn't understand why. In particular I was struck by the perverse glee that some at my university displayed when they recounted the death and destruction detailed in the novel; it almost seemed as if many at my school *wanted* the fictional plot to be realized, that they looked forward to apocalyptic chaos.

Second, in February 2007, when I was a graduate student at the University of Texas at Austin, I attended a research colloquium on the American invasion of Iraq. As the war entered one of its most violent years, one speaker offered a troubling explanation for all the deception, chaos, and bloodshed: cynically, our leaders were not that interested in "winning" the war—at least not in the traditional sense (defeating the enemy, handing over control of the country, and then withdrawing the troops). For those who saw the geopolitical advantages of maintaining massive military bases in the Middle East—as well as for the shareholders of Halliburton and Raytheon—the US actually *wanted to lose*. That explanation troubled me, for obvious reasons. Although I lacked the expertise to judge the merits of such a thesis, the larger conceptual point that the speaker put forth lingered with me. I had not considered that for particular individuals in particular communities, the passive acceptance—and even active manufacturing—of crisis, chaos, and disorder could serve a powerful constitutive function.

Third, on November 9, 2016, before the National Communication Association annual convention, a gray cloud seemed to hover over Philadelphia that had nothing to do with the weather. Donald Trump had just been elected president, and for many communication scholars his election reflected a repudiation of our life's work. For those of us who devoted our intellect and passion to illuminating the best obtainable version of the truth—and then sought to use that truth to inform public policies that make life less difficult for others—the Trump candidacy and election made no sense. How could a mendacious, inexperienced, ignorant reality TV star attract the support of sixty-three million Americans? Trump's election reminded me of the constitutive potential of chaos and disorder. It sounded a lot like Trump got elected by promising to reset hierarchies of power and return a "forgotten man" to his rightful position . . . by sowing chaos in American political life.

What methods were available to explore the rhetorical foundation of these interactions? As a rhetorical scholar, I knew that our tradition produced a set of well-developed critical tools for examining appeals to shared human progress. But many of these tools hinged on our desire to avoid crisis, chaos, and disorder; thus, rhetors can motivate by leading us toward a future without them. However, these three experiences reminded me that some communities are not constituted in this way. Some don't want to avoid chaos and disorder; some are willing to tolerate them—or even to participate in manufacturing chaos as a way to restore order to a disordered world; and, if that is the case, some may actively embrace the threat of chaos. In fact, they might even yearn for it. In an age when chaos and disorder function as dominant organizing rhetorics, this missing warrant—a yearning for chaos—severely inhibits modern rhetorical theory.

After more than two years of the Trump presidency, I am reminded almost daily—in the graduate seminars I teach, in NPR stories, and in conversations with my uncle—that we need a better vocabulary for explaining meaning-making outside of appeals to peace, order, shared human progress, and rational argumentation. While this book wanders across some dark messaging and cynical rhetors, I continue to be excited by the possibility that this inquiry can make a unique contribution to public conversation by identify the pernicious arguments propping up our chaotic urges. My hope is that this book will illuminate a politically urgent and theoretically rich exploration of the human condition. And for communication and rhetorical scholars, I hope the book assists with developing a fresh set of critical tools that can offer a more nuanced and comprehensive explanation of our bewildering world.

INTRODUCTION

Theorizing Catastrophe

> So convenient a thing is to be a rational creature, since it enables us to find or make a reason for everything one has a mind to.
>
> —BEN FRANKLIN[1]

IN 2016 the Oxford Dictionaries named *post-truth* its "Word of the Year." Describing post-truth as the "circumstances in which objective facts are less influential in shaping public opinion than appeals to emotion and personal belief," the levity of the award clouds its more troubling implications: post-truth reflects the presence of a community no longer committed to organizing society through the best obtainable version of the truth. Further, post-truth reflects a broader distrust in political institutions, the media, courts, colleges and universities, scientific organizations, as well as the people who participate in these institutions. Especially for traditionally empowered communities, post-truth points to a cultural moment when distrust, paranoia, fear, helplessness, and rage function as central organizing emotions.[2]

I do not mean to suggest that post-truth and the decline of rational argumentation are unique to our historical moment. Americans have long reacted to change by casting suspicion on institutional authority and intellectual elites.[3] But there is a difference today: distrust of the liberal order has moved off the fringes and into traditional avenues of power. *Donald Trump won!* And his election—itself a reason for distrust in conventional opinion polls that almost universally showed his 2016 opponent winning—needs to be situated in relation to the low levels of trust in traditional political institutions all over the world.[4] Joshua Gunn described 2016 as the "Fuck it!" election, as if millions of Americans looked at their options and thought, "Fuck it,

I'm voting for Trump."[5] Gunn compared voting for Trump to throwing chairs at a wrestling match—but in this case, the pit is the corrupt institution and the chairs reflect one's civic participation. "Fuck it!" illustrates post-truth rage and helplessness—the act of voting with one's middle finger. In context, then, Trump's candidacy and election reflect a culmination more than an aberration.

For scholars of communication and rhetoric, post-truth pushes us to an unsettling place: we may have overlooked a missing warrant. Chaos and disorder are often assumed to be harmful outcomes that rational people will wish to avoid. Therefore, rhetors should be able to motivate an audience by promising a future of order and progress. Drawing from Jürgen Habermas and his theory of communicative action, instead of bullying, lying, and scaring each other to reach mutual understanding, we coordinate our behaviors through speech acts that incorporate shared claims of validity—claims that facilitate prosocial public policy. Thus, democratic deliberation has hinged on a tacit commitment to reason-giving and the enlightenment principles of rational-critical argumentation.[6]

Rational argumentation offered profound epistemological and ethical value.[7] No individual would completely get their way in each dispute, but we could all be confident that resource allocation was reached under appropriate conditions.[8] We could trust the *process*, in other words: an inherently consensual form of social coordination connecting reason, language, and policy to the best obtainable version of the truth.

For an insecure discipline, communication scholars appreciated the primacy of language in facilitating social order and democratic governance. Consequently, our rhetorical tradition has produced a well-developed set of critical tools for examining how we are influenced by the enlightenment principles of empirical rationality, scientific fact, and deference to relevant expertise.[9]

The discipline's privileging of rational argument was never naïve about the ubiquity of conflict and difference.[10] All political actions—all attempts to socially organize, to build caves and condos, to construct bridges and websites—contain the potential for conflict and enmity. But our rhetorical tradition allowed individuals to disagree without slipping into helplessness and rage. Even more optimistically, rhetoric could leverage conflict and difference to push humans to new points of identification, cooperation, mutual aid, and solidarity.[11]

And it worked.

We pat ourselves on the back knowing that it is no coincidence that the most peaceful and productive moment in human history, in which billions have been lifted out of poverty and human rights have been expanded to formerly marginalized groups of people, emerged in association with the ascendancy of the enlightened principles of rational argumentation. When public persuasion was required, rational argumentation encouraged the deployment of more evidence, more science, and more expertise (along with less fantasy, less violence, and fewer witch burnings).

Circling back, Donald Trump and his post-truth presidency have contrasted and thus illuminated our scholarly tendency to oversubscribe reflexivity, open-mindedness, and sophistication to our political decision-making. The Habermasian version of rational argumentation neglected covert barriers, including social-institutional practices and economic disempowerment that blocked so many from participating in democratic deliberation. William Rehg suggested that in a polarized political context fueled by unreflective journalism and hyperventilated emotions, rational deliberation may be impossible—even for well-intentioned citizens.[12]

I want to press further here and suggest not only that may post-truth be an indication that rational argumentation is no longer the criterion of deliberation; it may be that the *rejection* of rational argumentation is the constitutive parameter for entrance into an alternative community. In the following pages, I develop the rhetoric of catastrophe to describe one such alternative.

OPERATIONALIZING CATASTROPHE

I was initially attracted to *catastrophe* because of its geological connotation: a definition from the *Oxford English Dictionary* describes a catastrophe as a sudden or violent change in the physical order, such as an upheaval or convulsion affecting the earth's surface and the living things on it.[13] As a discrete *rhetorical* process, catastrophe illuminates the discursive formations and symbolic resources drawing traditionally empowered individuals into constitutive communities bound by the acceptance and anticipation of chaos and upheaval as a way to restore crumbling hierarchies of power and advance the forward march of history.

However, to identity catastrophe as a post-truth alternative to rational argumentation also presents several methodological challenges. First, consider the critical quandary posed by catastrophe's dark and cynical launch-point. If we assume popular political, cultural, and religious rhetors cannot come out and directly advocate for upheaval and calamity—and remain popular for long—how might the rhetorical critic illuminate the inner workings of the unarticulated?[14] Second, audiences are famously nimble, fickle, and fluid in how they seek out resonating discourses. Subjectivity comes from various sources; no one is just a Christian fundamentalist or Trump supporter; they may also be vegans, alcoholics, and Chargers fans. As Maurice Charland put it, "We can live within many texts."[15] How might the critic weave frayed discursive strands into a coherent rhetorical system? Third, strong subjectivities—the type that may resonate with catastrophe's scandalous urges—may be unified at higher, unconscious, and disparate levels of abstraction. How, then, does the critic explore influence outside of critical awareness? Without focus groups or Likert surveys, how does the critic meet standards of reliability and validity? More personally, given the wide range of religious, ecological, cultural, and political discourses examined here, what prevents me from shoehorning my preferred conclusion into the discursive evidence?

As a graduate student, I had done some research with Barry Brummett on the rhetorical homology, and I began to see its potential for addressing these questions. Widely used in the STEM fields to identify formal connections that share a similar guiding structure, the homology can also function as a useful tool for rhetorical scholars interested in exploring controversial social issues we would rather not address directly. The rhetorical homology identifies a common reservoir from which shared arguments are formed. The homology catalogs and analyzes those shared arguments as points of formal correspondence capable of passing meaning and influence across disparate discourses. In turn, controversial issues can be linked by unconscious structural relationships that pass meaning across disparate texts and experiences.[16] For example, in his book on the topic, Brummett used the rhetorical homology to locate a subtle—yet influential—discursive pattern among professional wrestling, old Laurel and Hardy films, and public performances of injury. Identifying performances of injury as a common rhetorical reservoir can then inform how individuals may confront the real injuries and slights they face in daily life.[17] As Brummett's example illustrates, political implications are unearthed as the homology indicates *who* individuals are urged to become as they rhetorically merge into various communities.[18]

Returning to my initial interest in catastrophe, if we assume that advocating *directly* for chaos would be unfashionable—and I think we should—the value of the rhetorical homology becomes evident. In what follows, I want to show how new communities have been formed that are equipped to respond to threats and disorder in similar ways. More broadly, if those formal relationships are plausible, the rhetorical homology could also offer larger conceptual insights across a range of other religious, ecological, cultural, and political conversations. In brief, such is the purpose of this book.

CATASTROPHIC HOMOLOGY

We make sense of the world by connecting the unknown to the known. In *The Philosophy of Rhetoric*, I. A. Richards argued that even our most basic sense-making tools depend on *structures* of sensations. All human experience is meaningless until it is structured. "A perception is never just of an *it*," he suggested; "perception takes whatever it perceives as a thing of a certain sort. All thinking from the lowest to the highest—whatever else it may be—is sorting."[19] When we perceive something as familiar as a salt shaker or as mysterious as the afterlife, we are lumping those messages into pre-existing categories. In turn, all sensation interpretation—all meaning-making—must be *patterned* before it can be interpreted; all experiences, C. K. Ogden and Richards argued, have the character of recurrence: it comes to us only in uniform contexts.[20]

Kenneth Burke connected our need for structuring to the rhetorical function of *form*. Describing the psychology of the classification process in the minds of an audience, Burke wrote, "Form is the creation of an appetite in the mind of the auditor, and the adequate satisfying of that appetite."[21] Later he described form as "the creation and gratification of needs" and the "arousing and fulfillment of desires."[22] He suggested a work has form "in so far as one part of it leads a reader to anticipate another part, to be gratified by the sequence."[23]

Good teachers know the power of form: competent pedagogy is characterized by structuring the unfamiliar with the familiar in the student's mind. Good baseball coaches know this: teaching a young baseball player to hit a slider will be assisted by his or her existing experiences hitting a curveball. As a parent, I am trying to apply this basic sensemaking principle with my two-year-old son now: to help him make sense of the exotic animals at the San Diego Zoo, I draw on an existing reservoir of not-so-exotic animals with which he is already familiar. The Bengal tiger is technically categorized within the Felidae cat family, but for now I can be satisfied with my son making sense of this unfamiliar creature as a "big ruff ruff."

More to the point, good arguers know to structure the unknown with the known: as Thomas Goodnight suggested, persuasive arguments resonate with an existing mental apparatus already at work in an audience.[24] An argument that resonates with the structural expectations of an audience activates both familiarity and affinity in the minds of listeners.[25] For example, when George Washington gave the first inaugural address, he had no immediate examples to draw from, so he borrowed liberally from British monarchical history and Protestant religious texts because he knew what would formally resonate.[26]

Good critics know the power of form, too, and so they use existing expectations and constraints to analyze audience interpretations of messages. We call this generic criticism, and it became one of the most popular critical tools of rhetorical scholars in the twentieth century.[27]

GENRE CRITICISM

Genre criticism informs the rhetorical potency of what Gunn calls "the linguistic sedimentation of affective recurrence in code and meaning."[28] In other words, genre is the name of forms repeatedly felt. In general, genre criticism describes patterns of discourse and explains how unifying characteristics within a text conform or frustrate audience expectations. More specifically, genre criticism involves three steps. First, the critic identifies similar structure and content, and then isolates similar characteristics. Next, the genre critic explores how the rhetor confirms or frustrates the expectations established by structural similarities. Finally, the critic looks to expose larger societal and cultural truths beyond an isolated artifact capable of informing why an audience expected what it expected, and to what end. Jamieson cited the play *Waiting for Godot,* which was billed as a comedy but frustrated audiences when the laughs never arrived, and thus failed to conform to their generic expectations.[29] Most presidential inaugurals employee a dignified mode of address, Jamieson also argued, as in George Washington's first inaugural. Therefore, it was revealing when Jimmy Carter's inaugural sounded like a policy address to a DC think tank—or when Donald Trump's inaugural sounded like a *Breitbart* tirade—because these instances of genre-busting transcended the individual rhetor and lent insight into the expectations and frustrations of society at large.

As I briefly described in the preface, I will employ the rhetorical homology here, and so it may be useful compare to genre and homology. All share similar characteristics: genre and homology are critical tools capable of illuminating rhetorical potency by identifying formal patterns grounded in discourse that inform political and social consequences. However, in the following section, I want to show how these two methods diverge in ways that make the rhetorical homology particularly valuable for our post-truth moment.

RHETORICAL HOMOLOGY

Because our perceptions are the product of more than one unique experience, the sorting process—in order to be as comprehensive as possible—must stretch beyond one discrete pattern.³⁰ This is where form becomes homology. Form is given coherence, and homological analysis can occur, when the critic notices how formal patterns seep into different discourses, different texts, and different experiences. Barry Brummett showed the value of the homology, especially for a fragmented mediated climate, in its ability to "merge distinctions between traditional, expositional forms of rhetoric and the more fragmented, nonverbal forms of popular culture."³¹ In other words, the homology explains what makes a distant or fanciful text resonate with an audience in a more nuanced and sophisticated way.

For the rhetorical critic, it is the homological relationship between text and experience facilitating the work of form—for the distant or fanciful text to make sense of the unfamiliar, complex, or threatening.³² Once a formal pattern has been established that crosses disparate orders of experiences and a shared underlying structure is located, the implications of the formal parallels can be unearthed. This is where homology becomes rhetorical: homologies order experiences; they offer an explanation for how formal parallels appearing across texts may equip an audience with motives appropriate for their social situations; and they instruct audience members in how to respond to the larger social dimensions of their day-to-day existence.³³

An example might be helpful here. American comedy is full of white, male characters best described as *completely confident, yet completely clueless*. Think Homer Simpson and Peter Griffin (*The Simpsons* and *Family Guy*), David Brent and Michael Scott (*The Office*), and almost every character played by Will Ferrell (Ron Burgundy, Ricky Bobby). I had a German exchange-student once comment on the connection between our attraction to such characters in American popular culture and our attraction to such characters in American electoral politics. She was identifying a homologous relationship across disparate texts: television comedy is not electoral politics; and yet, in this case, a shared confident-yet-clueless reservoir may be influencing our sensemaking capacity across each discourse. The comment would not have been homologous if the German student described a relationship between our attraction to confident-yet-clueless characters in television sitcoms and similar characters in motion pictures, because she would not have identified a *disparate* order of experience.³⁴ She might be right—a formal connection might exist between sitcoms and movies—but the comment would fail to branch out in any meaningful way, and so it would have been of little rhetorical value.

Compared with genre criticism, the rhetorical homology relies less on audience awareness. The situational and substantive elements that inform genre expectations are implicated in homological criticism—but not completely. Generic confirmation and frustration depend on the *conscious* expectations of the audience. Homology does not. Homology refers to formal patterns ordering experiences and texts below the level of conscious awareness or observation.[35] Unlike my German student, one need not be aware of the homology for it to perform its rhetorical heavy lifting. For comparison, notice how Campbell and Jamieson use terms like *constellation of elements, manacles,* and *anchors* to describe how individuals consciously interpret new messages in relation to pre-existing generic expectations.[36] Brummett uses a different set of terms; he suggests that homological resemblances "cut across experience," operate "higher up the scale," and are based on the "triangulation of different dimensions of culture." Brummett warns the homological critic to be prepared to "jump the tracks laid down" by lower-level and more direct linkages across content.[37]

Accordingly, the rhetorical homology also relies less on similar formal patterns to determine rhetorical potency. Compared with genre criticism, the homology is more concerned with how *disparate* texts and experiences branch out—beyond generic confines—to pass meaning across eclectic points of formal correspondence. What counts as eclectic? Jason Edward Black noted how formal patterns in abortion and puppy-milling discourse share generic dimensions—while still maintaining disparate qualities at their base.[38] Kathryn Olson detected a formal parallel between sport hunting, "hate crimes," and stranger rape, which homologically connected to a larger mechanism of motivation in mainstream American discourse.[39] She argued that a common interpretive framework across these discourses can be traced back to the ways violent actors symbolically construe their victims as *worth dominating* in some shared hierarchy that the violent actors perceive as significant. In my own work, I noticed a homological connection in the recently popular caveman mythos formally linking representations of gay men and representations of black men.[40] The homology underpinning these formal parallels relates to the Othering process in which the complaints of an aggrieved minority are made to appear trivial and ridiculous. In another essay, I noted a formal relationship between grant writing in higher education and prosperity theology in American religious discourse. I argued these two discourses homologically drew from a shared rhetorical reservoir related to neoliberal modes of governance.[41] In each of these studies, the formal connections become more interesting (and more rhetorically powerful) because they branch out across widely disparate texts, objects, practices, and experiences equipping audiences for living and informing political attitudes in disparate ways.

My use of catastrophe here affirms this research in showing how upheaval and convulsion cluster individuals into coherent communities by reorienting identities in alignment with subjective, discursive, and fear-oriented messaging. But divergently, my use of catastrophe advances our theoretical tools for understanding post-truth appeals by identifying and cataloging five symbolic points of formal correspondence operating across disparate texts, media, and experiences. I categorize these five points of formal correspondence as follows.

Perceived Marginalization

Perceived marginalization positions individuals into a community defined by victimage, threat, and insecurity. This is not to suggest that feelings of aggrievement and fears of displacement felt by one community are any more or less real than the aggrievement and fears of another community.[42] I only want to suggest that *perceived marginalization* among the traditionally empowered—mainly straight, white, native-born men—offers an undeniable perversion of the term *marginalized* (especially when compared with more objectively marginalized communities, including immigrants, people of color, and women). As Ackerman and Coogan make clear in *The Public Work of Rhetoric*, anxiety is a ubiquitous part of the human condition, but some experience crisis in more visceral ways than others.[43] Because rhetoric reconciles contradiction, language must emerge to mediate the liminal spaces connecting baselessly marginalized subjects with an acute and motivating sense of aggrievement. And it does. In this case, on a local level, in appeals to "reverse racism" and a "war on Christmas" (or a "war on men"); and on a global level, including appeals to institutional distrust and conspiracy theory.

Perceived marginalization affirms and advances the extant conversation in two primary ways. First, perceived marginalization is untethered from objective metrics of oppression. In the following case studies, I encourage the reader to notice how marginalization is described as an objective, factual, occurrence—an observable result of incompetence and corruption.[44] But notice also how those appeals often contradict the material standing of the target audience. Such a contradiction aligns with Murray Edelman's description of "crisis" as a political act, not a recognition of a fact or a rare situation.[45] Likewise, *perceived* marginalization affirms Denise Bostdorff's argument that fear and insecurity need not be based on proximity of threat.[46]

The second way perceived marginalization affirms and advances the conversation is through its discursive potential. Bostdorff reminds us that, especially when confronted with crisis, we all lean heavily on a framework of interpretation that emerges from language and its cultural oscillations.[47] Edelman described crisis as a creation of the language for this reason.[48] Objective, material events occur—many fitting within the parameters of "the political" because they influence who has what and how much—but, as Bostdorff contends, those events only make sense when resonant language allows individuals to interpret political conditions as tenuous.[49]

Consequently, catastrophe is a perverse, reactionary rhetoric. The community has been betrayed, and it needs a language to react to that betrayal. In the forthcoming case studies, be on the lookout for subjective and objective descriptions of marginalization, especially where the liminal space between fears of looming threats contradict empirical reality.

Prophetic Perversion

Institutional distrust and elite betrayal also inform who assumes a prophetic voice and how grievances are described. Here, I use the term *prophetic perversion* to inform how the rhetoric of catastrophe reconciles a second pressing contradiction: catastrophe must react to the scorn coming from intellectual authority and traditional sites of expertise—including academic institutions, mainstream religious denominations, and political elites. But catastrophe must also carve out rhetorical space for a prophetic voice marked by top-down consolidation of power and authority. There is a *magisterial* dimension to catastrophe: the forthcoming rhetors are domineering, even dictatorial. Catastrophic prophets are men of strong egos, chafing against the institutional bits in their mouths; they are true believers feeding on supernatural hay. At the same time, prophetic perversion reconciles this dictatorial voice with a brand of *republican perspicacity* that encourages community members—regardless of training or education—to decipher the causes and effects of their marginalization *on their own*.[50] Following the lead of Asen and Gunn, my use of perversion should be contrasted with colloquial understandings of the term (i.e., the creepy old man wearing a trench coat into the porno shop).[51] Prophetic perversion—as I use the term here—informs a dense set of texts demanding specialized interpretations, not decipherable by everyone and, thus, suitable to divination by specialized prophets. But these texts are *perverted* because they inform the alteration of expertise and authority from its socially sanctioned course or condition; in this case, by distorting what counts as authoritative and prophetic.

Consider the defining rhetorical outcomes of prophetic perversion in the following case studies. First, notice how prophetic perversion allows catastrophic rhetors to define the terms of debate—to make the first move on the chessboard and to force the opposition to respond before making its case. Whether it is MS-13 gang members teeming across the border or transgender soldiers weakening our military, opposition to catastrophe must first describe the issue *against the existing frame*; in so doing, opposition inevitably reinforces the concerns of a target audience already fearful of declining racial supremacy and stable gender identities.

Second, notice how prophetic perversion facilitates the concentration of power. Catastrophic rhetors benefit personally, in the books they sell and the votes they garner, as we generally become more comfortable with autocracy during moments of upheaval.[52] As Levistky and Ziblatt make clear in *How Democracies Die*, authoritarian tendencies can then be unshackled from democratic constraints, and opponents can be silenced as disloyal or ignorant. Drastic times call for drastic measures.

Third, notice how prophetic perversion facilitates secure subjectivities in the face of elite rejection. The catastrophist winks at its target audience. In a hushed tone, it reassures the intellectually marginalized that those scornful, out-of-touch elites do not have a monopoly on knowledge.

Finally, notice how prophetic perversion leverages the betrayal of sacred documents and founding texts. The following case studies will be replete with references to the Bible, the US Constitution, and the Bill of Rights—in most cases, as the frozen bedrock justifying political and social prescriptions against the conventions of rational argumentation.[53]

Hermeneutic of Systematicity

Prophetic perversion is an internal rhetoric, focused on circling the wagons in defense of the target audience. My use of the term *hermeneutic of systematicity* complements prophetic perversion's internal focus by informing how the rhetoric of catastrophe seeks to develop external legitimacy in the face of intellectual marginalization.

Beginning in the mid-nineteenth century, the scientific method emerged to become the semantic currency of knowledge production.[54] Rational argumentation would come to draw much of its cultural force from this ascendancy. The *presence* of Young Earth Creationists or PizzaGate conspiracies is not a problem for the Habermasian public sphere—as long as the pseudo-scientific and conspiratorial cannot influence public policy.[55] In other words, myth, magic, and divine revelation were fine, as long as they stayed in their lane. Between the 1950s and 1990s, scientific knowledge production further demarcated the boundary between knowledge derived from scientific principles and knowledge invoked from mysterious or supernatural sources.[56] However, catastrophic rhetoric is not content with that demarcation. It does not want to stay in its lane. The hermeneutic of systematicity offers catastrophists the vocabulary required to enter the public sphere, and in so doing, advances on the claim put forth by James Darsey—that marginalized discourse often gathers rhetorical force by turning a society's most revered expressions back upon itself.[57] Rhetorical ju-jitsu.

Because *systematicity* is such a broad term, let me spend a moment describing how I plan to deploy it. Everyone thinks systematically at times: objectively, methodically, and deliberately. But we also think unsystematically as well: arbitrarily, randomly, and haphazardly.[58] Systematicity is defined by degrees, not absolutes. Astrology, creationism, and Marxism assume elements of systematicity, but not to the degree of evolutionary biology or the theory of relativity.[59] You will notice in the following pages how hard catastrophic rhetoric works to develop such degrees of systematicity. However, according to the conventions of scientific knowledge, catastrophe will always fall short. Science is *cumulative*: it assumes we don't yet know enough, and so it normalizes hypotheses into testable programs of research. Science is *risky*: it consists of an inductive progression from empirical observation to generalizable theory. Science is *contingent*: it tries to advance knowledge to new places, and, in so doing, science sometimes fails, regroups, and sets out again.

Catastrophe does nothing of the sort.

Catastrophe imitates scientific vocabularies through appeals to objectivity, induction, disinterest, and scientific data. It does not rely on myth, magic, and divine revelation alone. But cumulative, risky, and contingent knowledge production is never the goal. Instead, catastrophic systematicity will serve two important functions for the rhetoric of catastrophe. First, it offers a catastrophic community the vocabulary to claim participation in an honest, well-intentioned, intellectual disagreement among truth-seeking erudites. Catastrophe may not turn an evolutionary biologist into a creationist, but systematic vocabularies can muddy the waters of public conversation enough to influence public policy more so than complete acquiescence to the supernatural would allow.

Second, systematicity can police the constitutive boundaries of the community. Some readers may notice pale reflections of the children's tale *The Emperor with No Clothes*. Remaining ignorant of (or quiet about) the emperor's nudity is the price of admission into the community; articulating misgivings is grounds for dismissal. By uttering, for instance, that the Bible is not a science book, that the planet is warming, that bringing a gun into the home makes everyone less safe, and that Donald Trump is an incompetent Russian stooge functions as evidence that one is either too stupid or too evil to remain in the community.[60] Like professional wrestlers, audiences are urged to *keep kayfabe*—to deliberately misrecognize reality, an ideal rhetoric for a post-truth moment.[61] In other words, systematicity allows both the vocabulary to appreciate the emperor's clothes and the motivation to keep quiet if you do notice his butt-cheeks.

Militant Individualism

Militant individualism draws suspicious, distrustful, and fearful individuals into catastrophic communities. Specifically tailored to individuals who feel betrayed by traditional institutions, militant individualism encourages clear boundaries between the few insiders who can see the looming threats posed by changing social conditions and those too ignorant or evil to notice. Militant individualism encourages the disgruntled to withdraw and observe the looming calamity from a safe distance. Consequently, the institutions that have betrayed the target audience *deserve* to be sliced to the bone. The result is an icy form of social Darwinism where hierarchies of power are constructed through competition and aggression, devoid of collective networks and infrastructures.

What rhetorical value does militant individualism serve? For straight, white, native-born men, catastrophic rhetoric resonates within a community unaware of the relationship between collective interdependence, effective governance, and human progress. Consider the mental orientation required to think that militant individualism is the most appropriate response to our most pressing social and political challenges. Such ignorance is informed by the phenomenon that the social institutions that have long worked to privilege catastrophe's target audience have functioned so well that many fail to even notice their existence. "Keep your government hands off my Medicare!" they end up shouting.

I recently noticed a bumper sticker on a car parked at my university that illustrates this dimension. It read, "Man is not free unless government is limited" next to a picture of Ronald Reagan. I thought nothing of it until I looked closer and noticed the car had a US naval base parking pass on the windshield (thanks to a 700 billion-dollar military budget); it was parked in a disabled parking spot (thanks to the Americans with Disabilities Act), at a public university (thanks to the California Master Plan for Higher Education). As Michael Lewis described in his book *The Fifth Risk,* it is often immigrants who come from outside the US, carrying with them the most intimate experiences with institutional corruption, who recognize the US government as the most competent institution in human history. In contrast, catastrophe's target audience resonates with militant individualism because it has long taken institutional privilege for granted. Defining rhetorical outcomes will include derision of the federal government and intergovernmental organizations like the United Nations; a narrow focus on crime and immorality in urban areas; and the affirmation of hierarchy, even at the expense of democracy.

Telic Temporality

Finally, *telic temporality* positions individuals into catastrophic communities defined by a particular linear and determined understanding of time. There are many ways to understand time. When asked to sketch a visual image of "time" on a piece of paper, many in the West would draw a straight line, assuming one temporal trajectory that everyone is swept up into; ancient Greeks, however, would have drawn a circle, Hegelians a spiral, and Victorians a gradually rising line stretching to a utopia.[62] Babylonians understood time as a wheel, repeating in circles; Nietzsche also thought of time as a wheel involving a limited number of atoms, which could assume the same form again and again for eternity; Confucius compared the passage of time to a flowing river; Isaac Newton saw time as a rigid scaffold. In contrast, the rhetoric of catastrophe views time as a historical progression unfolding in a series of stages—marked by moments of crisis, to be sure, but ultimately leading to an advanced, utopian social condition.

Given the presence of conservative influences in the forthcoming case studies, the reader may assume the rhetoric of catastrophe, in contrast, reflects a regressive temporality—*a longing to go back in time*. I concede that the reader may recall other examples of regressive temporality in the forthcoming case studies. However, I aim to show how these appeals actually function as socially sanctioned cover for the more telic aspirations that occupy a fundamental place in catastrophic discourse—an aspiration marked by the desire to advance history forward toward a definitive end. In contrast to a regressive temporality that seeks to go back in time, my conceptualization of telic temporality also informs the distinction between crisis and catastrophe. "Crisis" reflects a point in the story, not the destination. The stages that mark the forward march of history—the launch of Sputnik, the Six-Day War, the terrorist attacks of 9/11, or Hurricane Katrina—reflect a *moment* in the narrative. Extending the work of Foust and Murphy, telic messaging encourages an orientation toward time that aligns the painful stages of crises with catastrophe's ultimate renewal and restoration.[63]

Consider the presence of alternative temporal outcomes. Hesford, Licona, and Teston's extension of precarity illuminates one example. The historical record shows that natural disasters and institutional failures can make possible a reinvigorated "politics of solidarity"—reminding us of both the vulnerability of the human condition *and* the power of collective resistance against calamitous forces.[64] In other words, precarity need not function as a telic step leading always to institutional distrust and cynicism. Crises can exhibit, at some level, evidence of interdependence and collective solidarity in the face of calamity. Public policy can evolve in response, as our efforts to redress the hole in the ozone led to banning CFCs, and millions of traffic deaths led to seatbelts and safe driving laws—saving millions of lives from skin cancer and car accidents. Catastrophe orients its audience in a temporal direction that rejects such efforts. Rather than prevent and redress, moments of crises are understood to be momentarily painful steps on the way toward catastrophic renewal.

CHAPTER PREVIEW

The following four chapters will further illustrate the divergence between genre and homology. But first, I do need to concede that structurally similar associations may appear across the forthcoming religious, ecological, cultural, and political discourses. Put another way, because the homology assumes the unification of strange bedfellows, it is fair to consider how disparate and eclectic my case studies actually are. In other words, are my bedfellows strange enough? Or could generic criticism based on other classification schemes unite these discourses more parsimoniously?

I will argue that despite the associations across these discourses, my inquiry conforms to the methodological expectations of the rhetorical homology by detecting unconscious formal structures performing heavy rhetorical lifting across disparate discourses at higher levels of abstraction. What's more, I will argue that the appearance of generic consistency across what are actually quite disparate discourses is evidence of the potency of the catastrophic homology already at work in public conversations. In other words, to suggest a generic association across religious, ecological, cultural, and political discourses reflects the outcome of a powerful rhetorical alchemy throughout one hundred years of American rhetorical history. Strange bedfellows have become familiar lovers.

Looking closely at "apocalyptic" and "conservative" associations illustrates this point. If either term describes my discourses completely, my inquiry would be better suited for generic criticism. But they don't. The dominant strand of apocalyptic discourse in America today is premillennial dispensationalism, which urges constituted audience members to yearn for a divine rapture that destroys corrupt institutions and restores hierarchies of power (I note the overlap between these apocalyptic urgings and catastrophe's telic destination in the next chapter). However, apocalyptic discourse incompletely describes the rhetorical homology because it operates at the level of conscious awareness in the minds of premillennial audiences, and so fails to "cut across"—in Brummett's term—to higher levels of abstraction. The reader may also notice the ubiquity of Republican rhetors in the following chapters and conclude that conservativism would work well as a site of generic exploration.[65] However, "conservative" is a more complex site of struggle than its misguided associations with the rhetoric of Jerry Falwell, James Dobson, Wayne LaPierre, Jim Inhofe, Steve Bannon, and Donald Trump would imply. From Edmund Burke to Dwight Eisenhower, conservativism once described prudence, deliberation, and moderation; it described institutional protection and deference to tradition and rule of law; and it steered a sober course between liberal excesses (from the French Revolution to 1960s American social movements) and political viability (the acceptance of robust New Deal and Great Society programs).[66] In that sense, my discourses are not conservative. Notice in the following case studies the dearth of respect for institutions, the rule of law ... or even democratic norms and majority rule. The catastrophic homology is represented by demolition-minded perverts—arsonists with Molotov cocktails seeking to burn down institutions to advance the march of history and secure stratified hierarchies of power.

To affirm such a cynical homological relationship requires abundant discursive evidence, ample examples derived inductively from relevant case studies, respecting the validity of the audience under analysis, and the consideration of the best arguments the discourse has to offer—not just the easiest to caricature. I ask the reader's patience as these methodological demands inform the length of this book. The catastrophic homology could not be supported with an article-length essay. I need to spend some time in the following pages both contextualizing each discourse and churning through the evidence to meet these methodological standards. I want to emphasize that the contextualization should not be misunderstood as mere background or setup for the "real analysis" that follows. Each case study chapter will link the catastrophic homology to historical conditions and then demonstrate how the five points of formal correspondence draw rhetorical potency from the catastrophic rhetoric in ways that align with the historical expectations of the time and place in which each emerged.

In what follows, I detail how a homological reservoir of catastrophe constitutes a fundamentalist orientation uniquely equipped to manage unfamiliar, complex, and threatening discourse through five points of formal correspondence. I begin in the next chapter by describing Christian fundamentalism as a deep and illustrative reservoir from which various disparate discourses draw catastrophic influences. For one hundred years, Christian fundamentalism has drawn individuals into *post-truth* constitutive communities "in which objective facts are less influential in shaping public opinion than appeals to emotion and personal belief."[67] Fundamentalism is not "rational" in the traditional sense. Nor does it try to be. Its influence comes not from its rational explanatory power; very few enter or leave a fundamentalist community because a rhetor assembled enough empirical data to move them.[68] Instead, fundamentalism relies on the affective defense of non-empirical and nonscientific values necessary for community constitution in a particular historical moment.[69] And we cannot understand the rhetorical reservoir fueling post-truth/catastrophe without Christian fundamentalism. I then locate those five points of correspondence in ecological catastrophe and the rhetoric of anti-environmentalism (chapter 2), cultural catastrophe and the rhetoric of gun rights (chapter 3), and political catastrophe and the rhetoric of Donald Trump (chapter 4). These discourses are united by a shared yearning for chaos and upheaval as a mechanism to reorder a disordered world. It can never accomplish this aim. Instead, the rhetoric of catastrophe thrashes and flails from grand promises to utter failure, but not without making life more difficult for millions of people. We ought to stand up and take notice.

CHAPTER 1

Christian Fundamentalism and the Catastrophic Homology

AMERICAN CHRISTIANS are generally united by a shared belief in the authority of scripture, the desire for a personal relationship with Jesus Christ, the belief in a spiritual rebirth through Christ's redemptive death and resurrection, the primacy of evangelism, and the expectation of a Second Coming.[1] Many religious historians suggest that Christian fundamentalism—the subject of this chapter and the rhetorical reservoir of the catastrophic homology—tends to diverge from this common ground more in tone and temperament than in doctrine.[2] Evidence of fundamentalism's rough edges is not hard to find. The late Rev. Jerry Falwell, an influential fundamentalist minister, put it well in his book *Strength for the Journey*, when he described a fundamentalist as "an evangelical who is mad about something."[3] However, to suggest that tone, temperament—even anger—describe the distinctiveness of fundamentalism too often produces an unsatisfying, cliché caricature of what is the central organizing rhetoric for millions of Americans. Instead, Christian fundamentalism went from political exile in the middle decades of the twentieth century to political dominance in the 1980s because it functioned as a potent alternative to rational argumentation. Recall that rational argumentation prioritizes empirical reality, scientific facts, and deference to relevant expertise. From that foundation, complex questions about political and economic distribution are reconciled in an attempt to affirm equality, tolerance, and shared human progress.

Christian fundamentalism prioritizes none of that.

Fundamentalism constitutes a community of conservative Protestant Christians through counterpublic speech that appropriates perceived marginalization, prophetic perversion, systematicity, militant individualism, and telic temporality in order to restore order and reconstruct fragile hierarchies of power in the face of modernizing forces.

This counterpublic potential was evident in 1920—as liberal, educated, and cosmopolitan Methodists and Episcopalians in the northern US, more likely to accept a positive conception of upheaval and change, began to develop new epistemologies to align with shifting avenues of political power. That counterpublic potential remains evident one hundred years later—as Christian fundamentalism still functions as a powerful site of rhetorical invention by aligning its points of formal correspondence with a worldview marked by catastrophe, lending valuable insight into our inability and unwillingness to redress our most urgent ecological, cultural, and political challenges.

To add texture to fundamentalism's rhetorical potency, consider the following exchange. Frances FitzGerald was researching for a book on the influence of ministers like Jerry Falwell when she interviewed Nancy James, a member of Falwell's Thomas Road Baptist Church. It was the early 1980s, so FitzGerald asked James about her thoughts on the Equal Rights Amendment. James was "totally against the ERA," she told FitzGerald confidently. FitzGerald, a Pulitzer Prize–winning historian and journalist, countered with a series of rational arguments supporting the ERA. James listened politely; at one point, James even apologized for not being able to respond to FitzGerald's counterarguments because she was so ill informed. Buoyed, FitzGerald assumed James's paralysis was a sign of progress. But as FitzGerald closed the interview and left the house, James ran out after her. James apologized again for her ignorance before saying, "I will find out more about the ERA. I know I'm against it. I'm just not sure exactly why."[4]

Larger conceptual insights regarding fundamentalism's rhetorical potency—far beyond Falwell's fulminations, James Dobson's disciplining, and Pat Robertson's hellfire and brimstones—are reflected in that exchange. James does not appear to be angry, caustic, or evil. She seems to be polite, sober, and thoughtful—and also unwilling to conform to the expectations of rational argumentation. I call that exchange *textured* because James and FitzGerald illustrate the depth and nuance required to get past fundamentalism's cliché caricatures. A task well suited for the rhetorical homology.

STOREHOUSES OF SOCIAL ENERGY

I want to begin by positioning fundamentalism's development in relation to the rhetorical techniques described in the introduction, especially the affective defense of the non-empirical and nonscientific. The emergence of that vocabulary can be traced back to the 1920s, when American Protestantism began to split into a liberal "modernist" camp and a more conservative "fundamentalist" camp. This split was not just doctrinal; it was philosophical—even paradigmatic.[5] Many evangelical Protestants who felt threatened by changing cultural conditions were drawn toward a deference to authority, a desire for rigid hierarchies, and a preference for order, individualism, and competition. Evangelical Protestant leaders, in particular, were men "of strong egos" who built up their own churches and Bible schools without the assistance of traditional denominational resources. These rulers of their own fiefdoms were less comfortable with denominational oversight or traditional religious trappings. In their understanding of history, science, biblical interpretation, and, more importantly, the nature of truth, they began to develop a divergent orientational apparatus. As a result, some individuals marked by these contextual features began to view changing social conditions as disorienting signals of degeneration.[6] Many were left without a vocabulary to explain rapid economic, ethical, and cultural changes. Myth, miracle, and tradition were harder to maintain in the centralized bureaucracy of modern industrial life, particularly in new urban centers populated by immigrants who did not look, eat, recreate, or worship like they were used to.[7]

Without knowing this history, fundamentalism is easy to misunderstand. Today, a significant number of fundamentalists reject Darwinian evolution for a Young Earth account of creation; many view the Bible as inerrant in matters of science, history, and geography. For those sharing this orientational apparatus, scientific, technological, and industrial advancements did not seem to reflect human progress; instead, these advancements were reminders of a failed sensemaking mechanism that left their community disordered and isolated.

Here, the central purpose of this chapter comes into focus: by deploying the rhetorical homology, I hope to show how fundamentalism created a coherent subjectivity within this rhetorical interaction by aligning its symbolic resources to resonate with a particular type of individual in a particular historical moment. Fundamentalism could only tap into existing "storehouses of social energy"—to adopt Christa Olson's phrase—by aligning generally accepted opinions with new explanations for an unfamiliar and chaotic world.[8] Otherwise, it would have devolved into an esoteric, separatist cult.

It didn't.

Instead, Christian fundamentalism emerged as a powerful site of rhetorical invention by aligning its points of formal correspondence with a worldview marked by catastrophe. I hope to show in the rest of this chapter how—in order to restore order and reconstruct fragile hierarchies of power in the face of modernizing forces—fundamentalism constituted a community of conservative Protestant Christians through counterpublic speech drawn from the catastrophic homology, including *perceived marginalization*—as it resonates with individuals through discourses of victimage and betrayal; *prophetic perversion*—an internal alteration of elite expertise balancing magisterial deciphering and republican perspicacity; *hermeneutic of systematicity*—an external lens based on the imitation of scientific vocabularies to aid scholarly engagement; *militant individualism*—promoting the derision of social institutions and the eschewal of white male privilege; and *telic temporality*—understanding time as advancing forward to a definitive endpoint defined by temporary pain but, ultimately, restoration.

THE EARTH IS TO GROW WORSE AND WORSE

Chantal Mouffe has shown that when we lose our firm linguistic footing we tend to also lose the desire to participate in the communities constituted by a dying rhetoric. We instead replace previous allegiances with other sorts of collective identifications that create new subjectivities and alternative social responsibilities.[9] Put more directly, we become new people. Fundamentalism's birth story begins with locating constitutional comfort by drawing heavily from the rhetoric of Dwight L. Moody (1837–99)—an evangelical revivalist popular during the second half of the nineteenth century. Moody grew up in Massachusetts, the seventh of nine children. He converted to evangelical Christianity at the age of seventeen after his uncle required him to attend church services as a condition of employment in the family's shoe-repair shop. Moody would grow to develop the discourse that resonated with conservative ministers seeking to form churches, seminaries, and Bible societies that could defend their version of traditional, evangelical Protestantism.[10]

Moody's vocabulary urged a catastrophic response to modernism. With a corpulent physique, full beard, and arched eyebrows, Moody articulated the sense of crisis reflected in modernism's impact, especially in the emergence of urban slums, poor working conditions, and moral decay. "I look upon the world as a wrecked vessel," Moody declared. "God has given me a lifeboat and said to me, 'Moody, save all you can.'"[11] He also asserted, "The Earth is to grow worse and worse, and that at length there is going to be a separation."[12] "Individual survivors might be rescued," he suggested, "but the vessel itself was beyond hope."[13] Crisis, chaos, and calamity—not economic development or shared human progress—marked the consequence of modernism.

Why was Moody so suspicious? Between 1790 and 1850 Protestant Christians enjoyed near-complete cultural dominance in the US, as little daylight could be found between Protestant institutions and other cultural and political avenues of power.[14] Catholic, Orthodox, Lutheran, Mormon, and Jewish faiths were not yet influential. Instead, Protestant ethics shaped legal and economic arrangements; colleges, universities, and seminaries prioritized Protestant moral instruction and clergy training; and scientific inquiry mainly focused on knowing more about the natural world so as to marvel at God's handiwork.[15] An American Protestant living in 1850 would find the militancy, anger, and insecurity of today's fundamentalism at odds with the comfort and prestige once enjoyed.

However, Protestant dominance began to fade after the American Civil War. Between the 1860s and the 1920s, as the war ended and the Industrial Revolution began in the US, evangelical Protestants faced a series of cultural, economic, and epistemic challenges. Culturally, thirty million new immigrants—many from Eastern and Southern Europe—arrived in the US, introducing Catholic, Greek Orthodox, and Jewish competitors to Protestant cultural dominance. Economically, the transition from agrarian to industrial modes of production introduced new forms of innovation, centralization, and bureaucratic control, offering massive corporations more influence over family farms and small businesses.[16] Epistemologically, Charles Darwin began to exert influence on methods of scientific inquiry. Religion was pushed out of the hard sciences and into seminaries and divinity schools; but concurrently, German biblical criticism was also beginning to change how religious scholars understood biblical authority by emphasizing the historical context of sacred scriptures, freeing theologians from the constraints of traditional biblical interpretation, and leaving far less space for conservative biblical hermeneutics.[17]

Were these challenges enough to constitute a *crisis*? Recall from the introduction that upheaval is never experienced objectively or independently. As Bostdorff and Edelman made clear, tumultuous political events of all kinds are linguistic constructions.[18] We only make sense of changing social conditions in relation to a complex confluence of endogenous and exogenous factors, including personality differences and relational affiliations. Put more simply, upheaval of any kind functions as a rhetorical site of struggle where emerging vocabularies compete to align with changing social conditions. For example, consider how modernism's upheaval could be a reflection of positive human progress. The US was largely a rural, agricultural nation when the Civil War began. But by the end of World War I, the US had become the world's dominant industrial and manufacturing power, with greater steel production than Germany and Great Britain combined, 200,000 miles of railroads, and an expanding network of public schools for native-born and new immigrants to contribute to an evolving economy. Immigrants filled the positions required for the shift from an agricultural to an industrial economy. And new epistemologies, especially Darwin's influence on scientific methods, offered new insights into our natural world.[19]

On the other hand, consider how an alternative worldview could make sense of all this change. Yes, technological innovation, increased productivity, and industrial development sparked massive economic growth—but not everyone shared in those benefits equally. Many family farmers lost control of their produce to the railroads, and many small businesses, especially in rural areas, were destroyed.[20] Religiously, many evangelical Protestants felt uncomfortable sharing their privilege with new indigenous sects like Mormons and Seventh-Day Adventists, or imported faith traditions coming from Jewish, Catholic, and even Lutheran traditions. Epistemological changes represented clear threats to the intellectual authority of Protestantism in the academy. Many conservative Protestant clergy and theologians were squeezed out of higher education, as myth, miracles, and religious traditions became less useful for explaining the world.

Two themes from Moody's vocabulary were particularly useful for affirming this threatened worldview. Theologically, Moody rejected German biblical criticism and Darwinian evolution. He also promoted the Princeton Theological Seminary's assumption that every word of the Bible was absolutely and literally true. He began one sermon by telling his congregation, "If I utter a syllable that is not justified by the Scriptures, don't believe me. The Bible is the only rule. Walk by it and it alone."[21] Although he avoided the term *inerrancy*, he was not confused about the comprehensive truthfulness of the Bible, saying, "If there was one portion of the Scripture untrue the whole of it went for nothing."[22] Moody was also one of the first premillennial dispensationalists. Premillennialism is an eschatology drawn from John Nelson Darby, a nineteenth-century English sectarian, who prophesied that civilization was marching toward an inevitable decline, culminating in the great battle of Armageddon. But before that, Christ would return to lift away believers before the Second Coming, at which time the kingdom would be restored and Christ would usher in the millennium.[23] Moody's vocabulary would be used to popularize this eschatology in the late nineteenth and early twentieth centuries.

Why did biblical literalism and premillennialism resonate in this historical moment? Both encouraged individuals to perceive changing social conditions as threatening. German biblical criticism left conservatives with fewer hermeneutic resources; in response, biblical literalism offered firm intellectual footing. Premillennialism encourages adherents to long for an alternative to their day-to-day reality. Fundamentalists, in turn, were much more likely to accept premillennialism because it resonated so well with their feelings of marginalization. In contrast, mainline Protestants were more likely to assume a postmillennial eschatology, assuming that God can redeem humankind without a violent Armageddon, and that Christians need not wait until society deteriorates to the point that it can only be salvaged by a gruesome apocalypse. Consequently, liberal postmillennials sought to invest in a more optimistic future in which they work to create stronger mechanisms of global peace and justice.[24] Historically, postmillennialism reflects American religion at its best: a social gospel optimistic about the progress of humanity and the potential to ameliorate social ills, as seen in historic efforts to abolish slavery, alleviate poverty, educate women, and reform prisons.[25] Most religiously inclined Americans want to improve the world, not hasten its destruction. Fundamentalism began to be marked by separation and withdrawal. It sought to root out the causes of the earth growing worse and worse, first looking inward and defining themselves against the accommodating mainline Protestant and Catholic religious practices. And then looking outward, fundamentalism began to eschew a history of Protestant involvement with social issues, including poverty, temperance, and suffrage, and to redouble energies toward conversion and evangelism. From this position of perceived marginalization came an exclusionary political and social agenda in which absolute binaries between the saved and the damned not only marked an unbreachable divide but also constructed hierarchies of power that granted moral rewards to the elect.[26]

This is not to suggest a direct through-line between Dwight Moody and Jerry Falwell. Moody was unlike the famous fundamentalist rhetors that followed him—he was not Falwell or Dobson; he never directly attacked liberal Protestants as enemies of the Christian faith; he ignored them.[27] In the late 1880s Moody was kept contained. For a time Protestant Christianity tempered Moody's outrage, allowing fundamentalists and liberal Protestants to maintain a peaceful—if tenuous—coexistence within the American Christian community. However, that changed after 1919.

Battle Royal for the Fundamentals

In 1919 William Bell Riley, later known as "The Grand Old Man of Fundamentalism," would be elected the first president of the World's Christian Fundamentals Association. Reflecting the initial divergence from Moody's contained discourse, Riley used his acceptance speech to connect the passion and number of participants at the conference (not to mention his own ascendancy) to the fact that a community of believers had not "succumbed to the interchurch 'tapeworm' that was infecting churches and denominations around the country."[28] A year later Curtis Lee Laws, editor of a conservative Baptist periodical, gathered together a group of three thousand ministers and lay leaders at the 1920 Northern Baptist Convention for a preconference gathering on the "Fundamentals of Our Baptist Faith." Laws described the attendees as people of faith "who mean to do battle royal for the fundamentals."[29] Pause for a moment and consider why Riley or Curtis Laws felt the need to organize conferences on the fundamentals of their faith. And why were so many interested? The answers reveal much about the developing perception of betrayal and victimage in conservative Protestants' mental condition at the time.

According to George Marsden's definitive history, fundamentalism took off in the US as Lyman and Milton Stewart, oil wildcatters who made a fortune in the Union Oil Company in California, conceived and financed the publication of a twelve-volume series of essays detailing what they thought to be the essential doctrines of Christianity.[30] They called the series *The Fundamentals: A Testimony to the Truth*, and it featured several responses to German biblical criticism, including a revealing description of its "unscientific" methods and its suspicion of the supernatural.[31] Affirming the contours of systematicity, *The Fundamentals* sought to develop external scholarly legitimacy—and react to intellectual marginalization—by deploying scientific vocabularies. For example, Canon Dyson Hague, a lecturer in liturgics and ecclesiology at Wycliffe College in Toronto, Canada, began the pamphlet with the chapter "The History of Higher Criticism," in which he decried German-influenced biblical interpretation: "It is notorious to what length the German fancy can go in the direction of the subjective and of the conjectural. For hypothesis-weaving and speculation, the German theological professor is unsurpassed."[32] Each chapter from *The Fundamentals* sought to offer the intellectual force needed to wage larger battles against modernism's cultural shifts. Conservative Protestants, mostly in the South, with less education and weaker denominational ties, deplored secularizing cultural forces and began to fight back against what they framed as an attack on their traditions and beliefs.

It is at this point that the difference between Dwight Moody in the 1890s and Jerry Falwell in the 1980s becomes relevant. Rather than separate, fundamentalism first attacked mainline Protestantism with a militant antimodernism that would characterize its discourse for decades to come.[33] Gone was the peaceful coexistence; in its place arose an organized effort to root out and destroy modernism in churches and schools.

Clear Borders and Few Entrances

The militancy, piety, and rigidity attributed to fundamentalists today first emerged in the 1920s.[34] A general suspicion of modernism's "worldliness" developed.[35] Contrasting their divergent beliefs with those of other denominations, fundamentalists sought to keep from losing authentic religious expressions. The result was a fundamentalism that put distance between themselves and apostate outsiders.

As it moved further away from other Protestant faiths, fundamentalism developed a marginalized identity based on betrayal and (perceptions of) victimage. Fundamentalism became an exclusive strand of Christianity, with clear borders and few entrances, reserved for those who have "prayed the prayer," acknowledged their personal sinfulness and their need for salvation, and could define themselves against liberalizing Protestant Christians. Because it was not wed to the liturgical rubrics, creeds, and common beliefs of Catholicism and mainline Protestant denominations, fundamentalism's community-constituting characteristics were more pliable. This is evinced in the vocabulary that developed into fundamentalism. More specifically, I want to connect fundamentalism with the characteristics of a *counterpublic*. Fundamentalist speech was marked by vivid, familiar plotlines, resonant villains and heroes, and gratifying conclusions forming the coherent discursive grounds of resistance to the threat posed by religious and political modernizing forces.[36] Fundamentalism, as a discrete movement constituted by shared speech, began to define itself and its constituency in opposition to the larger public transformations. Its withdrawn, privatized speech drew together precarious individuals in this moment as a way to overcome perceived marginalization, and then later, to reassert their demands for public legitimacy.[37] Appropriating rhetorical appeals to traditionally marginalized individuals, fundamentalism offered individuals in this moment the terrain on which to organize, cohere, and imagine resistant subjectivities in the face of modernizing forces.[38]

While the degree and severity might be questioned, evidence of marginalization was not hard to find. The religious and political institutions that once functioned to ensure their power now seemed like part of a larger conspiratorial plot hell-bent on destroying conservative Protestants and their way of life.[39] Fundamentalist speech repositioned the world as a dangerous, corrupting site of struggle. For those sharing this orientational apparatus, scientific, technological, and industrial advancements did not seem to reflect human progress; instead, these advancements were reminders of a failed sensemaking mechanism that left their community feeling disordered and isolated. Attempts by mainline Protestants and Catholics to adjust to these economic and cultural shifts looked like further slippage toward accommodation to the rest of the world's soiled institutions.[40] Many conservative Protestants saw a world robbed of stability by these changes, especially scientific advancements that encouraged doubt and uncertainty, economic shifts that disrupted an agrarian lifestyle, and a liberalizing Protestant theology that seemed to prioritize skepticism over faith. The result illustrates perceived marginalization based on an acute loss of order and a feeling that traditional institutions could no longer be relied on to explain a changing world.[41]

In the face of this fear, fundamentalism offered order, discipline, and community. Rather than evolving with modernizing forces, individuals and communities that would come to be known as "fundamentalist" developed a rigid, literal hermeneutic to combat liberalizing theology, a militant anger against changing cultural norms, and isolated defenses against the permeation of modernism into their traditional avenues of understanding. Consequently, other disparate discourses were realigned to mesh with this worldview.

In their understanding of history, science, biblical interpretation, and, more importantly, the nature of truth, Protestants began to develop an alternative sensemaking foundation. The more important historical lesson I want to emphasize here is that modernism's upheavals produced doxa without discourse, text without context. As a result, some individuals were more likely to view changing social conditions as disorienting signals of degeneration and an assault on their traditional way of life.[42] Many were left without a vocabulary to explain rapid economic, ethical, and cultural changes. Worse still, modernism's institutions could lure Christians away with the spoils of secularism. Fundamentalism repositioned their own churches—and later, Bible schools, bookstores, church camps, and seminaries—as places of refuge, protection, and security against a world that had forsaken God.[43]

From the decades between *The Fundamentals* and *Focus on the Family*, this counterpublic repositioning would run like a red thread through fundamentalist speech. Dwight Moody warned of a looming separation, a future that would grow worse and worse. For fundamentalists, he was prophetic. The social center would come to sanction sinful modernism, first with German biblical criticism casting doubt on the accuracy of sacred scriptures, and later the social revolutions of the 1960s and 1970s . . . all fueling the perception that the moral order was being subverted and the church and family under attack.[44] MTV and pornography were acceptable to the American public, but prayer in school and the Ten Commandments on the courthouse steps were not.

Consequently, fundamentalism worked hard to assume an identity akin to oppressed groups of people. Recall that I asked the reader in the introduction to consider whether material conditions have any influence on perceptions of marginalization. And note that in this case material marginalization seems less relevant for the development of counterpublic discourse than the *felt* marginalization—a worldview based on perceived wrongs only loosely associated with reality.[45] We know that the articulation of counterpublic speech does not depend on pre-existing exclusionary status. Fundamentalist churches did not ask for verification of oppression at the narthex. Keep in mind that most fundamentalists were straight, white, and native-born. They made their way through the twentieth century without experiencing the discrimination felt by many of the communities whose language they were appropriating. The political and economic success of American fundamentalism in the latter half of the twentieth century—including the growth of fundamentalist churches, the burgeoning strength of right-wing media, and their influence within the Republican Party—should remind us that marginalization need not be materially grounded. Rather, the articulation of marginalization functions as the constitutive cost of admission into this community.[46] Here is where scholars of communication and rhetoric are especially well suited for extending the contributions of disciplines like religious studies, sociology, and history. Discursive systems of justification were deployed to justify pre-existing arrangements; fundamentalist speech was not trying to change minds or convert outsiders; this counterpublic speech was designed to justify attitudes and behaviors already circulating in the social milieu.

For a contemporary example, consider the subordinate positioning of many fundamentalist Christians today in relation to the LGBTQ community. From the fringes of internet cranks up to the lofty legal opinions of Antonin Scalia, William Rehnquist, and Clarence Thomas, "homosexuals" and a "homosexual agenda" are understood to form a powerful cabal exercising disproportionate influence on American culture and politics.[47] I once had a job interview at Wheaton College where I had a lot of trouble explaining to the provost why rhetorical scholars focused so much of our counterhegemonic scholarly energy on LGBTQ issues. He seemed to understand our focus on race, gender, and class, but he couldn't understand why we would lump Ellen

DeGeneres and Elton John into that research program when it seemed to him like straight people were now the marginalized identity in so many public contexts. According to the standards of rational argumentation, however, such feelings of aggrievement are unhinged from material reality. According to the Williams Institute at the UCLA School of Law, LGTBQ Americans face much greater economic challenges that straight, cisgender Americans.[48] Controlling for gender, age, race/ethnicity, and education level, LGBTQ Americans and same-sex couples face greater risks of being in poverty than straight Americans; rates of food insecurity are 1.7 times higher in the LGBTQ community than in the non-LGBTQ, as 29 percent of LGBTQ adults were food insecure in 2012—compared with 16 percent of Americans nationwide.[49] And same-sex couples with children are more than twice as likely to receive food stamps. However, in the legal opinions of Antonin Scalia and the parenting guides of James Dobson, fundamentalism's counterpublic speech does not rely on the standards of rational argumentation or empirical economic data. Instead, many fundamentalists today see *Will and Grace* and the Obergefell decision with the same trepidation that Riley, Laws, and the Stewart Brothers saw Darwinism and German biblical criticism one hundred years ago.

Jonathan J. Edwards's description of fundamentalism as *an impossible majority* is illuminating here, as such tensions would follow fundamentalist counterpublic speech from the political wilderness after the Scopes Monkey Trial to its triumphant ascendance to the centers of American political power in the 1970s and 1980s. The impossible majority points to several lingering questions: What describes the discursive process by which a community of mostly straight, white, native-born, Protestant men articulate a precarious and insecurity identity with such force? And further, what happens when fundamentalism conquers the villainous center and moves from the wilderness to the White House? How does the counterpublic canine maintain constitutive force once it has caught up to the car?

Fundamentalist counterpublic speech would come to reflect the sophistication common to all strong discourses. Not confined to attracting Iowa corn-farmers worried about the implications of Darwinian evolution on their daily lives, fundamentalism would be reconstituted and redefined, replete with shifting plotlines, characters, and narrative arcs. The marginalization represented by the League of Nations in the 1920s would morph into the threats posed by the USSR, and then Al Qaeda and ISIS; Darwin would be replaced by Eleanor Roosevelt and then Hillary Clinton. Nonetheless, the felt marginalization of Moody, Laws, Riley, and *The Fundamentals,* and then later, Billy Graham, Jerry Falwell, Pat Robertson, and James Dobson, would remain coherent, marked by the appropriation of perceived marginalization in an effort to articulate grievances in the face of a changing world and restore order to a disordered world.

MASTER-MINDED BY SATAN

Fundamentalism was not limited to John Birch Society cranks and backwoods, snake-handling charismatics. Although never confined to the proverbial wilderness, Billy Graham's discourse offers a wonderful opportunity to examine fundamentalism's moderate articulations and to explore the best of fundamentalism's arguments (not just the easiest to caricature). Graham is not often lumped together with Dwight Moody, Oral Roberts, and Pat Robertson. He was likable, eloquent, and handsome. He looked like a Hollywood movie star, spoke like a passionate revivalist, and massaged political differences like a gifted pol. Serving as a counselor to every American president from Truman to Obama, Graham carefully avoided the cultural briar patch many fundamentalist figureheads dove into headfirst. And so, few journalists questioned him about the political implications of his message, and most religious historians do not examine him in relation to more fringe fundamentalist leaders. But, according to the doctrinal, philosophical, and paradigmatic features being explored here, Graham was fundamentalist to the core.[50]

Billy Graham leveraged the perception of marginalization felt by this community during the middle decades of the twentieth century. For example, when Harry Truman announced that the Soviet Union had successfully tested an atomic bomb, Graham used the news as the headline for his sermon the next day.[51] He was also quick to paint his community as besieged on all sides by cunning communists. In a 1957 sermon Graham said,

> My own theory about Communism is that it is master-minded by Satan ... I think there is no other explanation for the tremendous gains of Communism in which they seem to outwit us at every turn, unless they have supernatural power and wisdom and intelligence given to them.[52]

Consider the subjectivity required to resonate with a general description of the world that lumps together Satan and the USSR in an anti-American conspiracy. The presence of Sputnik in the sky over Detroit is less relevant for that resonance than a larger worldview marked by insecurity, detectable in a range of spheres from outer space and international affairs to the most intimate areas of domestic life. Worse, Graham's counterpublic speech resonated with a larger worldview devoid of a competent state apparatus to defend

America against the sieges of Stalin or Satan. Graham's fears are not an aberration: his conspiratorial urgings were also reflected in the rhetoric of Phyllis Schlafly, Barry Goldwater, Ronald Reagan, and James Dobson.

Built on Counterculture

James Dobson's Focus on the Family functions as a second illustrative case study in the evolution of fundamentalist counterpublic speech. A child psychologist with a PhD from USC, James Dobson founded Focus on the Family as a nonprofit organization "dedicated to nurturing and defending families worldwide."[53] Though he was never ordained, Dobson turned his popular parenting books and syndicated radio programs into an important touchstone for larger counterpublic struggles. Dobson articulated Dwight Moody's fears: he argued that the world had fallen so far and so fast that even the family—*especially* the family—was unsafe from modernism's threats. In his book *Dare to Discipline*, Dobson established his original critique, connecting permissive parenting to the larger cultural acceptance of feminism, fluid gender roles, pornography, abortion, and LGBTQ lifestyles. Kurt Bruner, vice president of Focus on the Family's publication and video productions, described Focus's aim as reinforcing Christian values in the home reflecting a broader mission "largely built on counterculture."[54] Focus on the Family's counterpublic speech would later urge resistance far beyond the home and family, including public battles over religious symbols in public places, curriculum in public schools, media bias, liberal-judicial establishment, and resisting efforts to curb climate change.

As Focus on the Family grew between the 1970s and 2000s, Dobson's discourse began to reflect the challenges of Edwards's impossible majority. Focus on the Family became a cultural force, marked by an 81-acre corporate campus in Colorado employing more than 1,400 people, a radio program that reached two million listeners on six thousand channels, ten magazines reaching 2.3 million homes, and a syndicated newspaper column appearing in five hundred newspapers. The cultural force accompanying that growth would not satiate fundamentalist anxiety, however. The goalposts shifted. While Dwight Moody's lifeboat sought to save individual souls, James Dobson's cultural broadside reflected a larger fundamentalist progression: modernism betrayed not just culture, media, the courts, and family, but the entire state. America's founding as a God-fearing pseudotheocracy had been betrayed by secular humanists. Consequently, Dobson expanded the mission: fundamentalists were not content to protect the family or even the state against liberalizing forces—they were to integrate themselves into the inner workings of the state.[55] Put bluntly, Dobson was not satisfied selling *Dare to Discipline* in the Religion & Spirituality aisles of Barnes & Noble. He wanted into the White House.

Perverting the Center

In his article "The Rhetoric of the True Believer," Roderick Hart illustrated the predictive potential that can emerge when rhetorical criticism is done well. Speech draws individuals into communities; speech calls out the conditions in need of response; speech even shapes speech. Thus, the rhetorical value of connecting a doctrinaire discourse like fundamentalism to an audience positioning itself against a secular public may allow critics the opportunity to speculate on future events—depending on the adherence to the discursive parameters being set up. Following Hart's lead, if Riley in the 1920s or Graham in the 1950s or Dobson in the 1980s constituted a dispersed and fragmented set of individuals into a coherent community by deploying such counterpublic rhetoric, it may be possible to examine fundamentalist speech across a range of disparate discourses and to trace their upcoming retreat to the wilderness, conspiratorial appeals, and eventual emergence into traditional avenues of power

Explaining why the most influential Christian since Saint Paul would see a satanic conspiracy in Sputnik or why a child psychologist—with a PhD from USC—would defend Roy Moore—and each attract huge audiences doing so—would indicate that fundamentalism could continue to thrive without modernism's standards of rational argumentation. However, the challenge of intellectual inferiority would linger for fundamentalists keen on transcending narrow religious spheres. For Dobson to gain entrance to the White House, a more intellectually rigorous, systematic hermeneutic far beyond the biblical literalism outlined by Moody would have to be developed. In other words, fundamentalist counterpublic speech would remain marginalized if it did not develop a satisfying discursive response to the intellectual challenges posed by the acceptance of Darwinian evolution, German biblical criticism, and New Revised Standard Versions of the Bible. Fundamentalism had to grapple with a public that was eschewing nonuniversal religious assumptions to guide public policy.[56] As Moody warned, the whole of it may go for nothing without such a rebuttal. That Dobson and Graham, and Laws and Riley, could influence domestic and foreign policy, from abortion to climate change, indicates that fundamentalist counterpublic speech reconciled that challenge.

PLAIN FACTS AND COMMON SENSE

While modernism did challenge the trustworthiness of the Bible, it is not accurate to assume biblical inerrancy dominated American Christian theology before the 1920s.[57] More saliently, some conservatives began to see liberal theological developments as one more example of institutional betrayal shutting their perspectives out of the intellectual centers.[58] Fundamentalism cohered around the assumptions that institutions of higher learning—including prestigious seminaries and divinity schools—were becoming training grounds for apostate biblical hermeneutics, silencing conservative voices and further fueling stereotypes of rural, conservative Christians as ignorant hillbillies. Consider how difficult it is to constitute a religious community—to offer a satisfactory explanation for how God intervenes in human affairs, to interpret sacred scriptures written thousands of years ago, and to explain the greatest mysteries of human life—when society's experts heap scorn on your way of thinking. Fundamentalism had to react to liberalizing theology. Its continued viability depended on it.

Fundamentalist discourse began to embrace the scorn and stereotypes of intellectual elites. Biblical justification for this reaction was drawn from the Apostle Paul's first letter to the Corinthians, in which he described the wisdom of the world as "foolishness in God's sight" and a trap that "catches the wise in their craftiness" (1 Cor. 3:19). Paul continued in the next chapter, further articulating a counterpublic position against the wisdom of the world: "We are *fools for Christ's sake*," he wrote, "but ye are wise in Christ; we are weak, but ye are strong; ye are honorable, but we are despised." With that divine charge, modernism's theological evolution looked to be producing worldly biblical scholars too smart for their own good.

William Riley—"The Grand Old Man of Fundamentalism"—illustrated the adoption of ignorance in the face of modern theological sophistication. He pushed back, portraying techniques of German biblical criticism as a ruse designed to confuse the plain truth of the scriptures.[59] Riley lauded plain churches, plain preachers, preaching to plain people in a way that still emerges one hundred years later.[60] Today, fundamentalists generally place less emphasis on high biblical criticism and instead have developed a more populist, anti-intellectual appeal. For example, fundamentalist preachers often taught without notes, used humor and plain reasoning, made more direct eye contact with their congregations, and featured short, cogent, colloquial expressions. They also emphasized dramatic biblical stories, especially concrete descriptions of hell, which served as an important rhetorical development in the face of what looked to many like a decaying world.[61]

Such an embrace would be a suitable response to modernism . . . if fundamentalists were content to remain on the margins. But embracing foolishness—even for Christ's sake—would turn out to be unsustainable when fundamentalists grew tired of the political wilderness. This is not to suggest that fundamentalists sought to convert everyone. The wholesale conversion of an outside world that scorns the community's way of thinking was never a priority. Nonetheless, margins are lonely places, and heaped scorn breeds insecurity.

Some fundamentalists may have tried to find comfort in embracing foolishness, but it does not seem that, as a whole, fundamentalism relinquished the desire to stay invested in public life or totally gave up on defending its theology in public conversations. Jonathan J. Edwards put it well: "Fundamentalist doctrine requires the believer to regularly speak to outsiders about the deepest facets of belief and being—risking not only loss of control but also loss of eternity in the process. It is a tension that Fundamentalist believers must continually negotiate—the command to speak against the risk of speech—and one that in various ways they attempt to control."[62] Extending Edwards, I think it is important to consider how the spoken engagement described here assumes a narrow connotation in fundamentalist communities. "Regularly speaking to outsiders" does not require adherence to the conventions of rational argumentation or deference to relevant expertise. That adherence—that deference—is too risky. Instead, fundamentalists were charged with maintaining constitutional viability in the face of modernism apostasies without risking one's soul to eternal damnation—either in hell or at Harvard.

In the 1920s most Protestants affirmed the inspiration, authority, and trustworthiness of scripture, but few would understand inerrancy or literalism as touchstones of their faith.[63] However, by 1976 more than eighty million Americans would affirm the Bible as "literally true" according to a Gallup poll.[64] What happened between 1920 and 1976?

As I argued in the introduction, fundamentalism is not "rational" in the traditional argumentative sense. What fundamentalism needed—to acquire a rigorous defense against modernism's apostasies—was the appearance of engagement, the look of "regularly speaking with outsiders" . . . without the risk of rational engagement.

I want to locate that vocabulary in the discursive evolution from biblical literalism to biblical inerrancy. Inerrancy offered the mechanism to extend the pre-existing conservative affinity for biblical literalism, but with a more sophisticated, internally consistent, rhetorically inventive, and intellectually legitimate retort to modernism's scorn. This began by synthesizing versions of Catholic exegesis with a particular strand of Puritan Calvinism.[65] I should note that strict five-point Calvinism did not inform the day-to-day lives of many of those drawn to fundamentalism; instead, it was a particular systematic hermeneutic derived by the Princeton Theological Seminary that had the most lasting impact.[66] Reflecting the principles of rhetorical invention, Calvinism was recalibrated to align with the new marginalized condition of this nascent community. More specifically, fundamentalists found in inerrancy a scaffold of rationality that could respond to modernist thought.[67]

As inerrancy developed, it offered fundamentalism a retort to modernism's theological advancements. No longer would fundamentalism be confined to foolishness: God's revelation could even take on the look of scientific rigor.[68] Fast-forward sixty years: Jerry Falwell would write in his best-selling book *Listen! America* that the Bible is "without error in all matters pertaining to faith and practice, as well as in areas such as geography, science and history."[69] Modernists from the 1920s would likely assume such a sentence written in 1980 must have come from a marginalized crackpot. That it came from one of the most influential Christians in the country, and that it was not at all scandalous, illustrates the inventive value that inerrancy would adopt in in the twentieth century.

Careful, Unbiased, Systematic

Fundamentalism resisted modernism's scorn and constituted an alternative community by appropriating secularizing vocabularies, especially the deployment of scientific, rigorous, and even falsifiable language. Fundamentalists had to know that few secular humanists would be converted by such appropriation; its systematicity could never meet the standards of scientific validity. But those limitations did little to prevent scientific and historical appropriations from shoring up the internal walls for many conservative Protestants in this moment. And this is an important illustration of systematicity in fundamentalist discourse: what matters is the appearance of rigorous, scientific vocabularies, not to convert outsiders but to constitute the already predisposed into the flock.

Inerrancy functioned as the bridge between fundamentalist theology and a scholarly veneer. In relation to the work of Moody and Riley, fundamentalist rhetors such as J. Gresham Machen, Reuben Torrey, and Charles Hodge laid the rhetorical groundwork for Falwell's taken-for-granted appeal that would come decades later. As J. Gresham Machen, a Presbyterian theologian known for leading a revolt against modernist theology at Princeton, put it, "We refuse, therefore, to abandon to the student of natural science the entire realm of fact, in order to reserve to religion merely a realm of ideals; on the contrary, theology, we hold, is just as much a science as is chemistry."[70] Machen was not to be confined to the realm of the cosmic or the magical. It was only in subject matter—not epistemology—that religion and chemistry differ; both were sciences "concerned with the acquisition of orderly arrangement of truth." He wrote, "The historic continuity of the Christian religion is based upon its appeal to a body of facts—facts about God, about man, and about the way in which, at a definite point in the world's history, some nineteen hundred years ago, a new relationship was set up between God and man by the work of Jesus Christ."[71] He continued, "Christianity is based not merely on ethical principles or on eternal truths of religion, but also on historical facts."

Dwight Moody's closest associate and eventual heir, Reuben Torrey (1856–1923), thought of himself as a scientist pursuing what he called the "careful, unbiased, systematic through-going, inductive study and statement of Bible truth."[72] One book, *What the Bible Teaches,* was a five-hundred-page tome collecting biblical "propositions" written in the style of an encyclopedia. Torrey adopted the language of a scientist; he claimed to "assume absolutely nothing." One of the three editors of *The Fundamentals,* and founder of what became Biola University, Torrey argued that "true science does not start with an a priori hypothesis that certain things are impossible, but simply examines the evidence to find out what has actually occurred."[73]

In 1871 Charles Hodge, a prominent Princeton theologian, published *Systematic Theology,* which assured its readers that God's sacred scriptures do not mislead. He wrote, "The Bible is to the theologian what nature is to the man of science. It is his store-house of facts."[74] In 1909 Cyrus Scofield published an annotated version of the King James Bible that appealed to many because it taught its readers to conduct their own systematic textual analysis, a feature that aligned with a more republican approach to biblical analysis.[75] Scofield's annotations offered the reader the chance to connect current events and scientific trends in a way that bolstered the appearance of systematicity.[76] Recall also how the publication of *The Fundamentals* featured several responses to German biblical criticism, including a revealing description of their opposition's "unscientific" methods based on "hypothesis-weaving" and suspicion of the supernatural.[77] In contrast, *The Fundamentals* detailed the archeological and historical evidence for the divinity of Christ and supernatural events described in the Bible. Fundamentalists could engage in biblical criticism. W. H. Griffith Thomas argued:

> We do not question for an instant the right of Biblical criticism considered in itself. On the contrary, it is a necessity for all who use the Bible to be

"critics" in the sense of constantly using their "judgment" on what is before them. What is called "higher" criticism is not only a legitimate but a necessary method for all Christians, for by its use we are able to discover the facts and the form of the Old Testament Scriptures. Our hesitation, consequently, is not intended to apply to the method, but to what is believed to be an illegitimate, unscientific, and unhistorical use of it. In fact, we base our objections to much modern criticism of the Old Testament on what we regard as a proper use of a true higher criticism.[78]

J. J. Reeve, in another essay in *The Fundamentals,* wrote, "The scientific spirit which gave rise to it is one of the noblest instincts in the intellectual life of man. It is a thirst for the real and the true, that will be satisfied with nothing else."[79]

The appropriation of scientific, historical, and archeological language served several important functions. Fundamentalist interpretation could appear more stable than liberal theology. As Machen wrote, "The Christian religion is based upon a body of truth, a body of doctrine, which will remain true to the end of time."[80] Machen's assertion must be understood in direct contrast to liberal theologies that also considered unfolding revelation, historical and social context, and "the shared experience of the believers."[81] Resonating with the anti-intellectual outlook of this community, fundamentalists often referred to their developing hermeneutic as reading the "plain facts" of the Bible based on "common sense."[82]

Plain facts and common sense were not acquired through advanced education. Instead, fundamentalism developed through what FitzGerald called a mental "faculty that existed prior to, and independent of, reason and experience."[83] Reflecting the distinction between *science* and *pseudoscience* that I discussed in the introduction, fundamentalism adopted eighteenth-century Scottish philosopher Thomas Reid's description of "mind furnishing"—a metaphor alluding to a pre-existing cognitive faculty that produced knowledge, sensibility, and even memory. For Reid, knowledge was produced by the "will of the maker," sensibility was "part of a furniture of the mind," and memory was produced by "the inspiration of the almighty."[84] Already present in the hearts and minds of believers, God's truth did not require the intellectual defenses developed in modernist epistemologies.[85] In the fundamentalist tradition, God is understood to speak directly to the hearts of the born-again. As such, fundamentalist readers searching for biblical insights did not worry too much about the difference between the expositions of a trained theologian and those of an enthusiastic layperson—as long as the message meshed with their own understanding of how the world worked. God's word should be decipherable by those who receive it. Again reflecting the lessons of *The Emperor with No Clothes*, fundamentalism's systematicity sought to leverage the motivating power of insecurity to urge the suspicious to keep their reservations to themselves. If you needed to rely on an elite-sanctioned interpretation, you either did not have enough faith or you were so sinful that you could not hear and respond to God's call (an either-or conclusion that will emerge throughout this book).[86]

J. Gresham Machen offered a useful illustration when he compared knowledge of God to knowledge of China: "God has made us capable of receiving the information which He chooses to give. I cannot possibly evolve an account of China out of my own inner consciousness, but I am perfectly capable of understanding the account which comes to me from travelers who have been there themselves. So our reason is certainly insufficient to tell us about God unless He reveals Himself." Because God is not China—a physical location that I can know by learning from others, even if I have never been there—a pre-existing mental capacity must make us "capable of believing" in God, a capacity that could not be developed by elite education.

A revealing tension emerges here: from one angle, inerrancy evoked stable, pre-existing mind furniture to urge individuals to take every word of scripture at its literal and historic meaning—that if God stopped the earth's rotation in the book of Joshua that means *God literally stopped the earth's rotation*. But concurrently, inerrancy also leaned heavily on allegory, adoption, and rearticulations to fit changing social, cultural, and political conditions.[87] Put another way, fundamentalism urged common sense and plain facts but left unresolved what to do when common sense is not at all common, and the plain facts are not at all plain. Repositioning fundamentalism as a mechanism of rhetorical invention, such a tension was reconciled in the same way that all strong discourses remain sophisticated, timeless, stable, and viable: fundamentalism adjusted its formal plotlines, recurring characters, and conflict resolutions depending on the social conditions.

This sophistication has long drawn liberal accusations of hypocrisy and contradiction.[88] Many mainstream religious authorities criticize fundamentalist instruction for relying heavily on stories that interpret the Bible unevenly and appropriate ancient Jewish and pagan traditions. Critics have also noted the inevitable proof-texting this hermeneutic encouraged: the Bible was treated like an encyclopedia or dictionary where ideas could be extracted from anywhere in the thousands of pages, shorn of context or history, and thrown together to inform a wide range of complex social and political issues—from World War I to the New Deal to the civil rights movement to, more recently, same-sex marriage.[89] The Bible is actually quite cryptic, liberal theologians responded, and it must be to remain vibrant across generations. Biblical authors may be inspired witnesses to spiritual truths, but they felt no need to convey the scientific or historical truths of that inspiration. Like all good writers, they relied on myth, narrative, allegory, and poetry to offer as much insight and inspiration as possible. As mainline critics have pointed out, the Bible is not a book; it is a library. The "plain facts" are sometimes not facts at all, and no one interprets the Bible literally.[90] Fundamentalists suggested the Bible was inerrant in its "original autographs," but critics noted how opportunistic this argument was when the original autographs could not be found.

However, such criticisms miss the inventive and constitutive value of fundamentalism. First, inerrancy was valuable because it offered a strong intellectual defense. Conservative evangelicals looked at modernist forces, especially in terms of biblical scholarship, and saw an example of slippery-slope accommodation. For fundamentalists, even a minor relaxation of dogmatic rigidity often seemed to herald the dissolution of the community.[91] Describing fundamentalist inerrancy, Sharon Crowley wrote, "In rhetorical terms the ideology of clarity opens few spaces for invention; the only modifications permitted are those necessary to adapt the structure to new historical developments."[92] But I need to quibble with Crowley's assertion here because "the only modifications" is a subtle but massive qualifier. If inerrancy foreclosed invention, fundamentalism would have broken off from Protestantism into a separatist, esoteric cult. It didn't. Instead, it became one of the most creative religious movements in American history.[93] Inerrancy helped, not by conforming to the demands of rational argumentation but by allowing fundamentalism to reflect the movement, flexibility, and contingency so vital to rhetorical invention. More broadly, the doctrine of inerrancy reflects what Russian Bolsheviks did with Marxist rationalism, Islamic radicals do with the Koran, and constitutional originalists do with the law: in the face of upheaval, fundamentalists tried to ground their identity within the enduring guise of orthodoxy when in fact they could not (and cannot) escape the ephemeral world of rhetoric. Modernism not only posed a theological threat to conservative Protestants; it exposed a rhetorical deficiency. Conservative evangelicals were robbed of the vocabulary for explaining the world in persuasive ways. Thus, inerrancy was as much a response to this discursive deficiency as it was a method of scriptural interpretation (and in so doing fundamentalists are doing what we all do). Further, each fundamentalist group can be distinguished by their need to assert a singular authority, to ground allegiance in that authority, and to define social conditions accordingly.[94]

This transcendent feature points to a second rhetorical function: Christian fundamentalism reconciles conflicting conceptions of prophetic authority. Mind furnishing means *anyone* can read the plain facts. And these plain facts were not confined to the pages of scripture. Fundamentalism empowered its audience to detect connections between the plain facts on the page of the Bible and the events on the pages of the *New York Times,* offering what Jonathan J. Edwards would call "a new investment in current events and a new role as interpreters of the political and social landscape."[95] Furthermore, if fundamentalists could make their own connections, then elite, seminary-trained clergy—a relative rarity, especially in the rural South—were not needed. Inerrancy offered certainty, purity, and comfort: rather than consult people with more education—and open themselves up to further intellectual challenge—fundamentalists, with the help of the Holy Spirit, could interpret scripture themselves.[96]

Did this republican perspicacity make prophetic witness unnecessary? Jonathan J. Edwards suggested that in contrast to the elitism outside the community, fundamentalism forced lay readers to remain independent of Bible teachers and ministers.[97] Instead, Edwards argued, more local fundamentalist congregations could cohere around an immediate, situated version of sovereign, prophetic authority unencumbered by denominational sanction or elite credentials.

I agree with Edwards here, in part. But what he may be underemphasizing is that fundamentalism's republican perspicacity also allowed *anyone* to assume the role of prophetic witness. This is an unresolved tension in fundamentalism. While biblical interpretation is open to all, some community members still deferred to fundamentalist prophets when their theological capacities failed them. And those capacities often do just that. Until he died in 2016, readers of the best-selling *Left Behind* series wrote to fundamentalist prophet Tim LaHaye asking for assistance in navigating the "common sense" of Revelation.[98] The mind furnishing of such letter writers seems to be insufficient. But, paradoxically, Christian bookstores are full of deciphering guidebooks, and fundamentalist churches often feature prophetic rhetors interpreting the "plain reading" for a thirsty audience. On a poster with the prompt "What Do We Teach?" *Answers in Genesis* tells visitors to the Creation Museum in Petersburg, Kentucky, that they will learn that "the evidence from *observational science* confirms the Biblical account of history every time."[99] Notice how *observational,* as the operative term, illustrates the vocabulary reconciling authority—what *we* teach at *our* museum—with the capacity of lay visitors to observe biblical history in their own lives. Reflecting James Darsey's work on the prophetic ethos, fundamentalism's tension here allowed the development of republican prophetic witness, not confined to individual heroic rhetors, but open to anyone, especially reluctant voices who could not deny the radical calling put on their mind furnishing. It is even more potent, as forthcoming chapters will illustrate, if the reluctant prophet is one who infiltrates the elite but then returns to expose the lies to the true believers.[100]

An explicit mandate often follows closely behind the articulation of inerrancy. As Gresham Machen wrote, "If these views are true, they must determine our every action, in our capacity both as men and as ministers in the Church. God has placed us in the world as witnesses, and we cannot, in the interests of ecclesiastical harmony or for any other reason, allow our witness to become untrue."[101] Ecclesiastical harmony and shared experiences cannot make the witness untrue. You could forsake inerrancy, as Episcopalians or Methodists did because that is where the context led them, but it didn't change the biblical truths.

In July of 1925, in the grass outside a sweltering courthouse in Dayton, Tennessee, the inventive capacity of fundamentalism was put to the test. In what came to be known as the Scopes Monkey Trial, William Jennings Bryan—fundamentalist, ardent opponent of modernism and Darwinism, and three-time presidential candidate—helped prosecute high school teacher John T. Scopes for teaching evolution in a public school. The national attention drawn by Bryan's duel with Scopes's famed defense attorney Clarence Darrow offered the American public an opportunity to witness both the opportunities and the challenges of fundamentalist systematicity.

THE SCOPES MONKEY TRIAL

The Scopes Monkey Trial was an embarrassing defeat for anyone associated with fundamentalism and inerrancy, especially William Jennings Bryan.[102] According to the primary and secondary accounts of the trial, Clarence Darrow's science textbook overpowered Bryan's Christian Bible.[103] Despite their legal victory, most accounts furthered the connection between Bryan and his version of fundamentalism to stereotypes of ignorant, Bible-thumping fanatics and dirt-farming hillbillies. Everyone associated with inerrancy was tarred with the same brush: despite the efforts of Princeton Theological Seminary, J. Gresham Machen, and *The Fundamentals* pamphlets, fundamentalism looked like an outdated religion for simple people with simple beliefs who would soon have to adapt to modernism's forces or be relegated to history's dustbin.[104] The Scopes Trial became a turning point in the fundamentalist/modernist split because it shifted authority to secularists and liberal Christians and pushed fundamentalists to society's margins. As George Marsden wrote, "No longer could fundamentalists raise the level of discourse to the plane where any of their arguments would be taken seriously. Whatever they said would be overshadowed by the pejorative associations attached to the movement by the seemingly victorious secular establishment."[105] When Bryan died five days after the trial, the symbolism was obvious: fundamentalism had been killed not by a heart attack but by the forces of modernism.

Conventional explanations for fundamentalism's humiliation tend to focus on Bryan's concessions in the face of Darrow's rational examination. Darrow began chipping away by starting with a reasonable concession from Bryan: *humans are not made of salt*. Citing Jesus's statement in Matthew 5—"Ye are the salt of the earth"—Bryan affirmed a metaphorical reading: Christians should function like salt by saving God's people. He said, "I believe everything in the Bible should be accepted as it is given there; some of the Bible is given illustratively." Citing Matthew 5, Bryan continued, "I would not insist that man was actually salt, or that he had flesh of salt, but it is used in the sense of salt as saving God's people."[106]

When Darrow moved on to less metaphorical questions about the historical accuracy of the Bible, Bryan did seem to contradict inerrancy's demands. Darrow asked Bryan, "Do you think the earth was made in six days?" Bryan replied, "Not six days of twenty-four hours."

Darrow smelled blood.

When pressed, Bryan again conceded the metaphorical potential of the creation story in Genesis, admitting that the days could have been longer than twenty-four hours—up to and including millions of years each. But here is where the conventional explanation for Bryan's humiliation falls apart. The *New York Times* described the audience gasping in response to Bryan's concession. Not long after, the *Times* reported, the audience in the courtroom was laughing at Bryan's absurd responses to Darrow's questions. According to the *Times*, no one should pity Bryan and his ilk for being mocked; his "admission of ignorance of things boys and girls learn in high school, his floundering confessions that he knew practically nothing of geology, biology, philology, little of comparative religion, and even little of ancient history" should draw no sympathy. Scholars tend to concur with this interpretation, including George Marsden, who described Bryan's performance as a "debacle," as he was unable to "answer the standard village-atheist type questions regarding the literal interpretation of Scripture."[107]

These accounts need to be quibbled with. Bryan's performance, and the Scopes Trial more broadly, reveal important lessons for the eventual development of fundamentalism and its preferred hermeneutic far beyond concession and contradiction. As Erik Doxtader and Jonathan J. Edwards have pointed out, fundamentalism—first and foremost—demands engagement, investment, and the rigorous defense and marshaling of evidence. Bryan met these obligations.

First, he made his purpose clear: he cared little about John Scopes or the public educational curriculum in Dayton, Tennessee. He was there to defend the Bible against the threats of Darrow's ridicule. As Bryan put it on the witness stand, "I am not trying to get anything on record. I am simply trying to protect the Word of God against the greatest atheist or agnostic in the United States." After prolonged applause, he went on: "I want the papers to show I am not afraid to get on the stand in front of him and let him do his worst." Returning later to the same theme, Bryan said, "The reason I answer is not for the benefit of the superior court. It is to keep these gentlemen from saying I was afraid to meet them and let them question me, and I want the Christian world to know that any atheist, agnostic, unbeliever, can question me at any time as to my belief in God, and I will answer him." And, in a final example, "I answered the question in order to shut his mouth so that he cannot go out and tell his atheistic friends that I would not answer his questions. That is the only reason, no more reason in the world."[108] Bryan fulfilled the fundamentalist demand for worldly engagement.

Second, Bryan reflected how the ridicule of the world was to be accepted—and even embraced—by fundamentalists. Being laughed at by Darrow and ridiculed in the *New York Times* or by H. L. Mencken in the *Baltimore Evening Sun* meant nothing to Bryan. In a prescient way, many conservative Protestants shrugged off the humiliating accounts of Bryan's performance as a 1920s version of fake news: some assumed the *Times* and the *Sun* converted a few awkward responses into overblown fodder for the liberal media to attack the Bible.[109] Instead, Bryan expressed the telic assurance that would come to comfort a fundamentalist community immune to the world's scorn, suggesting in his posttrial comments that "the case was of little consequence," as the issue will "one day be settled right"—no matter what H. L. Mencken would write in his East Coast newspapers.[110]

Third, concessions and inconsistencies seemed to matter much more to liberal attackers than to fundamentalist defenders. For example, Anne Janette Johnson took Bryan's metaphorical concession of the six-day creation story as an example of Darrow "trick[ing] him into acknowledging that he himself sometimes turned to *interpretation* of the Bible rather than *literal acceptance* of the Bible."[111] But again, the standard of consistency set up by Johnson (and George Marsden) means little to fundamentalists, then and now. To confine inerrancy to its most literal and narrow sense—that every word of the Bible is absolutely true, scientifically and historically—is to perpetuate a caricature that does little to illuminate how this community was constituted.[112] Only outsiders would think it useful to bang fundamentalists over the head with the scientific inconsistencies of the Creation story. For many insiders, it was not a heretical error to adopt metaphorical readings of scripture, including understanding the six "days" of creation as "ages."[113]

Fourth, ignorance of worldly affairs did not matter to Bryan. Standards of rational argumentation, that one pursue the best obtainable version of the truth and use that knowledge to guide policy (in this case, the educational curriculum in Dayton, Tennessee), are insignificant. Bryan admitted to Darrow that he had never heard anyone speak of the number of people living in Egypt or China five thousand years ago before Darrow asked him about it on the stand; Bryan couldn't say whether there were thousands of books in the library on such subjects because he had never considered it, much less found them and read them; Bryan admitted that "he had never tried to find out" where Cain got his wife; he admitted that he had never given the geocentricity of the Joshua story "much thought"; and he admitted the geological implications of God stopping the earth's rotation never occurred to him. Bryan also didn't have much interest in examining the claims of other religions; nor had he considered critical accounts regarding the origins of scripture.[114]

Darrow asked Bryan about God's ability to make the earth stand still, as the Old Testament book of Joshua details.[115] When Bryan said it was possible, Darrow replied, "Mr. Bryan, have you ever pondered what would have happened to the earth if it had stood still?"

"No," Bryan said, "The God I believe in could have taken care of that, Mr. Darrow."

Darrow replied, "Don't you know it would have been converted into a molten mass of matter?"

In such a response, Darrow betrayed the ignorance common to the fundamentalism opposition: Bryan's response was not scientific; it was theological. Giving the scientific implications much thought meant nothing to him. Instead, in response to Darrow's probing, Bryan would have Darrow read aloud from the Bible in the courtroom, and then affirm what was just read as his position.

What do these exchanges add up to? Bryan's rhetorical performance not only met the existing demand of fundamentalist inerrancy in its infancy; he lent insight into fundamentalism's primary discursive plot points for decades to come. Why, then, as Harding made clear, did the primary and secondary accounts of the trial, even those written for sympathetic audiences, conclude that Darrow humiliated Bryan and his ilk? Keep in mind that the court ruled in Bryan's favor. And Bryan surely did not think Darrow humiliated him. There is no record, even from his wife, of Bryan admitting defeat.[116] Right after the trial, Bryan went on a victory tour across Tennessee, drawing huge crowds and predicting that other state legislatures would follow the lead and also prohibit teaching evolution in the classroom.[117] Those attracted to the victory tour were quick to forgive Bryan for his concession to a metaphorical account of the six-day Creation story. Why, then, were scholars and journalists so confident in his humiliation?

Here is one possible explanation, informed by the hermeneutic of systematicity: fundamentalist inerrancy demands, above all else, the articulation of absolute confidence, even if you must deny the material reality right in front of your face. This is the primary constitutive demand, the price of admission into the community; further, this is the standard by which fundamentalists police the constitutive boundaries of the community. The higher moral ground always goes to the inerrantists who could articulate a "more literal" confidence than anyone else.[118] Thus, Bryan's performance, and the larger historical sensemaking apparatus built up around it, begins to show signs of cracking in meeting these constitutive demands.

First, systematic inerrancy demands absolute confidence—the calm assurance that can only come from divine certainty—even in the face of withering rational assaults. But courtroom accounts describe Bryan losing his cool at times, even snapping at Darrow when he heard the laughter of an audience that he thought he controlled.[119] Second, fundamentalists demonstrated their constitutive potency by gathering allies. But Bryan seemed to lack instrumental evidence of his inventiveness. The presiding judge was a religious man who doubted evolution, but even he felt the need to step in during Darrow's cross-examination of Bryan and halt the trial to salvage his reputation; and the next day he expunged Bryan's testimony and stopped Darrow's continued examination of Bryan.[120] In a vivid example of Bryan's seepage, even Bryan agreed with the judge's decision: "I fully agree [with the judge's expunging] with the court that the testimony taken yesterday was not legitimate or proper."[121] While it mattered little if the *New York Times* or the *Baltimore Evening Sun* mocked you, if you also lost the support of conservative Protestant journals and bulletins, you were in trouble. Finally, the symbolism of Bryan's death just five days after the trial cannot be overlooked. Future public conversations about Scopes had to include Bryan's death, and the symbolism was undeniable (despite Bryan's legal victory and short-lived victory tour). Imagine, for instance, how different the historical narrative would be if Darrow had been struck by lightning the day after the trial.

Bryan could not frame the debate from the grave, and the symbolism of his death functioned as another example of fundamentalism in retreat. Harding went as far to suggest that "Bryan's death proved even Bryan knew the Bible was not literally true."[122] The emperor's nudity had been exposed—not by a clear-eyed little boy, or even by the performance of a declining three-time presidential candidate. Instead, Scopes lends insight into an important inflection point in the development of fundamentalist inerrancy: the emperor's nudity was exposed through a complex confluence of insiders and outsiders, messaging, and social conditions. All that—not just Bryan's concessions or heart attack—shattered the fragile illusion of inerrancy in a way that reflected a broader betrayal of American culture against the community.

Fundamentalists faced an encounter with disbelief.[123] They were beaten, and were left with only two possible responses: adjust their hermeneutic in accordance with modernism's demands, or beat a hasty retreat into the theological wilderness. Many fundamentalists did quit their denominations, especially in the northern US, and those who remained fell silent or retreated from civic affairs.[124]

Fundamentalism could have withered away at this point. Indeed, many fundamentalists assumed they would become irrelevant. Speaking of their lost cause, some adopted the language of martyrdom; they accepted their position on society's margins just as Christ was rejected during his time on Earth. Many fundamentalist leaders fulfilled this prophecy by fading into extremism and irrelevancy.[125] However, as the historical record reveals, fundamentalism and its most prominent rhetors did not remain on the margins for long.

RETREAT TO THE WILDERNESS

While the discursive source of fundamentalism's humiliation is often misunderstood, the outcome was undeniable: fundamentalism was not ready to cohabitate with modernism's rational argumentation as the sensemaking mechanism for institutional avenues of power. Many fundamentalists examined the terrain, saw the shifting religious, cultural, social, economic, and political momentum, and decided to withdraw.[126] Most of what could be considered "political" for fundamentalists meant shoring up the internal walls of their own subculture. Fundamentalism fell into a defensive crouch: if the secular world was doomed to decay, why bother with it?

Although Dwight Moody was long dead, his legacy again offered rhetorical guidance. Moody had built a series of institutions in the nineteenth century, including a summer conference for conservative ministers to fortify themselves against modernist liberalism and a Bible institute that would later become the premier school for fundamentalist training. Later, Reuben Torrey, Moody's heir, built up the Moody Bible Institute as a training ground in the "aggressive methods" of countering liberalizing seminaries and divinity schools such as Harvard, Yale, and Union. Torrey's effectiveness revealed that separate institutions could steel Christian workers against modernizing forces without compromising their faith.[127] Later in the twentieth century, conservative evangelicals began socializing mostly with friends from church groups, donating money mainly to evangelical agencies, reading material from Christian bookstores, and sending children to Bible camps in the summer and to Bible institutes or evangelical seminaries for higher education.[128]

Exile suited fundamentalism. Many equated their marginalized position with a martyrdom struggle in which the steadfast and faithful battle a wicked and modern world.[129] Fundamentalism also sought to address the weaknesses exposed by Scopes, and to sharpen its offensive tools in a way that would, one day, allow it to enter traditional avenues of power. Already aligned with a hierarchical, authoritarian, and marginalized outlook, fundamentalism adopted vocabularies marked by militant individualism. Recall that before the modernist/fundamentalist split in the 1920s, liberal Protestants were considered part of the collective Christian community. However, fundamentalists soon redrew sharper boundaries, not only against secular culture but also against anyone or any idea associated with modernism. This encouraged fundamentalists to push liberal Protestants outside the fold.[130]

Nothing Short of a Great Civil War

The revolutions of the 1960s further cemented fundamentalism's marginalization. For many drawn to this community, it looked like a conspiratorial alliance was forming among secular humanists in academia, media, popular culture, and political institutions, each keen on further marginalizing conservative Protestants.[131] As evidence, prominent fundamentalist rhetors such as Jerry Falwell, Pat Robertson, and James Dobson pointed to feminism, shifting gender roles, campus unrest, sexual promiscuity, abortion, cloning, euthanasia, gambling addictions, and pornography—each representing a frontal assault on the intimate private sphere of the nuclear family and a larger assault on society. As Dobson wrote, "Societies can be no more stable than the social foundation on which they sit. That foundation is the traditional family, defined as one man and one woman living together in a committed, loving marriage. If that institution crumbles, the entire superstructure of ordered society is destined to collapse."[132] The battle lines were made clear. Liberal secular humanists and their amorality were determined to betray America's pseudotheocratic foundations, attack the most intimate confines of marriage and family, and, publicly, "remove every evidence of faith in God from this entire culture," Dobson warned.[133] In contrast, he continued, fundamentalists drew their strength from the "wisdom of the Bible and the Judeo-Christian ethic, rather than from the humanistic notions of today's theorists."[134]

Dobson would describe the decline of universal, biblical law as like "a cancer that's spread through this entire nation."[135] Cancer evokes a militant response.[136] Jerry Falwell would phrase this response well as a war "not between fundamentalists and liberals, but between those who love Jesus Christ and those who hate Him."[137] Fundamentalist discourses were aligned accordingly, and the result was the development of a language of militant individualism. For instance, Francis Schaeffer, an intellectual heavyweight in fundamentalist circles, wrote, "Again we must see that what we face is a totality and not just bits and pieces. It is not too strong to say that we are at war, and there are no neutral parties in the struggle. One either confesses that God is the final authority, or one confesses that Caesar is Lord."[138] Schaeffer then compared the struggle against modernism to the American Revolution, in which "the colonists used force in defending themselves."[139] Pat Robertson insisted, in a 1992 message, "Either [America] returns to her Christian roots and then to further greatness, or she will continue to legalize sodomy, slaughter innocent babies, destroy the minds of her children, squander her resources and sink into oblivion."[140] As FitzGerald argued, Robertson kept calling for the return of Christian nation and he never quit connecting diversity and pluralism to utter chaos. James Dobson wrote in his book *Children at Risk*: "Nothing short of a great Civil War of Values rages today throughout North America. Two sides with vastly differing and incompatible worldviews are locked in bitter conflict that permeates every level of society. Bloody battles are being fought on a thousand fronts, both inside and outside of government. Open any daily newspaper and you'll find accounts of the latest Gettysburg, Waterloo, Normandy or Stalingrad."[141] It is, Dobson wrote, "a war over ideas. And someday soon, I believe, a winner will emerge and the loser will fade from memory."[142]

The discourse does indicate, however, that fundamentalism's retreat to the wilderness would only be temporary. Notice how the symptoms of godless secularism were not confined to the private sphere of the home or family; those attacks were supplemented by, or reflective of, larger public struggles. But if fundamentalists were focused only on saving souls, as Moody's "wrecked vessel" passage recalls, why worry about cloning, pornography, or the Ten Commandments on the courthouse steps? Consider one answer: because fundamentalist discourse reflected a concern with the symbolic constructions of Christian symbols—not as acts of faith or as conversion mechanisms—but as sites of public struggle against crumbling hierarchies of religious dominance, traditional gender roles, and social status.[143] Dobson, Falwell, Schaffer, and

Robertson would represent a constitutional potency far beyond saving individual souls, viewing their felt rejection from public spaces as a site of counterpublic potential.

Note also that fundamentalists could compare their marginalization with the direct political effectiveness of liberal Protestants within the social movements of the 1960s and 1970s. Because liberal Protestants were more engaged in the civil rights, women's rights, and anti–Vietnam War movements, fundamentalists viewed liberal political intervention with envy, and soon they began to supplement their focus on saving souls with resentment for neglecting the political sphere. As Falwell put it, the idea that religion and politics should be separate "was invented by the Devil to keep Christians from running their own country."[144] Falwell shifted political focus from isolation to engagement by equating cultural conflicts with grand battles between good and evil.

Although only temporary, fundamentalism's post-Scopes marginalization facilitated the development of a more militant vocabulary that would come to resonate with individuals uneasy with the cultural revolutions of the 1960s and 1970s. Witnessing symptoms of moral decay, fundamentalism began to leverage the assumption that the US was once a Christian nation but was now falling away.[145] Fundamentalists assumed renewed responsibility for aggressive political action to defend their faith, to protect public and private morality, and to restore America's Christian past.[146] As FitzGerald put it, Jerry Falwell "constructed a jeremiad that conservative Christians had to get into politics or see the destruction of the nation."[147]

However, I think we need to be careful in assuming militancy allowed fundamentalism to "re-emerge" from the wilderness. The re-emerging metaphor implies a referential approach to sensemaking—as if masses of coherent fundamentalist audiences moved from the center before Scopes to the margins, and then back to the center through this militant discourse. But that is not how *communities* are constructed. Instead, discourse functions in oscillation with shifting social conditions and potent rhetors, like Dobson and Falwell, equipping dispersed and fragmented individuals with an orientational compass that guided them toward a constituency of fundamentalists—a constituency that did not, and would not, exist apart from the following discursive themes.

First, fundamentalism reflected the confidence of true believers. Telic confidence would not be disrupted by social upheaval. Dobson described a "law written on the heart of every human being"—not just those who listened to his radio program or bought his parenting books. The "universe has a boss," he would go on to say: a boss who "has very clear ideas about what is right and what is wrong."[148] History advanced in a telic destination based on these laws and this boss, and America could heed it or temporarily divert toward godless secularism. Additionally, fundamentalist discourse appropriated scientific vocabularies. William Jennings Bryan and the confident ignorance he displayed in the Scopes Monkey Trial would become supplemented by the appearance of systematic rigor. It had to be. Bryan's inability to converse with Darrow revealed the limits of unsystematic, dogmatic vocabularies. For example, Focus on the Family saw threats to the family not only as a betrayal of the law written on the hearts by God but also as a contradiction to the abundance of social scientific studies affirming the traditional nuclear family against the harmful impact of cohabitation, divorce, contraception, abortion, and same-sex marriage.[149] Fundamentalist discourse also appropriated the aggrieved subjectivity of marginalized communities, especially as the civil rights movement and its leaders—decades later—would evolve into courageous symbols of truth spoken to power. For example, James Dobson went to Montgomery, Alabama, to support Chief Justice Roy Moore's two-and-half-ton monument to the Ten Commandments at the state courthouse. Dobson drew clear parallels from the historic location to his community's marginalization: "It is very, very ironic that this event and this confrontation is occurring in Montgomery, where a little black lady by the name of Rosa Parks, in 1955, had no power. She had no influence. She had no money. She was not a political leader, but she saw something that she felt was evil."[150] Like Rosa Parks, Dobson and his community seem to be without power, influence, money, or political clout, facing off against an empowered evil. For Parks that evil was white supremacy; for Dobson it was "the total displacement of Christian imagery by a godless secularism."[151]

CLOSER TO MIDNIGHT

In fundamentalism's telic conceptualization, a cosmic momentum drives time forward toward a definitive end. Events and experiences are inevitable, unalterable, and determined by external forces beyond human control.[152] Marginalized and disempowered communities, in particular, are encouraged by this telic temporality to reinterpret chaos as a sign of divine progress. Consider the comfort telic temporality provides an audience that looks out onto the world and sees nothing but upheaval and disorder. Telic temporality not only portrays disorder as inevitable; it also portrays suffering as a reminder of impending redemption. In this process, geopolitical turmoil, demographic shifts, social upheaval, natural disasters, and ecological crises are reframed not as random events but as part of a complex narrative that drives history forward. Ultimately, even the most tragic events connect to future redemption. The more cataclysmic the event and the more painful the suffering, the better the future appears.[153]

Consider how common clock-watching metaphors are within fundamentalist discourse. True believers can detect the events that reflect the clock's hands moving closer to midnight.[154] For instance, the 1972 movie *A Thief in the Night* opened with a clock ticking against a black background. The viewer then saw the clock on the nightstand coming gradually into focus as a message from Jesus Christ appeared on the screen: "Keep a sharp lookout! For you do not know when I will come, at evening, at midnight, early dawn or daybreak. Don't let me find you sleeping!"[155] Additionally, each chapter in Tim LaHaye's first book about biblical prophecy, *The Beginning of the End*, begins with a clock face and the hands getting closer to midnight as the reader is led through the complicated symbols of Christ's Second Coming. John Hagee, pastor of the fifteen-thousand-member Cornerstone Church in Texas and a prominent fundamentalist, began his book *Daniel to Doomsday: The Countdown Has Begun* thus: "God has a similar clock, my friends, and its hands *never* moved backward. Doomsday—the stroke of midnight is coming."[156] Notice how, within fundamentalism, chaos and disorder do not align with a "secular" narrative arc.[157] Instead, signs of the looming apocalypse are real only when they are situated within the proper dispensationalist stage. Jerry Falwell was known for connecting chaotic events on the front page of the newspaper with a pre-existing historical narrative featuring familiar protagonists and antagonists.[158] In one sermon series, Falwell is shown in Israel walking out Armageddon's battle lines and warning viewers that the time of Tribulation could already be occurring.[159]

Following the next step in this telic progression, I want to explore how fundamentalism's vocabulary repositioned chaotic social and political events as unavoidable, acceptable, and even preferable as a mechanism to restore order and justice to a sinful world.[160] Rather than prevent or mediate chaos, it seems fundamentalism's telic urgings encourage audiences to hasten the progression of history. Telic implications are reflected in the fact that a significant population of Americans may resist efforts to avoid crisis and chaos; indeed, many view chaos as a necessary reordering mechanism. Notice how fundamentalism does not shy away from pain and suffering: as the world collapses around them, fundamentalists take comfort in knowing their temporary suffering will be rewarded. For example, Falwell often preached that his brand of fundamentalism meant followers would face outright hostility from the world: "Learn to pay the price. If you are going to be a champion for Christ, learn to endure hardness . . . You won't always have the applause of men." In another sermon, he said, "You will have Satan as your archenemy. The moment you entered the family of God, Satan declared war on you. The Christian life is to be a competitive, combative life."[161] Consequently, fundamentalism limits opportunities for democratic deliberation, cooperation, and identification. Even more troubling, the points of correspondence detailed in this chapter align with a clear propensity toward violence as a way to achieve redemption. There is nothing wrong with breaking a few eggs to cook this telic omelet.

Fundamentalist rhetors began to advocate directly for domestic policies whose consequences could hasten their telic preferences, such as gutting government support for the poor, displaying a cruel apathy toward redressing the AIDS epidemic in the 1980s as a way to punish gay men for their immorality, and, more recently, supporting immigration policies that would dissuade asylum seekers by making the process so miserable.[162] Bob Jones, founder of Bob Jones University and an ardent fundamentalist, summarized the political implications in this way: "The church is not told to change the moral climate of the world. The commission of the Church is to save men and women out of the world. Anybody who knows and believes the Scripture recognizes that the moral situation of the world is going to grow worse and worse as we go further and further into the apostasy."[163]

Internationally, few actions can foment catastrophe like large-scale violent conflict. Reflecting Roderick Hart's assertion that rhetorical criticism contains predictive potential, it should surprise no one that fundamentalism tends to align with hawkish attitudes toward American military intervention.[164] These political leanings stand in sharp contrast to the ecumenical and collective engagement in social issues marking the history of American Christianity, including active involvement in poverty aid, temperance, and suffrage.[165] Additionally, collective solidarity, including ecumenical relationships with people of other faiths and large-scale intergovernmental organizations, such as the United Nations, are treated with suspicion by fundamentalism. Many anticipated the rise of a world government run by elite liberals as a sign of the consolidation of power that must precede the Rapture.[166] Finally, a central theme of fundamentalism was the reassurance that justice will be served and that dissenters will suffer when the world ends.[167] The Creation Museum in Petersburg, Kentucky, features an illustrative image: a large poster titled "The Lake of Fire" features the Apostle John exiled on the Island of Patmos looking down on "the Judgment of the wicked." Beneath him is a pit full of tormented, shapeless figures, along with a passage from Revelation 21:8: "But the cowardly, unbelieving, abominable, murderers, sexual immoral, sorcerers, idolaters, and all liars, their place will be the lake that burns with fire and brimstone. This is the second death."¹⁶⁸ Such representations, however disconcerting, reflect a required step to make way for the Second Coming of Christ and, even more urgently, for the supreme reign of fundamentalists, on Earth, now.¹⁶⁹

Militant Half-Wish

I want to circle back now and consider how someone like Nancy James would make sense of such messaging. Would the humble, apologetic, and patient Nancy Jameses of the world be comfortable equating Christians marching in civil rights protests with hatred for Christ and love for Caesar? Would Nancy James be comfortable with James Dobson equating the crumbling of the structural integrity of her family with Roy Moore's monument to the Ten Commandments? As a meaning-making exercise, such dark and cynical messaging informs Charles Strozier's use of the term *half-wish*—a useful description of the inevitable tensions that emerge when fundamentalism's telic aspirations confront pragmatic social and political realities. A confluence of human compassion and democratic mechanisms can contain such telic consequences. Put another way, Dobson or Falwell uttering it does not make it so. Many fundamentalists would recoil if confronted with the pragmatic consequences of these telic urgings. Adhering to the principles of rhetorical invention, fundamentalist rhetors, instead, fill pews and sell books by tossing arguments against the wall to see which ones stick. Rhetorical slippage is evident when fundamentalist rhetors have to issue public apologies for scandalous statements—which is not at all uncommon. Jerry Falwell's remark about the cause of the 9/11 terrorist attacks, for instance, functions as a vivid case study of Strozier's half-wish. On September 13, 2001, in an appearance on Pat Robertson's *700 Club,* Falwell said, "The abortionists have got to bear some burden for this because God will not be mocked. And when we destroy 40 million little innocent babies, we make God mad. I really believe that the pagans, and the abortionists, and the feminists, and the gays and the lesbians . . . the ACLU, People for the American Way, all of them have tried to secularize America. I point the finger in their face and say, 'You helped this happen.'" Pat Robertson responded, "Well, I entirely concur."¹⁷⁰

Falwell's remarks were criticized in religious and political circles, and he was forced to apologize.¹⁷¹ It soon became clear that Falwell's argument would not stick. But one may wonder whether Falwell should be faulted for throwing the argument that lesbians helped cause 9/11 against the wall. Remember that he lived in a community that gobbles up eighty million copies of the *Left Behind* novels, equates school lunch programs with Joseph Stalin, and wears eschatological timepieces that see political progress as humanistic efforts to delay Christ's return. Rhetoric that equates the USSR with Satan (Graham), diversity with chaos (Robertson), scientists with enemies of the American Revolution (Schaeffer), females in the workplace with Gettysburg and Stalingrad (Dobson), and efforts to redress racism with government overreach (Bob Jones) may not be irrational. A more useful avenue of research would focus on exploring how the rhetorical dimensions of Nancy James's life are informed by such dark and cynical appropriations and associations. Can such discourse account for all who may be within the fundamentalist community? And how strong are the links between this militant—even catastrophic—urging and the fundamentalist community produced? Exploring these questions offers the underlying force for this entire project.

Twenty-five hundred years of rhetorical theory and criticism remind us that the *intent* of fundamentalist rhetors is less relevant than the consequences produced by its constitutive potential. Rhetoric induces attitudes, intended or not. Ideas have consequences. Words matter. People suffer and die as a consequence of such utterances, even if they produce "half-wishes."[172] New social arrangements are constructed and affirmed when fundamentalist discourse equates MTV with ISIS. As Chantal Mouffe argued, productive discourse reconceives the friend–enemy relation so that those with different opinions and perspectives are understood to be respected adversaries (rather than satanic enemies). Mouffe wrote that, ideally, opponents are "no longer perceived as an enemy to be destroyed, but as . . . somebody whose ideas we combat but whose right to defend those ideas we do not put into question."[173] During its time in the wilderness, fundamentalism developed in opposition to these argumentative ideals. Instead of legitimizing opponents, fundamentalism developed clear, interchangeable enemies who needed to be vanquished rather than engaged.

Catastrophe and Redemption

Fundamentalist counterpublic speech makes clear what redemption looks like for insiders: telic confidence in the catastrophic reordering of a sinful world. But what does redemption look like for the pluralistic and the secular? Can secular humanists and liberal Protestants alike be redeemed through telic catastrophe? If so, what rhetorical function does that mechanism of shared redemption perform?

Rhetorical scholars have yet to fully examine how the answer to these questions informs pragmatic political practice in the US far beyond religious discourse. Grappling fully with the political implications of fundamentalism is not easy. I think many scholars and journalists avoid all that by assuming that fundamentalism's telic endpoint includes the conversion and redemption of the entire world, including secular humanists. Jonathan J. Edwards, for example, argued that fundamentalist redemption narratives "establish the discursive framework bringing together the spiritual work of the Fundamentalist church and the political redemption of the pluralistic and secular world."[174] More specifically, Edwards located three routes for redemption in fundamentalist discourse: unbelievers can be saved, cured, or eradicated.[175] For insiders, the first two options dominate fundamentalist discourse. Fundamentalism urges redemption for insiders by adopting the counterpublic speech and norms of the community. However, there is little evidence in fundamentalist discourse that those first two redemption mechanisms are available to the pluralistic and the secular. Recall that this *impossible majority* demands protection not just from the state but from the entire edifice: the courts, the political leadership, even the popular culture. And because it cannot ever meet such a standard, fundamentalism will always stand in opposition to the collective efforts to redeem the world.

Redemption and Regression

The reader may be aware that fundamentalist discourse is replete with regressive temporal references and assume that a fourth option is available to the secular world: redemption through regression. Karma Chávez, for example, described such nostalgic vocabulary as "countermemory." Fundamentalism looks back fondly on the period before the upheaval of the 1960s, when America was good, gender roles were more traditional, sex occurred only in marriage (missionary style), everyone went to church on Sunday mornings, and the social fabric had yet to be stained by the revolutions of the 1960s, media devolution, and various forms of family experimentation.[176] In a 2005 *Focus on the Family* magazine article titled "Our Father Knows Best," Tom Minnery responds to liberal critics who have accused Focus on the Family of trying to take the country back to the 1950s. "Is that so bad?" he asks. "It was a time when two-parent families were the norm and children could pray in public school classrooms. It was a time when children were safe to play in the neighborhood and laws protected pre-born children." Additionally, "Our society acknowledged God, valued families and protected innocent human life."[177] James Dobson also illustrated this regressive nostalgia well when he described his own upbringing:

I attended high school during the "Happy Days" of the 1950s, and I never saw or even heard of anyone taking an illegal drug. It happened, I suppose, but it was certainly no threat to me. Some students liked to get drunk, but alcohol was not a big deal in my social environment. Others played around with sex, but the girls who did were considered "loose" and were not respected. Virginity was still in style for males and females. Occasionally a girl came up pregnant, but she was packed off in a hurry, and I never knew where she went. As for homosexuals and lesbians, I heard there were a few around, but I didn't know them personally. There were certainly no posters on our bulletin boards advertising Gay Pride Month or Condom Week. Most of my friends respected their parents, went to church on Sundays, studied hard enough to get by, and lived fairly clean lives. There were exceptions, of course, but this was the norm.[178]

Rather than characterize the 1960s with advancements in social and racial equality, regressive references in Focus on the Family discourse emphasize "Five Bads": drugs and rock music, the sexual revolution, feminism, divorce, and "God is dead" theology.[179] Some have cited such nostalgic references as evidence for fundamentalism's regressive political urges. Carrie Anne Platt described Focus's logic as "hope for the future [that] can be restored through a return to the family values and rituals of the past."[180] Richard Popp argued, "This notion of time was instrumental to Focus's family-centric ideology: rearing children in a climate steeped in the past's values ensures the regeneration of values for the future."[181]

I want to concede regressive allusions in fundamentalist discourse but also to transcend those by noting a series of pressing tensions that actually makes the nostalgic longing for a bygone era less constitutively potent than a catastrophic telic temporality. First, regression to the 1950s seems like a quaint and impractical solution in the face of fundamentalism's portrayal of the post-1960s world. Fundamentalist discourse is so bleak; could returning to the Happy Days of the 1950s really salvage the family, culture, or state? In a January 2000 newsletter, Dobson seemed to indicate that society may be too far gone: "I wish it were not necessary to share these discouraging trends and predictions about the family in North America, but this is a reality. If traditional marriage and parenthood continue to lose ground year by year, marriage and parenthood as we have known them will soon die. That would mean absolute chaos for mankind."[182] Second, there is little historical evidence linking the Bible-based family to the building blocks of a righteous society. The plotlines and characters of Dobson's Happy Days are not reflected in the Bible. And the romanticized, sentimental Victorian family is a historical fiction. As most social histories make clear, the family has always been a dysfunctional work-in-progress, and nostalgia for a golden age of the American family draws on a past that never was.[183] Further, in 1948, 69 percent of white men said they had paid for sex, and two-thirds of Americans were not involved in religious activities before the 1950s (I know of no data on preferred sexual positions).[184] Third, fundamentalism's political associations linking the private to the public sphere seem tenuous. Even the sentimentalized version of the nuclear family—where it did exist—was facilitated by many of the policies fundamentalists tend to vehemently oppose, including robust government support programs for education and housing.[185] Instead, nostalgic appeals to family align with the rejection of the structural remedies to broken families, such as limiting mass incarceration and redressing institutional racism.[186]

Rational argumentation could debunk and expose inaccurate and misguided rhetorical connections. Focus on the Family's grasp of history is cloudy, their use of social science research misguided, their systematic hermeneutic nonfalsifiable, and their proof-texting opportunistic. Dobson and his community are not marginalized. Fetal tissue research did not cause the decline of Happy Days. Furthermore, the political associations seem like a shameless attempt to exert fundamentalism's political will on the Republican Party, especially those threatened by the inevitable liberalizing forces and historical arc bending away from their interests. Again, Dobson and his ilk could have splintered into an off-brand AM radio program and self-published parenting books that no one bought. They didn't, in part, because such appeals depend on a standard of rational argumentation that means nothing to them. Instead, they want secure walls and few entrances. They want prayer in schools and the Ten Commandments on the courthouse steps. They want Gorsuch and Kavanaugh. And they want Donald Trump.

Recall Edwards's three redemptive options: saved, cured, or eradicated. The latter seems to be the only option for those outside the fold. Fundamentalists are encouraged to withdraw, remain uncorrupted, and wait for the Second Coming. Fundamentalism is clear about what it will look like when the unbelieving world is redeemed through eradication. This discourse is replete with thick, gory descriptions of the secular world being hunted, caught, and tormented before it is cast into a lake of fire as true believers watch from the cliffs above. This does not mean fundamentalists are politically apathetic. Rather, fundamentalists further their paradoxical affinity for chaos by expending their political energies on projects designed to pave the way for the Second Coming.[187] Those actions rarely involve improving social conditions, like marching to increase the minimum wage or advocating for peace through UN intervention.[188] Such efforts are likely to be seen as misguided or pointless. Instead, fundamentalism encourages the most pernicious type of political activity: the anticipation of perpetual chaos.

Return from the Wilderness

Many have assumed the humiliation of the Scopes Monkey Trial sent fundamentalists into the wilderness for most of the twentieth century . . . until they were inspired by a group of potent rhetors and threatening social revolutions to re-emerge from the margins and to enter the public sphere with full-throated force in the 1970s and 1980s. Susan Harding articulated this account when she suggested that the events of the 1970s revealed a "hidden Protestant majority that was already in some sense manifesting itself in high political places."[189] She continued: "Once they saw themselves, and were seen, as related to one another and, taken together, as the Protestant majority, their marginal days were numbered." Harding was referring to a combined effect that included the rise of prominent fundamentalist rhetors, such as Jerry Falwell and Pat Robertson, along with a number of changing social conditions. Frances FitzGerald suggested that Falwell, in particular, "introduced the fundamentalist sense of perpetual catastrophe, and of war between the forces of good and evil, into national politics, where the rhetoric has remained ever since."[190]

Harding and FitzGerald represent a common but misguided perspective. Their empirical data is not wrong, and these historical events are not fabricated. Rather, as sociologists and historians, they neglect to consider the powerful constitutive role of rhetoric in fundamentalism's evolution.

Consider the limitations in these accounts. First, it seems to Harding and FitzGerald that fundamentalism's return from the wilderness was almost inevitable. It was not. Christian fundamentalism could have died a slow death in the wilderness, akin to a branch of the FLDS in rural Mexico or the Branch Davidians outside Waco, Texas. It did not. It ended up in the White House. Consider James Dobson's response when the White House called to thank him for helping to elect George W. Bush: Dobson told the caller many Christians believed the country was "on the verge of self-destruction" but that "God has given us a reprieve." "I believe," he added, "it's a short reprieve."[191] Moody, Schaeffer, Falwell, and Robertson had been sounding similar themes for one hundred years—to no avail. Now these vocabularies were being articulated into Karl Rove's ear.

Second, Ronald Reagan's rise, the IRS's attempt to desegregate southern Christian schools, and Focus on the Family's dominance can all be mistaken for endogenous explanations for fundamentalism's ascent; in fact, those rhetors and those conditions could also function as after-the-fact, exogenous explanations for deeper, subtler, constitutive developments.

Third, already *manifesting, re-emerging,* and *returning* are problematic terms to describe fundamentalism's position. Such labels assume a static, referential approach to fundamentalism. It is important to stress that there were no "fundamentalists" in the nineteenth or early twentieth century—at least not the type assumed by Harding that would be drawn to Falwell and Dobson. Fundamentalists were not at the center of power in the nineteenth century . . . *because there were no fundamentalists*. Few believed the Bible was literally true, and even fewer cared much about stem cells, same-sex attraction, pornography, feminism, or even abortion. A "hidden Protestant" of the type that Harding describes could not look around and see other conservatives worried about the IRS desegregating their schools, fetal tissue research, or welfare shirkers—those symbolic dimensions contained no constitutive potency. The iterative impact of these points of formal correspondence reveals an important finding: there is no essential fundamentalism. There are no social conditions that inevitably unite this community. And there are no rhetors—no matter how dynamic—that can "introduce" fundamentalist vocabularies into national politics. That is not how sensemaking works.

George Gallup did not find a hidden group of inerrantists hiding in a church basement in Denton, Texas. A third of Americans in 1976 may have articulated a literal belief in the Bible, but precisely zero Americans consistently operationalized that belief. Instead, fundamentalism creates audiences that would not otherwise exist. There is no fundamentalist discourse apart from the audience it produces, and no audience apart from its discourse. Without that dynamic oscillation, without an audience, each rhetor examined here and their messaging would have faded into obscurity—unless, of course, they end up being burned alive outside Waco.

CONCLUSION

We live our lives among complex strands of discourse.[192] While fundamentalism may be one important strand, there is nobody who is totally and completely a "fundamentalist." When such a subjectivity enters a room, a whole host of inseparable individual identity markers tag along, each reliant on various discourses to also produce coherent regional, political, cultural, economic, and social affiliations. As a critical tool, the homology informs how discourses can unite at a common, shared, foundational source, especially when one feels threatened by an unfamiliar and complex set of messages and conditions. In other words, the subjectivity required for an individual to resonate with inerrancy is not confined to biblical interpretation of the Jonah and the Whale story. The subjectivity required for an individual to explain their expectations of a divine rapture through premillennialism is not confined to an actual apocalypse. The subjectivity required for individual to explain the orbit of Sputnik as a product of an alliance with Satan is not confined to the USSR's space program. The subjectivity required for conspiratorial suspicion of intellectual elites is not confined to the biblical interpretations coming from Duke Divinity School. And the subjectivity required to orient dispersed individuals toward a catastrophe-minded direction is not limited to the threats posed by gun control, climate change, or Hillary Clinton.

For rhetorical critics, fundamentalism's constitutive potential points to sites of further exploration. In the following chapters, I want to show that from higher—even undetectable—levels of abstraction this formal branching-out potential can be detected in constructing catastrophe-oriented individuals far beyond the confines of religious interpretation. I make that argument in the following chapters by describing how the central point of formal correspondence described here can also be detected in ecological, cultural, and political discourses.

CHAPTER 2

Ecological Catastrophe and the Rhetoric of Anti-Environmentalism

IF YOU were ever to confront a wandering traveler interested in learning more about who Americans are, what we value, and how we make sense of the world, public conversations about climate change would be an instructive place to begin. Climate change is the quintessential issue of our historical moment. It engages the entire human condition. And it combines narrative elements of big business, global economies, religion, politics, science, and media—all with the possible fate of civilization itself on the line.

As I work to demonstrate the political and theoretical utility of the homology, climate change is instructive because it reflects the human need to attach symbolic resources to unfamiliar, complex, and threatening messaging; and climate change informs how pre-existing worldviews influence our ability to make sense of warnings from scientific experts about a changing planet and the reactions to such warnings. For example, climate change skepticism is not limited to the technical or the scientific; rather, it engages deeper and broader elements of culture, religion, and society.

The purpose of this chapter is to deploy the catastrophic homology to illuminate the source of those deeper and broader elements by exploring the relationship between Christian fundamentalism and anti-environmentalist discourse (I use the term *anti-environmentalist* intentionally; as this chapter will show, the range of discourse under examination here does not fit the term *climate change denial* because much of the discourse *does not deny that climate is changing*. The discourse does not support efforts to redress it).

I begin by positioning scientific efforts to enlist public support to redress a warming planet with the findings of environmental communication scholarship. This brief overview will illustrate both the limitations of rational argumentation and the value of the catastrophic homology in explaining decades of missed opportunities to redress climate change. I then explore a range of anti-environmentalist discourses that reflect the shared points of formal correspondence identified in Christian fundamentalism, before concluding with a short discussion of how the catastrophic homology affirms and extends our understanding of climate change communication.

COMMUNICATING CLIMATE CHANGE

Despite a well-earned reputation for disagreement, the scientific community reached near-complete consensus in the 1980s on one issue: the earth was warming, greenhouse gases were the cause, and humans were responsible.[1] Developing a meaningful response to this ecological crisis became the next challenge. Redressing climate change would engage complex issues of national sovereignty and challenges of global governance in an interconnected world. Internationally, redressing climate change would require an altruistic, sacrificial, and collective governing philosophy under which powerful countries such as the US and China would surrender some economic development so that poor countries such as Kiribati, Nauru, and the lowest Solomon Islands don't flood. Closer to home, climate change mitigation would have to be politically mandated and enforced within a social, economic, and political climate increasingly oriented toward market supremacy. More precisely, redressing climate change would pit human collectivity against the profitability of an energy industry that created millions of jobs and trillions of dollars in commerce all over the world. Nonetheless, many took comfort in the simplicity of the objective: either burn less carbon or fry the planet. Redressing climate change would be impossible otherwise. And the state had to be willing to deploy all its legal and coercive resources to ensure the long-term viability of our only home. Although it was clear that not everyone would accept their prescriptions, many assumed that with the fate of the planet on the line, scientific warnings and remedies would be noted, understood, and acted upon.[2]

Into the 1990s climate messaging adhered to a model of rational argumentation where scientific data supported a claim, and that claim was linked together by a warrant. The argumentative logic was not complex: overwhelming scientific evidence indicated that a warming planet will cause social, economic, political, and ecological harm; because harm should be avoided, we should take direct action to mediate ecological calamity. For this to happen, the public needed experts to educate them on the topic; education would increase public engagement; and increased public engagement would then lead to support for the policies needed to redress climate change. In the initial media coverage of global warming, scientists were not the primary source of information; *they were the only source of information*. As such, it was assumed that scientists—and their media partners—could deliver this critical message and shape public deliberations about climate change. Keep in mind that, at this point, dissenting politicians, conservative think tanks, and energy industry interest groups were not yet engaged in the conversation; global warming was not covered in the media, and when it was, journalists just reported what scientists said.[3]

But it was not to be.

Between the late 1980s and the election of Donald Trump, efforts to redress climate change devolved into a caustic, divisive reflection of American ignorance.

No political issue—not even immigration, abortion, or gay rights—became as polarizing as climate change.[4] More recently, a significant proportion of Americans now believe global warming is real and consider it a serious problem, but that urgency does not translate into redressing its causes.[5] By 2009, while awareness increased, little more than one-third of Americans thought that immediate, drastic action was needed.[6] A Pew public policy poll that same year found that global warming came in last among all surveyed issues.[7] Pew conducted a comparative survey of the perception of the global warming issues in twenty-five countries and found that Americans were less likely to consider global warming an urgent problem than those in developed countries; the percentage of Americans who agreed that "global warming is a very serious problem" (45 percent) lagged behind those in other countries, such as France (68 percent), Japan (65 percent), Germany (60 percent), and the United Kingdom (50 percent).[8] A 2009 comparative study of nineteen countries conducted by the University of Maryland's Program on International Policy Attitudes found that Americans were near the bottom in their desire for government action on climate change.[9] By 2017, 70 percent of the American public believed that climate change was already occurring, with growing percentages of people also believing that the consequences of climate change would pose a serious threat to humans within their lifetimes. Sixty-one percent of Americans agreed that the effects of global warming have begun.[10] But as Frank Newport reported, only a third reported worrying about it a great deal—a fraction that is about the same as when Gallup asked the same question in the 1980s.[11] Even as climate reporting and awareness increases (and we begin to see the physical effects of a rapidly changing planet), Americans remain reluctant to redress climate change.

The Trump administration's political response to the threat of climate change connected with many Americans' perspective on the issue. While the candidacy and election of Donald Trump reflected the general limitations of rational argumentation, his administration's approach to redressing climate change offers a vivid and specific example of such limitations. Sixty-three million Americans voted for a person who called climate change a Chinese hoax.[12] In office, the Trump administration reflected American unwillingness to take the causes of climate change seriously. Mick Mulvaney, Trump's director of the Office of Management and Budget, made clear the administration's priorities: "As to climate change, I think the President was fairly straightforward saying we're not spending money on that anymore. We consider that to be a waste of your money to go out and do that."[13] Note that Mulvaney said nothing about *believing* in climate change. Belief was not relevant. What mattered was the public's willingness to devote resources to redress it.

Few Americans would have been willing to support the policies addressing climate change if they did not believe it was real; however, increased awareness and belief did not lead to changed behavior—at least in this case.[14] Paradoxically, the recent shift away from climate change skepticism has not led more Americans to push for substantive action. Most now believe that climate change is harmful, but we have *normalized* the knowledge rather than acted on it.[15]

Climate research has tried to account for this regression. Susanne Moser and Lisa Dilling's research illustrated the clear distinction between grabbing attention and inspiring action.[16] Christina Foust and William Murphy also showed how knowledge did not translate into belief, and how more fear did not translate into more urgency.[17] Instead, the more people knew about climate change, the less they seemed to care: respondents with higher levels of information showed less concern.[18] Paul Kellstedt, Sammy Zahran, and Arnold Vedlitz even found that respondents who were better informed about climate change felt less responsibility for it. This stands in clear contrast to the assumption that redressing climate change requires more knowledge about the issue. Other scholars have gone further, showing that individuals will often stop paying attention to climate change when they realize there is no easy solution for it.[19]

Accordingly, climate change communication is plagued by a missing warrant. Rational argumentation urges us to assume that Americans would be motivated by the desire to avoid widespread destruction.

But what if we're not?

A scientist may see a computer model showing the earth warming as a reason to join the Paris climate accord or to ride her bike to work, while many others faced with the same evidence might see the hand of God beginning to restore order to a sinful world.[20] In the rest of this chapter, I examine a range of anti-environmentalist discourses that illustrate how that latter perspective reveals the rhetorical potency of the catastrophic homology.[21]

RESISTING THE GREEN DRAGON

Anti-environmentalists draw on the memory of a formerly empowered status that is now being threatened by an elitist scientific community trying to push them to the intellectual margins. Anti-environmentalists position themselves as the bulwark. Consider the Cornwall Alliance, a public policy organization tailored to evangelical Christians: they described global warming as "one of the greatest deceptions of our day."[22] Calvin Beisner, the national spokesperson for the Cornwall Alliance, identified his opposition as the "powerful forces" telling us that the science is settled.[23] Beisner asserted that environmentalism functions very much like its own religion, with its own God, doctrine, gospel, creation story, sin, and ethics.[24] A book and DVD series put out by the Cornwall Alliance titled *Resisting the Green Dragon* is not subtle: "Green" represents environmentalists and their associates; "Dragon" represents Satan. The dust jacket described its opponents this way:

> Environmentalism has become a new religion.
>
> Environmentalism's policies are devastating to the world's poor.
>
> Environmentalism threatens the sanctity of life.
>
> Environmentalism is targeting our youth.
>
> Environmentalism's vision is global.[25]

Resisting the Green Dragon's website articulated its marginalized status thus: "Without doubt one of the greatest threats to society and the church today is the multifaceted environmentalist movement. Although its reach is often subtle, there isn't an aspect of life that it doesn't seek to force into its own mold."[26] Anti-environmentalist Timothy Ball recalled how he received death threats for opposing environmentalism.[27] James M. Taylor, anti-environmentalist and vice president of the Heartland Institute, complained that their position as "climate deniers" was too often equated with "Holocaust deniers"; he also lamented being "painted into a corner and cast as a demon."[28] Richard Land, who ran the policy arm of the Southern Baptist Convention, wondered aloud whether Christians were allowing "themselves to be manipulated" and "duped" by powerful scientific forces.[29]

Reflecting a basic appeal to marginalization, anti-environmentalists note the financial resources of their opposition. Timothy Ball said, "In the U.S., it's a hundred billion at last count, federal money going to funding, trying to prove the theory."[30] Ken Chilton, anti-environmentalist director of the Institute for Study of Economics and the Environment, complained,

> The funding, for government funding, for grants, is skewed now towards those who believe that climate change is a problem. After all, why would you fund research on something that's not a problem? And so there has been a war chest built up for those who supposedly represent the consensus view.[31]

Anti-environmentalism draws on victimage, threat, and insecurity, suggesting that all human rights are under attack by environmentalists. Elizabeth Kolbert's *The Sixth Extinction: An Unnatural History* is used as a touchstone. In it, Kolbert adopts a secularized version of original sin, arguing that humans have an innate flaw that mistakenly places them above the natural world.[32] Anti-environmentalists distort this view until it becomes a trees-above-people caricature, which is then used to explain the marginalization of their views. In other words, redressing climate change reflects misplaced priorities in which humans are subordinate to nature. Hal Lindsey pointed to a conspiracy theory called "Agenda 21"—which he calls a blueprint for global environmental dictatorship supported by President Clinton and the United Nations to "rewild" half the US.[33] Lisa Vox showed that Lindsey's concern is that the program is premised on the assumption that human society is a cancer, which must be surgically removed if the earth is to survive.[34] Roy Spencer, anti-environmentalist and research scientist at the University of Alabama, suggested, "There are a lot of people who won't allow humans to have the same rights as trees."[35] Richard Land cited the Harvard biologist E. O. Wilson's claim that "humans are the enemy of nature."[36] John Christy said, "I've often talked to environmentalists who truly have the view that humans are bad for the planet, the planet would be better off without humans, and so it fits their view of what we can do to cease development, to help human life expand? They see those as bad things."[37] Spencer felt compelled to remind the audience that "humans come first." Richard Land assured the audience that humans are "not irrelevant" in God's creation. John Christy asserted that if you read Genesis, "you'll see that human life is at the peak of the pyramid and it is human life that has the greatest value in terms of what you see in creation. And, therefore, what you do to preserve, protect, grant security, and health to, in terms of human life is the number one thing you can do."[38] Even Billy Graham equated environmental care with misplaced priorities, writing in *Storm Warning,* "Supporters of the movement calling for 'environmental stewardship' often appear to worship, not the God of heaven, but the God of nature. This is a dangerous form of idolatry in itself."[39] This chilling quote illustrates the iterative potency of the homology: Graham is directly antagonizing environmental efforts, even within evangelical communities, by synthesizing the fear of betrayal evinced in perceived marginalization with the alteration of scientific expertise evinced in prophetic perversion.

Sacrificed at the Altar of Environmentalism

Anti-environmentalism positions itself against an illusory cabal of global elites—a favorite bogeyman of fundamentalist conspiracy theorists.[40] Astronaut and anti-environmentalist Walter Cunningham said, in the documentary *Where the Grass Is Greener,* that as Christians "we believe too much of what we are being told by politicians, newspapers, and things like that."[41] Cunningham also said, "Right now the issue of global warming is becoming the biggest scientific hoax in history."[42] Additionally, Calvin Beisner warned pastors that his opponents "infiltrate evangelical churches with environmentalist propaganda" and that "pastors need to be aware of this and warn people about it."[43] The threat of infiltration by powerful environmentalist forces resonates with a marginalized community defined by betrayal and insecurity. This theme recurs throughout the catastrophic homology: infiltration functions as a compelling retort to authority figures that seem to have betrayed the cause. Rooting out internal enemies within Protestant Christian communities has long been a fundamentalist concern. As a result, those who are open to addressing climate change are often lumped together with other enemies such as liberal Protestants and secular humanists.

Remember that fundamentalism had to work very hard to construct a marginalized position against its material advantages. Regarding anti-environmentalism, this discourse attempts to use the perception of a marginalized position to combat the accusation that powerful energy companies are backing their efforts. "Carlton"—a character featured in a television ad attacking cap-and-trade legislation—represents an elite enemy important for perceptions of marginalization. The ad begins as Carlton, assuming all the aesthetic dimensions of a spoiled slacker, says to the camera "Hey there" as he picks at a plate of canapés:

> I'm Carlton, the wealthy eco-hypocrite. I inherited my money and attended fancy schools. I own three homes and five cars, but always talk with my rich friends about saving the planet. And I want Congress to spend billions on programs in the name of global warming and green energy, even if it causes massive unemployment, higher energy bills, and digs people like you even deeper into the recession. Who knows? Maybe I'll even make money off of it![44]

Environmentalism is positioned as a contributor to poverty, as its policies enrich Carlton and his ilk while prohibiting the world's poor from using traditional energy sources to rise out of destitution. In contrast, anti-environmentalism tries to ally with the most marginalized. References to the Bible verse from Matthew 25:40 ("Truly I tell you, whatever you did for one of the least of these brothers and sisters of mine, you did for me") are woven throughout this discourse. Images of poor Africans gathering firewood and Indians burning dung in their mud huts as their children scavenge the dump for food are often featured in anti-environmentalist videos and literature. These images would be familiar to many evangelicals, as they resemble the images used in evangelical missionary promotional material. The poor are being sacrificed "at the altar of environmentalism," according to *Global Warming*, a documentary made by the Creation Museum.[45] Furthermore, "We Get It"—a national campaign describing itself as "an evangelical response to climate change"—suggested that the implementation of the Paris climate accord would reduce global average temperatures in 2100 by only 0.3 degrees, but at a cost of 70 to 140 trillion dollars, money that "would be far better spent providing pure drinking water, sewage sanitation, electricity, nutrition, health care, and better housing for the world's poor." The website continued, "Implementing the treaty would trap billions in poverty around the world and force millions in developed countries—especially the poor and elderly—back into poverty through skyrocketing energy costs."[46] H. Sterling Burnett of the Heartland Institute warned the audience, "These policies kill. People will die."[47] Larry Vardiman of the Institute for Creation Research said, "One of the unintended consequences of trying to do an all-out war on global warming is that it is going to cause the developing countries not to be able to develop as they need."[48] Jim Inhofe in *We Get It* reflected the double-move necessary to connect his community's (perceived) marginalization with the (objective) marginalization of the world's poor. Echoing a recurring theme, Inhofe claims that he is tired of "being misrepresented by people who don't bother to get their theology, their science, or their economics right." He continues, "Consequently, they put millions of the world's poor at risk by promoting policies to fight the alleged problem of global warming that will slow economic development, and condemn the poor to more generations of grinding poverty and high rates of disease and early death."[49]

Inhofe was attempting to combat the accusation that he is a shill for Big Oil. Thus, he aligns himself with the poor, the marginalized, and the least of these; he links his own disempowered position in the face of the Big Science cabal to the most marginalized in the African deserts and Indian slums. His comments also illustrate an important conservative point of reconciliation related to the role of the state and the market. Whether Jim Inhofe actually cares for the world's poor is not relevant; what's important to notice is how his discourse strikes an attractive balance between the altruism of redressing grinding poverty and disease with a general demand to limit government regulation. In other words, Inhofe's discourse affirms public policies that look to benefit *the least of these* in developing countries without antagonizing the American oil tycoons that fund his political campaigns.

COME LET US REASON

Like Christian fundamentalism, anti-environmentalism must reconcile a lurking paradox: how can it balance its marginalized position against the prophetic authority needed to accurately interpret technical scientific evidence? The science of climate change is complex; so it is with the theology employed to interpret it. Reflecting a recurring theme, anti-environmentalists are not willing to confine themselves to the supernatural or to concede the terrain of science to their opponents. The systematic hermeneutic is simply too important in shaping public conversations. Therefore, the ability of anti-environmentalism to strike the proper balance between marginalization and prophetic authority determines whether it can become the rhetorical agent trusted to make sense of the climate debate.

Anti-environmentalism employs two discursive strategies to reconcile this paradox. First, anti-environmentalism features the technical expertise of its prophetic rhetors. Although comfortable on the scholarly margins, anti-environmentalists do concede their willingness to infiltrate traditional intellectual institutions to receive the advanced education required to be proficient in the scientific details of climate change. However, they always return to their marginalized home to reveal the truth to their audience. For example, Calvin

Beisner introduced his documentary *Where the Grass Is Greener* thus: "We really have gathered some of the very top minds in the field here."[50] Beisner is intentionally using the broad term *field*; later in the film, the audience sees that the climate experts featured come from a variety of disciplines. An impressive list of credentials appears after each rhetor is introduced: doctoral degrees, military ranks, NASA experience, and Nobel prizes. Further, anti-environmentalists are positioned far from the urban effete of the "Carlton" character in terms of their aesthetic dimensions. They display the symbols of traditional stylistic expertise: their voices, vocabularies, attire, grooming, and comportment all match the expectations of credibility for this community.[51]

Second, these rhetors offer the appearance of scientific systematicity in their rebuttals to the threat of climate change. Again, anti-environmentalism does not limit its arguments to the supernatural or the magical. For instance, the We Get It website said, "Our stewardship of creation must be based on biblical principles and factual evidence."[52] Additionally, Jay Wile, president of Apologia Educational Ministries, in the *Global Warming* documentary, says, "The Bible tells us that we have to reason. 'Come let us reason together,' says the Lord. So it's a Christian responsibility to reason through these things. It's not enough to simply listen to the propaganda and believe it. We have to actually reason through it."[53] Michael Oard, in the Creation Museum's book *Global Warming*, writes,

> I think Christians should apply 1 Thessalonians 5:21, which says, "Examine everything carefully but hold fast to that which is good." And that has been my research principle for 40 years. I believe in holding fast to that which is good—to the Bible as God's word, to Jesus as my Lord and Savior. But then I examine everything that the world has out there from the environmental movement to a lot of different controversial issues, but we're to examine everything carefully. So based on that, I believe Christians should look at the data and examine this issue at more than the superficial level.[54]

This systematicity seeks to reframe environmentalists as if they are unwilling to engage in reasonable debates. Further, Beisner reflects the gaslighting vocabularies of Tucker Carlson and Jordan Peterson when he asks, "Why is so much of the environmental movement frankly antirational and irrational?" He later asked why his opponents "reject logic and become thoroughly irrational."[55] Jay Wile wondered why the "radical environmentalist movement has to ignore science." Beisner followed by suggesting environmentalists have found that the "easiest way to persuade people is not to argue the evidence."[56] The We Get It website accuses environmentalists of basing their "grossly exaggerated" claims "on computer models rather than empirical observation—which is the hallmark of true science."[57] The website also cited a 2009 US Senate report describing "700 prominent scientists [who have] disputed claims of dangerous man-made global warming." Calvin Beisner suggested his film featured "outstanding scientists" who use the "the best scientific evidence" to question whether we need to redress climate change.[58] The film is comfortable using quasi-technical language: it suggests that "empirical evidence does not support catastrophic warming" and cites research finding that of the 114 climate models that predicted how global warming would impact the planet, 111 could not predict what actually occurred.

Gridlock and the Appearance of Systematicity

Throughout this discourse, prophetic experts offer empirical observations and scientific evidence to counter environmentalists' arguments about the fate of the planet. Consider how these vocabularies adhere to rational argumentation. A cadre of intelligent old white men with suits, ties, and impressive credentials seem to be engaging in logical deliberation.

Is that not rational argumentation at its finest?

Recall how the homology leans on the *appearance* of systematicity rather than on the substance. While the academic titles and astronaut experiences of the anti-environmentalists can seem impressive, a closer look reveals much weaker credentials. *Where the Grass Is Greener* does feature a retired professor of climatology. But almost everyone else commenting on the technical details of climate change have little to no relevant experience or expertise on the topic. The documentary *Where the Grass Is Greener* features self-described experts like Dr. David Kreutzer, who has a PhD in economics; Matt Briggs, who has a PhD in mathematical statistics; Ken Haapala, who has an MS in quantitative economics; Harold Doiron, who has a PhD in mechanical engineering; Jay Richards, who has a PhD in philosophy and theology; James Taylor, who is an attorney and vice president for External Relations and Senior Fellow for Environment and Energy Policy at the Heartland Institute; James Tonkowich, who has a doctorate in ministry; Anthony Watts, who runs a popular website; Marc Morano, who is an aide to Senator Jim Inhofe, and who lists his BA in political science; and Tom Wysmuller, who is a candidate for a master's in political science. Two other attorneys are featured, with their titles after their last names listed as "Esq., J.D.," including Elizabeth Yore, the former General Counsel for the Illinois Department of Children and Family Services, and as of this writing the General Counsel for the National Center for Missing and

Exploited Children. Lord Christopher Monckton, "3rd Viscount of Brenchley," is prominently featured along with his "M.A. Classics; Dip., Journalism." Jock Allison has a PhD in reproductive studies and worked with the New Zealand Ministry of Agriculture and Fisheries; and Walter Cunningham is supposed to be credible because, along with his MA in physics, he is a retired US Navy colonel. Such an alteration of scientific expertise informs how anti-environmentalist systematicity perverts rational deliberation to make climate change seem like an unsettled controversy requiring further intellectual discussions. As it assumes the appearance of honest scientific skepticism about an uncertain issue, anti-environmentalism aligns with Leah Ceccarelli's description of a *manufactured scientific controversy*.[59] These vocabularies suggest an ongoing debate about an issue long since settled by an overwhelming scientific consensus. Under the guise of honest scientific skepticism, this manufactured controversy perverts the uncertainties inherent in the scientific paradigm to create the impression that the evidence is more suspect than it actually is. The goal is not to champion legislation or even to change anyone's mind; instead, anti-environmentalism is merely "trying to stop stuff," according to Jim Inhofe's spokesperson, Marc Morano.[60] Success is defined by obstruction, and gridlock is the goal.

Manufactured Scientific Controversy

This discourse is not the first to employ a manufactured scientific controversy with such impact. Historian Milena Wazeck, in her book *Einstein's Opponents: The Public Controversy about the Theory of Relativity in the 1920s*, described how individuals with some scientific training, but generally not in physics, joined a group of disgruntled scientists in the early twentieth century to challenge the theory of relativity.[61] They maintained the appearance of an ongoing public debate even though the experts had long accepted the theory. More recently, in the 1960s public relations firms for tobacco companies leveraged a manufactured controversy to slow public acceptance of the causal link between smoking and cancer.[62] Like the fossil fuel industry, the tobacco companies funded a network of institutes with scientific-sounding names to produce counterresearch and to emphasize the impression that this was a scientific debate among like-minded scholars. Additionally, Stephan Lewandowsky described how AIDS researchers in Africa had to defend their work against pseudoscientific challenges during the 1980s and 1990s, as the disease was killing millions.[63]

The manufactured scientific controversy is an important component in the perversion of systematicity. Anti-environmentalism avoids looking as though it *wants* the planet to burn; instead, it appears patient, as though merely awaiting more information. Climate scientists often struggle to respond to arguments like these. In a fascinating role reversal, wealthy conservative foundations and think tanks such as the Cornwall Alliance and the Heartland Institute come across looking like David to the Goliath of climate science. Affirming their marginalized position, anti-environmentalists assume the role of curious truth-seekers wanting to know more about the issue; they attempt to claim the moral high ground in their battle with the greedy, dogmatic, and entrenched "climate establishment." Climate scientists became associated with unpatriotic, ivory-tower academics and global elites intent on destroying American sovereignty—all to keep the Solomon Islands from flooding twice a year.

THE COURAGE TO DO NOTHING

As I showed in the first chapter, Christian fundamentalism is well primed for a defense of "religious liberty." In climate change discourse, secular scientists with an environmentalist agenda are grouped with other threats to fundamentalist individualism—everything from legal mandates to bake wedding cakes for gay couples to bureaucratic rules requiring the use of certain lightbulbs. Calvin Beisner warned his audience, for example, that environmental regulation from elites will soon be all-consuming: "The anointed [will tell us] everything we need to do in our lives," he said, including what showerheads to install and which toilets to use.[64]

Threats to individualism resonate with the Manichean binaries of fundamentalism. For anti-environmentalists, the Green Dragon is just one example of a larger attempt to consolidate power in the secular state. This is a potent fear for a community who already thinks they are alienated from traditional avenues of power. When faced with an existential threat, militant individualism becomes a fitting response. "Government"—with its feckless and corrupt bureaucrats and bloated and wasteful agencies—seems unable to redress massive social problems like climate change. Lisa Vox showed how new threats of environmental harm being circulated in the 1990s led to a decline in perceptions of scientific authority; and this trend was prevalent in conservative Christian communities.[65] Consequently, many Americans made sense of unfamiliar, complex, and threatening climate change discourse not by relying on the strength of empirical evidence and relevant expertise but "according to whether they meshed with their own sense of how the world worked."⁶⁶ Vox's extrapolation illustrates the dynamic oscillation between text and context underpinning this entire ecological conversation.

Pushing Their Agenda

The enemies of individualism are familiar to the fundamentalist audience. Beisner cited "Pres. Barack Obama, other world leaders, and leaders of the United Nations" as the opposition intent on adopting "a global agreement to reduce carbon dioxide emissions."⁶⁷ In *Where the Grass Is Greener,* Robert Carter also identified the United Nations as the enemy when he suggested, "the world's most powerful political lobby group has now become the global warming alliance."⁶⁸ Even the neutral organization charged with maintaining international piece and harmonizing the actions of nations seems to be pushing fundamentalists to the margins. Timothy Ball equated the environmentalist movement with "people that have a political agenda [using] it to push their agenda."⁶⁹ Marc Morano identified the opposition as "people with an agenda, people that want to centrally plan an energy economy."⁷⁰ Calvin Beisner said, "There are some environmentalists who are just basically anti-capitalism, anti-political freedom, anti-wealth, anti-industrialization, and they see the promotion of fears about global warming as a way to serve their own agenda."⁷¹ John F. McManus of the John Birch Society wrote:

> Behind the seemingly innocuous environmental movement lurks a plan to destroy the industrialization that has led to marvelous machines, great comforts, better health, and a higher standard of living. Its leaders want neither personal freedom nor national independence. If they have their way, these neo-pagans will usher in a return to poverty, filth, heat in summer, cold in winter, and the misery of earlier centuries.⁷²

Lord Monckton equated redressing climate change with "addressing a non-problem purely to give the governing class more power and the rich more wealth."⁷³ Monckton went on to argue that "the global warming scam represents the largest, most ruthless, most unprincipled transfer of wealth from the poor to the rich." Paul Driessen suggested that environmentalists want to "replace capitalism with government control . . . [redistributing] the wealth in the world: taking wealth from those who have it and giving it to someone else." Marc Morano deployed a mafia reference when he equated efforts to redress climate change as "essentially a protection racket: pay up now or bad things are going to happen." These vocabularies are likely to resonate with a community that aligns government intervention with the evils of collectivism.

Fitting with this individualistic position, courageous individual scientists, theologians, ministers, and lay Christians are left alone to defend religious freedom from the oncoming crush of environmentalism's central planning. Timothy Ball proudly noted, "When I saw that misinformation being used to control and bully people, I pushed back." And Calvin Beisner started *Where the Grass Is Greener* by introducing the experts featured in his film as "people who are not only brilliant but also courageous enough to question what powerful forces tell us is 'settled science.'"[74]

Natural Solutions

In contrast to the quasi-socialistic aims of environmentalists, anti-environmentalism offers solutions more aligned with militant individualism, including policies that affirm market orientations. Patti Lalonde, a fundamentalist evangelist, wrote, "Let us remember that while this world is suffering an environmental crisis it is suffering a far worse sin crisis."[75] Calvin Beisner conceded that proper Christian stewardship could include picking up trash along the roadside or along the stream.[76] Marc Morano advocated for individualistic policy solutions: "The greatest solution, if we did face a problem, which I don't believe we do, is not central planning, is not putting U.N. bureaucrats in charge—it's innovation and technology." He continued, "If we really do face a crisis, the solutions will just happen naturally. You don't need all this alarm. Whatever's going to happen to address the problem, if there is a problem, is going to happen on its own."[77] Morano went on, "Everything that needs to happen is happening. It's going to happen naturally . . . If you're concerned about global warming, sit back and watch the innovation happen. It's amazing." He concluded, "We just have to have the courage to do nothing."[78]

Consider a few of the following solutions promoted by We Get It:[79]

1. Bring in a speaker to teach your congregation about sound Biblical stewardship.
2. Conduct a Bible study examining scriptures which concern stewardship.

3. Organize a group from your church to partner with people in lower income communities to remove trash and debris from their neighborhoods where children live and play—and work to ensure that the areas stay clean. This is a great avenue for evangelistic outreach!
4. Participate in a mission's project to help bring development to impoverished communities overseas, and encourage your church to undertake long-term relationships that combine evangelism, pastoral training, church planting, economic development, and environmental restoration and protection.
5. Partner with organizations such as the Boy Scouts, Adopt a Highway, Adopt a River, Keep America Beautiful, or other local civic organizations to take part in local trash and litter pickup campaigns.
6. Construct bird houses in partnership with organizations such as the North American Bluebird Society or Hummingbird Society.
7. Help plant and restore threatened tree species with the Elm Research Institute, American Chestnut Foundation, or Arbor Day Foundation.

Anti-environmentalism offers individualistic solutions as alternatives to international agreements like the Kyoto Protocol and the Paris climate accord. In May 2017 Beisner co-authored a letter to President Trump urging him to withdraw from the Paris climate accord and to stop funding United Nations global warming programs.[80] Unfortunately, this individualistic approach—and its appeals to stewardship—is unlikely to slow the speeding train of climate change. Michael Mann, director of the Earth System Science Center at Penn State, referred to "solutions" like these as examples of the *procrastination penalty* in which stalling was actually quite effective for anti-environmentalists. Climate scientists had to convince the public to take drastic, sacrificial action—to leave money in the ground for the sake of a distant, intangible, and creeping threat. Anti-environmentalism just had to raise doubts.

Individual action is important: no one wants garbage in our streams, and we should restore threatened tree species in our local communities. But militant individualism illuminates a more troubling implication when this homology informs political action: if the secular world is hedonistic and immoral—and if only a series of cataclysmic events can restore order—what motivation would I have to support the collective actions necessary to confront ecological harm? Reflecting the scope and reach of this discourse, the political consequences of once-marginalized voices will become even more apparent in relation to the presence of telic temporality in anti-environmentalist discourse.

THE DETERMINED MARCH OF HISTORY

Redressing climate change on a collective, global scale may mediate the threat of ecological harm. But consider how this realization sits with the telic urges of the catastrophic homology. According to this view, history is controlled by an underlying order; as time passes, we move closer to the telic fulfillment of that order. An omniscient God controls how and when history lurches forward, including at the cataclysmic stages that often accompany progress. For example, John Nelson Darby long ago connected premillennial references to the disastrous impact of sin in the Garden of Eden, the Flood in the story of Noah and the ark, and the torture and crucifixion of Jesus. For a more recent example, the Creation Museum featured a poster-timeline stretching from the beginning of time (4004 BC) to the present that read, "God's intervention at key periods of history explains most of the world we see today."[81] From a fundamentalist perspective, how arrogant must humans be to think they can alter this determined march of history? More specifically, are we so bold as to assume that human actions can influence God's plan for the planet?

Telic temporality encourages audiences to take comfort in a community that is part of a preconceived, divine plan in which the forces of good will defeat the forces of evil.[82] A cataclysmic disaster is thought to prompt the battle that will reveal humanity's sinfulness but also cleanse the wicked and spare the worthy.[83] Consequently, redressing climate change on a collective scale looks more like apostate degeneration than like our only hope for saving the planet. For example, James Tonkowich, in *Where the Grass Is Greener,* called it an "insult to God" to think that "you can add a little carbon dioxide to the mixture and you can destroy everything that he so carefully put together."[84] Jim Inhofe, while promoting his book *The Greatest Hoax: How the Global Warming Conspiracy Threatens Your Future,* told a Christian radio program, "God's still up there. The arrogance of people to think that we, human beings, would be able to change what He is doing in the climate is to me outrageous."[85] Calvin Beisner said, "We think that an infinitely wise God designed, and an infinitely powerful God created, and an infinitely faithful God sustained the Earth and its various subsystems for the benefit of all the living creatures in the Earth."[86] Jay Wile encouraged us to stop worrying about how we are affecting the planet because God built in "feedback mechanisms"; consequently, Wile suggested, the earth is "not fragile, but robust."[87] The We Get It website read:

> The earth and all its natural systems are the product of an infinitely wise Designer, an infinitely powerful Creator, and an infinitely faithful Sustainer.

We should expect them, therefore, to be robust, resilient, and self-regulating, not prone to catastrophic collapse due to relatively minute changes.[88]

Ralph Drollinger, a fundamentalist minister who holds a weekly Bible study for members of Congress, offered a formal link between fundamentalism and anti-environmentalism when he suggested that anthropogenic climate change is impossible because God made a covenant with Noah after the Flood. Drollinger wrote, "To think that man can alter the earth's ecosystem—when God remains omniscient, omnipresent and omnipotent in the current affairs of mankind—is to more than subtly espouse an ultra-hubristic, secular worldview relative to the supremacy and importance of man."[89] James Wanliss, author of the book version of *Resisting the Green Dragon,* argued that historical progression is "not a matter of fate, conservation, or man's ability" but "of the decree of God."[90] The Creation Museum features an exhibit titled "7 C's in God's Eternal Plan." Seven pivotal events are described from the beginning—Creation, in six 24-hour days—to the end—Consummation, in which God creates a new heaven and new earth and "destroys death and casts out the disobedient." The third "C" is Catastrophe, in which "Adam's race became so wicked that God judged the earth with a great catastrophe—the global Flood—saving only those on the Ark built by Noah."[91] Confusion results (the fourth "C") before Christ (fifth) and Cross (sixth) ultimately lead up to Consummation. Consider how the ecological catastrophe represented by the story of Noah's Ark and the great Flood functions as a disastrous but necessary stage for the redemption. Note also the exclusivity of this redemption—*Consummation* is limited to "those who trust him," as the disobedient are "cast out." Visitors who can remember the earlier Lake of Fire image will know exactly where the disobedient would be cast.

Telic temporality emphasizes an alternative perspective regarding our rightful relationship with nature. Anti-environmentalism locates that relationship in select biblical passages that suggest humans have *dominion* over creation: we assume the God-given charge to shape, shepherd, and subdue all living things.[92] References to the first two chapters of Genesis, for example, are featured in anti-environmentalism: Richard Land said, "In Genesis 2, Adam was put into the Garden to keep it and to till it. To keep it means to guard and protect it. To till it means to cause it to bring forth its fruit to develop it. For what purpose? For human good."[93] James Wanliss defined dominion as God's commandment for "men to take dominion in the name of Christ, to fill the earth and multiply."[94] Jason Lisle encouraged Christians to "not [be] overly worried about it, because God has given us dominion over this earth." He continued,

> We know that God takes care of the earth as well and it's something ... that it's self-maintaining to some extent, and it's not something that we should

sort of jump on the bandwagon of all the people that have a lot of hype about this issue. I think we need to have a balanced approach as Christians.[95]

In general, I suggest that anti-environmentalism cannot be understood without accounting for its formal connections to Christian fundamentalism. More specifically, the theology of dominion informs why this messaging resonates so well with fundamentalists. As I argued in the introduction, we need to be wary of assuming a generic relationship between Christian fundamentalism and anti-environmentalism. Their formal relationship is not inevitable. Some Christian fundamentalists care about the fate of the planet, and some anti-environmentalists care nothing about fundamentalist theology. Rather, the political consequences are informed by the homological connection occurring at a higher level of abstraction—across disparate orders of experience—each drawn from the same catastrophic reservoir.

More specifically, a perspicacious reader may wonder why the argument that climate scientists "put trees ahead of people" contains rhetorical force. Exploring that question affirms the emerging composition of the catastrophic homology in three specific ways. First, efforts to redress climate change marginalize the fundamentalist audience by overlooking dominion as an important contextual dimension. In advocating for meaningful efforts to redress climate change, environmentalists may even appear to be subverting God's preferred hierarchy. Second, dominion informs a hermeneutic of inerrancy, as their literal interpretation of the creation story in the book of Genesis places humans over creation, subjugating the planet to human desires.[96] Third, dominion informs militant individualism, as only individual salvation can respond to the threat of ecological doom. James Wanliss wrote that human care of the earth is "not possible without a wholehearted embrace of Jesus Christ, on a global scale . . . Rather than seeking to save the planet on terms dictated by the Green Dragon, Christians ought to be preaching the only message that can save the planet—the gospel of liberty in Jesus Christ."[97] We Get It advocated for Christian environmental stewardship focused on spreading the gospel: "As the gospel spreads and more people are reconciled to God through faith in Christ and learn from Scripture to do justice, love mercy, and walk humbly with Him and to understand and use His creation as He intends, we can practice increasingly good stewardship of the earth and everything in it."[98]

CONCLUSION

We might initially expect rational argumentation to reveal to the public that a warming planet will cause ecological harm, and, in turn, that we would support meaningful political efforts to redress climate change. However, as I argue in this chapter, that line of argument was built on a missing warrant: it assumed that ecological doom is something we would all want to avoid. In fact, the public did become aware of the scientific consensus that the planet was warming. In 1981, 38 percent of the public had heard of "global warming." By the end of the 1990s, that number had reached near-saturation levels of 88 percent.[99] Many assumed that as journalists reported more on climate change—and the effects became more obvious—ignorance, denial, and hesitancy would fade.

But that did not happen.

Increased awareness—even increased *fear* of harmful consequences—did not seem to translate to democratic support for redressing its causes. This is not to cast blame on science or scientists. Instead, these findings illustrate how efforts to redress the threat of ecological disaster may be mediated by a catastrophic homology.

The points of formal correspondence located in anti-environmentalist discourse points to five summative conclusions.

First, climate change science is vulnerable to rhetorical deconstruction. Scientists have long struggled to bridge the gap between their findings and their political advocacy. Thomas Kuhn acknowledged that the scientific epistemic paradigm comes together as an esteemed source of knowledge by way of incremental research, residual uncertainty, and the recognition that findings are only and always temporary.[100] Anything that is overtly political, anything that advocates for specific public policy solutions, stretches beyond the objectivity of the scientific method. Thus, the paradigm of putative objectivity from which scientists derive their credibility can be turned back against them when they move into political advocacy. And yet, given the enormous cost of addressing climate change, certain alliances between scientists and politicians are all but inevitable. The political efforts encouraged by the science will cost billions of dollars and impact the daily lives of everyone on Earth. Scientists can objectively show that the planet is warming, but they cannot—with the same degree of confidence—support specific policy recommendations to redress its causes.

Further, as understanding improves, science often reveals new and more complicated questions. The cautious, contingent language of science is far removed from the real-world practicalities of political decision-making. *Politics* determines the distribution of goods and resources—how we collectively decide who gets how much of what, and when. Those resources are often finite. Whenever science is used to justify a political decision, anyone who disagrees with the finite political outcome can exploit the uncertainty inherent in science to discredit it.

Second, our collective failure to appreciate the constitutive potency of catastrophe led many to assume that more persuasive evidence would automatically lead to attitudinal and behavioral changes in the American public. It should have been clear—especially after climate change became a politically polarized issue in the early 2000s—that the public was not suffering from an information deficit problem. We did not need to be overwhelmed with charts and graphs. Instead of locating the deeper, contextual dimensions producing climate skepticism, we were too quick to attribute the American public's frustrating reaction to a lack of scientific evidence.[101] Anti-environmentalism knew better.

Knowledge is necessary but not sufficient to motivate action—especially with an intangible and complex issue like climate change. What has become clear during the following decades is that increasing the public's knowledge base does not help motivate enough of us to agree to the sacrificial political action needed.[102] The information deficit assumption is only useful when there is genuine ignorance related to a topic, such as tobacco and cancer in the 1950s, or HIV and unprotected sex in the 1980s. Consider, then, how misguided it was to talk about climate change as a "highly threatening disease attacking our planet" or to make public service ads that tried to change public attitudes and behaviors about climate change in the same way that twentieth-century public health advocates increased awareness about the dangers of smoking or HIV/AIDS.[103]

Third, the findings revealed by this discourse encourage a re-examination of *credibility* and its communicative function. By failing to account for the constitutive potency of catastrophic rhetoric, we were left to assume that a credible and authoritative community of experts could influence behavior. Kari Marie Norgaard, in her book *Living in Denial: Climate Change, Emotions, and Everyday Life*, argued that declining scientific authority reflects a unique and changing political and cultural landscape in the US.[104] However, the historical record suggests otherwise. Science does not set the conditions for public policy in a vacuum. As Leah Ceccarelli argued, scientific findings, and the new knowledge they produce, are bound together with cultural beliefs, symbolic resources, and our pre-existing mental apparatus.[105] Without reducing science to *mere rhetoric*, Ceccarelli has shown that much of our scientific environmental communication misunderstands how the sensemaking process leads to collective action.[106] Scientific epistemology is culturally privileged and often limited to technical spheres where meaning is made in relation to rules of evidence and specialized forms of reasoning. A complex relationship between culture, cognitive psychology, and risk perception influences how individuals make sense of scientific messaging through a cultural filter that colors attitudes, beliefs, and behaviors. Consider the lessons from the flawed information deficit assumption; we receive information depending on individual differences, and we can react differently to the same information. Many individuals engage with climate change discourse as the product of a humanitarian pursuit that flows from scientific expertise; but for others, the legislative proposals associated with sound climate science were part of a Chinese plot to curb American power.[107]

Fourth, these findings encourage a re-examination of fear-based appeals. Climate change was too often portrayed as a crisis in the hopes that alarming messaging would motivate enough people to listen and respond to their warnings. However, humans do not always respond rationally to messages of this sort. For instance, the sight of a snake in one's path is enough to trigger a fight-or-flight reaction; and this reaction makes sense even when the snake turns out to be harmless.[108] There is an understandable sociobiological reason for this: as primate brains evolved, poisonous snakes were a threat that we adapted to address, including specialized brain cells that are sensitive to snake images. However, climate change is different; the human brain is not adapted to connect ecological crisis to pragmatic political action.

Only a small part of our prefrontal cortex worries about the future, so when confronted with a message about rising sea levels in 2050, we do not have the cognitive capacity to muster the appropriate amount of concern. The kinds of threats our brains have evolved to deal with concern imminent dangers—such as a snake on the sidewalk—and they often involve a malevolent force going against our moral code. Hearing and responding to the threat of looming ecological harm caused by invisible gases requires the complete recalibration of our evolutionary development so that we consider the warming of our planet to be as ominous and urgent a threat as an unidentified snake.[109] Failing to redress climate change is, from this sociobiological perspective, not as illogical as it appears. The development of the human brain explains why certain fear-based appeals failed to motivate meaningful public policy redressing climate change.

A series of studies showed how these fear-based appeals might have had the opposite effect of what scientists intended.[110] The most dramatic fear-based appeals suffocated opportunities for a collective political response to the threat of climate change. Climate scientists ended up framing their dire warnings as ultimatums: act now or die. But that ultimatum leads many to resignation and inaction. These grave warnings demand such a massive response that any individual's behavior seems inadequate—so why bother?

Finally, the discourse examined here encourages a re-examination of how we understand hegemony and consent. Moser and Dilling articulate the frustration of many scientists, journalists, scholars, and concerned citizens when it seems as though the American public is too stupid or lazy to understand the gravity of climate change.[111] Focusing specifically on American Christians magnifies that frustration. While few studies isolate "fundamentalist" from "conservative evangelical Christian," we do know that older conservative evangelicals with "individualistic" values tend to express higher levels of doubt about the scientific consensus on climate change; they are most likely to deny that human activity is the cause; and they are least likely to think a changing planet merits a political response.[112] James Guth and Lyman Kellstedt found that conservative evangelical ministers and laypeople cared less about the environment than did Catholics or mainline Protestants.[113] Two factors, according to Guth and Kellstedt, predict whether a Christian will reject efforts to care for the planet: premillennial dispensationalism and identification with fundamentalism. Their findings would have us consider whether Christian fundamentalists—in particular—are too stupid to see what is happening, too lazy to care, or just too selfish to do anything about it.

As I hope this chapter has shown, those are flawed questions. Fundamentalists' unwillingness to redress climate change is not constructed and affirmed in direct, expositional discourse. Instead, the significant percentage of Christian fundamentalists who believe in the scientific reality of climate change but not in the collective efforts to redress its consequences align text and context, discourse and doxa through more subtle, disparate rhetorical reservoirs. Recall Charles Strozier's use of the term *half-wish* to describe how individual Christian fundamentalists often pull back when presented with the real-world consequences of their theology.[114] Most fundamentalists don't want to rape the earth, as Ann Coulter once urged.[115] However, the catastrophic homology's ability to bridge religious and ecological discourse reveals how a particular worldview can be fertile ground for these alternative discourses. The political commitments produced by the catastrophic orientation branch out in ways that contradict climate scientists' urgings. A worldview receptive to the discourse described here aligns with stronger system-justification attitudes, individualistic values, and support for more stratified hierarchies. Anti-environmentalist discourse calls audiences into a community that does not view climate change as an imminent and harmful threat to the future of humanity.

Even more troubling than ecological passivity, this formal connection is potent because it encourages audiences to reframe ecological harm as a path leading to the divine restoration of global order in a disordered world. Recall that the catastrophic homology is affirmed by audiences drawn to upheaval and chaos. When environmentalists warned of ecological harm, fundamentalist audiences were more likely to align that discourse into a familiar worldview. Put another way, when environmentalists argued that society would face grave consequences *unless* the government acted to ban DDT, *unless* Americans limited population growth, and *unless* we reduced carbon emissions, they were attempting to leverage a nonexistent warrant in the minds of many fundamentalists.[116]

CHAPTER 3

Cultural Catastrophe and the Rhetoric of Gun Rights

AMERICANS HAVE MORE GUNS than any other developed nation—almost four hundred million. We also have more gun violence than any other developed nation—roughly thirty-three thousand Americans die each year by gun violence, a number fifty-one times higher than for the United Kingdom.[1] But the trauma evoked by the prevalence of gun violence in the US does not point to policy solutions.[2] And like other discourses examined in this book, the prevalence of gun violence does not engender sober assessments and productive public deliberation about how best to redress it. Novelist Stephen King compared Americans talking about guns to drunks arguing in a bar, too busy thinking about what to say next to actually listen to anyone else.[3] Empirical evidence related to the impact of gun legislation, for instance, has been shown to have almost no effect on public opinion.[4] Guns are part of a larger sense-making process in which individuals tend to only accept information that confirms what they already believe; we apply stricter standards to information challenging those beliefs; and those with more extreme views are more likely to feel like they understand an issue (even when they don't). These dysfunctional tendencies are exacerbated when we mainly socialize—at National Rifle Association (NRA) conventions, in Reddit discussion threads, and at March for Our Lives protests—with those who confirm our opinions.[5]

Scholars examining this deliberative dysfunction have found that we lack the critical vocabulary to talk about guns, gun violence, gun control, and gun rights.⁶ Gun-control proponents too often conform to the stereotype of the out-of-touch elitist.⁷ Gun-rights discourse—the focus of this chapter—responds with its own confusing arguments, anecdotal evidence, senseless fear appeals, wild exaggerations, and historical revisionism.⁸ I concede the presence of such messaging, but following the lead of Michel Foucault, I also want to assume that a community as powerful as gun owners and their allies could not be constituted only by fallacious discourse—at least not for long.⁹ As a group, gun owners are not uniformly unstable or deranged. And well-intentioned American gun owners are not all being duped by the NRA.

A better approach is to consider the dynamic oscillation between gun-rights discourse and the conditions faced by gun owners that work together to produce a political subjectivity oriented toward catastrophe. And so, I want to suggest that the messaging that has and continues to come from the NRA and the most prominent pro-gun rhetors, including Charlton Heston, Wayne LaPierre, Chris Cox, Sarah Palin, and Donald Trump, can add further texture and nuance to a developing rhetoric of catastrophe. I consider in this chapter what symbolic resources are developed in gun-rights discourses that orient gun ownership toward a more stable political subjectivity. Put more specifically, what are white American men getting from hearing and responding to pro-gun messaging? And what does such messaging get from them?

I begin by summarizing the reactive arguments of gun-rights discourse. I focus specifically on the historical evolution of the NRA from an apolitical organization concerned with target shooting competitions to a dominant force in American politics and a rich source of gun-rights discourse. I then examine the formal relationships characterizing gun-rights discourse before concluding with a discussion on improving public conversations about gun violence in the US.

GUN CONTROL'S MISSING WARRANT

On the Left, many assume that gun owners and their allies are ignorant or indifferent to the thirty thousand Americans killed by gun violence each year. The empirical evidence does indicate that guns are a deadly solution in search of a nonexistent problem. On an aggregate level, when controlling for all other factors, including socioeconomic variables and other crime statistics, more guns means more gun violence. Put simply, the US has more lethal violence *because* its citizens have more guns. The moment a gun enters a home, everyone becomes less safe, including the curious toddler, the teenager sneaking in after curfew, the depressed dad, and the abused mother. Many gunshot victims are shot with their own guns. Guns in the home are often an enticement for thieves rather than a deterrent because they are universally valuable and easy to sell. More so than other instruments of violence, guns are force multipliers. In other countries, people routinely get depressed, or angry, or jealous, just like they do in the US; however, the threat of these situations becoming deadly is much less. Given the ubiquity of guns in the US, it is much easier for normal, daily conflicts to escalate from a verbal altercation or a fistfight to murder.[10]

In turn, efforts from the Left to redress gun violence tend to follow a familiar argumentative structure: first, the need for gun-control legislation is affirmed by the ample empirical evidence revealing a clear relationship between more guns and more gun violence; then, state interventions addressing this need for gun control are proposed, including legislation supporting stronger background checks, magazine limits, increased research funding, a ban on cheap handguns and assault weapons, restrictions on the number of guns an individual can buy during a specific period, and the prohibition of gun sales to criminals.[11] Gun-rights discourse then responds to the Left's gun-control arguments. The rhetoric of catastrophe offers a chance to explore—in relation to different rhetorical domains—how such responses build toward a shared homology.

The lack of a warrant inhibits productive public conversations about gun violence in America. Gun-control arguments from the Left mistakenly assume that *reducing violence* is a shared aspiration linking empirical evidence to public policy. Scholars, journalists, and politicians aiming to better understand gun violence in the US often lack the critical equipment to theorize such a mistaken assumption. And here is my point of intervention: the manifest content of gun-rights discourse—including some cartoonish messaging from the NRA and its sympathizers—is secondary to the formal patterns of the demand and affect they organize.[12] As one of the most powerful forces in American politics, the NRA functions as a rich source for exploring cultural catastrophe in relation to religious and ecological discourses.[13]

THE POLITICS OF GUNS

For most of its history, the NRA was a moderate civic organization for hunters and target shooters.[14] In 1958 the NRA's mission was carved onto its headquarters: "Firearms Safety Education, Marksmanship Training, Shooting for Recreation."[15] Further, the NRA developed, as Adam Winkler wrote, "with the assistance of generous government subsidies."[16] But in the 1970s the NRA altered its focus. Robert Spitzer noted how the NRA first focused its political efforts on specific legislative races.[17] The NRA then used its initial legislative success to prioritize political lobbying and consolidate its efforts into the creation of the Institute for Legislative Action. Guns became a mechanism of self-defense, not just for sport, hunting, or collecting. The new NRA, led by Harlon Carter and Neal Knox, wanted to stop new gun laws and roll back existing laws. A new motto was etched on the NRA's headquarters in all-caps: THE RIGHT OF THE PEOPLE TO KEEP AND BEAR ARMS SHALL NOT BE INFRINGED.[18]

The more militant NRA grew to become the most powerful political lobby in the country. Membership tripled, fundraising grew, and political influence soared.[19] However, the popularity of the new NRA would come to illuminate a lurking paradox related to guns, gun violence, and political power. Elites once deployed gun-control laws to keep the marginalized in their place. Indeed, firearms do offer the marginalized disproportionate opportunities to defend themselves relative to their size and numbers. Guns offer long-distance attack capabilities freeing the out-matched from the natural inhibitions of face-to-face combat against a more powerful foe. Guns can be used at a distance; guns require minimal time and physical effort; and guns symbolize an understood threat. Consequently, guns can be a potential victim's last line of defense.[20] This is especially true for those who cannot rely on the police or other state agencies for protection. Thus, gun-control laws aimed at blunting the violent potential of the disempowered have long been deployed by authorities to maintain social order. More precisely, patriarchal white supremacy has been maintained by keeping guns out of the hands of slaves, women, Native Americans, and even Catholics. Stretching as far back as the 1600s, almost every English colony on the East Coast passed laws forbidding ownership (or restricting the sales of firearms) to women, slaves, and indigenous people. Adam Winkler noted that Catholics, as well as colonists unwilling to affirm allegiance to the British Crown, were subject to confiscation.[21] Racial fears have also been deployed to justify gun-control laws. Slaves and free black Americans alike were forbidden from owning guns in the eighteenth century. After the Civil War, Black Codes in southern states prohibited newly freed slaves from owning guns, and the Ku Klux Klan prioritized gun confiscation.[22] Even after the passage of the Fourteenth and Fifteen Amendments—indeed, up through Jim Crow—restricting firearm ownership for black Americans was thought to be central to maintaining order.

But for the modern NRA, gun-control laws were seen as a mechanism of oppression. What changed? Adam Winkler suggested a correlation between

NRA membership, rising crime rates, and the proportion of NRA members buying guns for personal protection.[23] But given the empirical evidence, we know that buying a gun to enhance one's safety is misguided.[24] Instead, I want to suggest in the forthcoming section that white American men were being drawn into a powerful community constituted by familiar catastrophic appeals to aggrievement and betrayal.

The Black Panthers and Expanding Marginalization

The rhetorical potency of perceived marginalization hinges on spreading perceptions of anomie, disorder, and victimage far beyond the audience affected most by social change. This strategy of amplifying feelings of marginalization through appeals to betrayal and victimage was used in the discourse of conservative religious leaders in the 1920s and energy companies and their anti-environmentalist allies in the 1980s (and, as I examine in the next chapter, this strategic amplification of marginalization has been used in the political messaging of Donald Trump and Steve Bannon). Gun-rights discourse aligned with a similar rhetorical objective. And it did so by adopting the aggrieved messaging of an unlikely source: The Black Panthers.[25]

Modern gun-rights discourse—reflecting the Black Panthers' message of marginalization—resonated with aggrieved white American men by drawing them into a constitutive community marked by the perceptions that gun owners have been betrayed by the institutions once responsible for their defense and affirmation. The result was a more coherent community of gun-rights advocates who perceived themselves to be under attack. This is not to suggest that gun-rights rhetors deliberately adopted Black Panther messaging. Further, the actual victimage felt by black Americans during the 1960s did not spread to white American gun owners in any significant way. Rather, the social, economic, and political conditions of this target audience evolved in a particular historical moment to align fragile white American men with messaging already circulating in Black Panther discourse. Let me begin by identifying the most relevant themes being developed in the Black Panther messaging of the 1960s before connecting those themes to gun-rights discourse.

First, black Americans were made vulnerable by the precise institutions mandated to ensure their safety. The police, with their monopoly on legal violence, are supposed to be the primary source of safety and protection for all Americans. Too often betrayed by their putative defenders, many black Americans, instead, viewed the police as a source of oppression and insecurity. The Black Panther Party for Self-Defense initially formed to redress that betrayal. Free breakfasts sought to remedy a lack of social services, and firearms to remedy the oppressive function of law enforcement.²⁶ From their marginalized position, the symbolic and instrumental use of firearms by the Black Panthers reflected a history of disempowered Americans struggling to defend themselves and to bolster their communities.

These dual symbolic and instrumental purposes reflected a second theme of the Black Panthers that would appear in gun-rights discourse. As Robert Scott noted in his 1968 analysis of black power rhetoric, violence was a dominant discursive touchstone for black Americans.²⁷ Even many civil rights activists understood the instrumental value of firearms. Guns also served a powerful symbolic function. As Bryan McCann notes, the rhetorical representations of violence have long served a constitutive function for black Americans.²⁸ Symbolic appeals to violence forged lines of identification between those resisting white violence in the racist American South and people of color resisting oppression elsewhere. For the Black Panthers, walking around in public with loaded .357 magnums, 12-gauge shotguns, and .45-caliber pistols, even inside the California State Capitol at one point, constituted a stronger, more militant community.²⁹ Reflecting a technique that gun-rights discourse would later replicate, black Californians appreciated the public display of power, strength, and militancy symbolized by firearms on the bodies of Black Panthers roaming the halls of the California Capitol building. As Huey Newton later recalled, black Californians flocked to the Black Panthers' offices in Oakland seeking more information about starting new chapters in their neighborhoods. White Californians were horrified. Led by Governor Ronald Reagan, California enacted some of the strictest gun-control laws in American history in response.

Consequently, a third theme of Black Panther messaging emerges: Black Panthers reacted to the gun-control laws supported by Reagan the same way many white American men would soon react to gun-control laws supported by the Left. Many Black Panthers felt that Reagan's new gun-control laws were not aimed at preventing crime or increasing safety. Portending what was to come when perceived marginalization expanded, these laws were understood as tools of legal oppression to keep a disempowered community in its place. Soon after, white rural California gun owners also looked upon the new laws with suspicion. They also believed these laws did nothing to make anyone safer. Initially driven by race-based fear, these laws sparked a backlash that would later become the modern gun-rights movement.³⁰

Citizen-Protectors and the Anti-Gun Axis

Before the 1960s many white Americans understood guns as part of an important cultural tradition of self-reliance and recreation. Accordingly, guns were mainly used for sport, hunting, and collection. But in the 1970s and 1980s, as changing social conditions threatened white male hegemony, crime rates rose, and civil unrest proliferated, more white Americans began to view guns as a necessary means of self-defense. In *Citizen-Protectors: The Everyday Politics of Guns in an Age of Decline,* Jennifer Carlson showed how such a shift must be understood within a larger worldview marked by decline, loss, sadness, and despair for many white American men.[31] As these men felt betrayed by the state, guns began to serve a familiar set of instrumental and symbolic functions.

Instrumentally, guns offered the protection the police could not. The data confirm this eventual shift from sport to protection. For instance, a Pew survey from 2017 found that 67 percent of respondents cited protection as the major reason for owning a gun—only 38 percent cited hunting and 30 percent cited sport shooting.[32] Symbolically, owning and displaying guns and gun accoutrements functioned as an important rhetorical response to perceived marginalization. Guns filled a void for threatened masculinity, informing what it meant to be a good man—a citizen-protector, in Carlson's term—who could take care of his family. A new apparatus of gun culture developed. Attending NRA conventions, reading *American Rifleman* magazine, and putting the organization's iconic red sticker on one's vehicle became important public symbols fulfilling that constitutive function. In her examination of gun culture in Michigan, Carlson wrote that many of the men she interviewed carried because guns "said something important about who they were and what they wanted to become."[33]

Pause for a moment and reflect on that quote. Carlson is misguided, of course. She is not describing how sensemaking actually works. Guns were not a passive display of extant masculinity. The symbolic act of carrying a gun did not "say" who these men were. Instead, owning guns, carrying guns, and talking and thinking about guns constructed and affirmed a new subjectivity that would otherwise not exist.

An urgent question then emerges: who were white American male gun owners urged to become? Carlson deployed the term *citizen-protector* to describe this new identity. For these men, to profess a willingness to use guns in self-defense was to affirm a new, coherent identity.[34] For Black Panthers, structural white supremacy induced a general distrust of many American institutions, including law enforcement, the courts, media, and politics. Reflecting a fourth discursive theme, white American men also adopted a suspicion of institutions that spread from law enforcement to "government" writ large.[35] Consequently, justification for gun ownership expanded; it moved beyond protection-from-criminals to protection-from-government-tyranny. For these communities, gun-control laws, such as the Gun Control Act of 1968, began to look more like government infringement on the rights of the individual.[36] As I discuss next, a new interpretation of the Second Amendment developed providing legal justification for the right to revolt against the government. There would have been little need for such an interpretation if these men still felt essential. If one cannot have a hand on the levers of power, one can at least have a finger on the trigger of a gun.

A confluence of enemies emerged to align with this marginalized and defiant perspective, including "gun grabbers" and "government thugs" who seek to confiscate firearms, consolidate power, and destroy liberty.[37] "Government" would grow to represent the conspiratorial interests of individuals such as Janet Reno, Sarah Brady, George Soros, Michael Bloomberg, Barack Obama, Nancy Pelosi, and Bill and Hillary Clinton. Institutions such as the United Nations, the Bureau of Alcohol, Tobacco, and Firearms, the Justice Department, and even the Centers for Disease Control and Prevention acquired the same taint.[38] Chris Cox, director of the NRA's lobbying arm, the Institute for Legislative Action, began referring to opponents as an "anti-gun axis."[39] And Wayne LaPierre warned, "The U.N. is the most lethal threat ever to our Second Amendment rights" and suggested that the UN wants nothing less than to impose "total gun prohibition" on the US.[40] Any attempt at gun-control legislation became interpreted as an infringement on the right of Americans to revolt against a tyrannical government. Universal background checks were decried as facilitating the creation of a master list of gun owners—a critical precursor to the confiscation of firearms and the imposition of martial law.[41]

Laura Collins offered a useful illustration of how perceived marginalization emerged within the lives of gun owners in her analysis of gun-rights discourse. Examining reactions to a 2013 request by Starbucks CEO Howard Schultz that patrons not openly carry firearms in their coffee shops, Collins located feelings of aggrievement and victimage as gun owners were unable to perform their citizen-protector identity when they bought their morning coffee.[42] One person noted, "You have said in the letter that the US Constitution is not worthy of honoring in your store." Others referenced "blatant discrimination against our Second Amendment rights"; "denial of the Constitution"; "anti-Constitutionalist" actions; "throw[ing] the Constitution under the bus"; and "trying to take away something that doesn't belong to [Starbucks]." Collins also found that gun-rights discourse often leveraged legitimate victimage to justify more expansive readings of the Second Amendment. Many of the gun-rights commenters positioned themselves as a minority group, using analogies to racial and sexual orientation to justify their marginality. "What's next, a memo stating that black people are not welcome because they scare some of your customers?" asked one pro-gun commenter. Another asked, "Just wondering if you're going to ask gays or blacks to stop coming in your stores next?"

The decision to open carry allowed gun owners to position themselves as victims of bigotry. Open carry was not just a practice one engaged in from time to time. It was a permanent state of being, an immutable identity that formed the basis of a protected class. The discomfort of a Starbucks customer, anxious about drinking her latte in the presence of other customers who are openly carrying guns, is thus equated with racist and homophobic bigotry.

The perceived marginalization within gun-rights discourse activated political potency. Allegations of misconduct unjustly positioned gun owners on the margins. This prompted a demand: Howard Schultz—along with all the other bigots—needed to apologize and stop trying to infringe on the rights of a constitutionally protected class. Beyond Mocha Frappuccinos, a unified community of aggrieved citizens was formed. They felt traumatized by the bigotry, even resentful. However, because the politics of trauma and resentment do not urge an isolated political response, perceived marginalization needed to be connected to a sacred value.[43] Perceived marginalization prompted a new interpretation of the Second Amendment as a vulnerable site in need of protection, and its noble defenders formed a new constitutive community.[44] Rather than mitigate trauma and resentment, gun-rights discourse cultivated it, located scapegoats and all-powerful villains, and positioned gun owners and their allies as afflicted by those enemies' evil designs—unless they could respond in a potent manner.[45] As Brett Lunceford argued, constructing an identity in this way kept the focus on an all-powerful enemy, and allowed gun-rights advocates to position themselves as members of a unified, marginalized community.[46] And because the gun-rights community is reconstituted by feelings of victimization, larger connections to other betrayals and slights—such as not being allowed to say "Merry Christmas" or Chinese currency manipulation—would resonate in powerful, new ways.

Jackbooted Thugs

The rhetorical construction of government tyranny as a constitutive touchstone produced pro-gun messaging as fallacious as it was effective. Prominent gun-rights rhetors began warning of government officials going door-to-door and confiscating guns from law-abiding citizens. The late NRA president Charlton Heston cited the confiscation of guns as the prelude to the "bloody terror by the dictatorships of Napoleon, Mussolini, Stalin, Hitler, Fidel Castro, and Pol Pot—all of whom began their reign by confiscating guns."[47] One NRA mailer reminded readers, "The first thing Communists do when they take over is register all the guns." Another mailer began, "Imagine a knock at the door. It's government agents come to confiscate your guns. Are you in Gorbachev's Lithuania? Think again. It can happen right here."[48] An article in *American Rifleman*, the official magazine of the NRA, warned readers that hostile government agents would soon begin to "go house to house, kicking in the law-abiding gun owners' doors."[49] NRA executive vice president Wayne LaPierre wrote in a fundraising letter that a semiautomatic weapons ban would give "jack-booted thugs more power to take away our Constitutional rights, break in our doors, seize our guns, destroy our property, and even injure or kill us."[50]

Most white American men had little to fear, of course. Men of color are disproportionately much more likely to be victims of gun violence. And if the state does come to the door, they usually knock first. As the 1971 story of Ken Ballew illustrates, government officials usually only kick in the door during emergencies, in this case after police were shot at from the home of someone stockpiling homemade grenades. Furthermore, private gun ownership would do little to slow down a tyrannical government with a $700 billion annual military budget.[51] But notice the degree of systematicity within gun-rights discourse connecting guns to personal safety. If guns were associated with security, and not just sport, hunting, or collecting, then gun-control laws could be framed as infringements on the inalienable right to protect oneself.[52] The legal right to own firearms—and, more deeply, to protect one's family in tumultuous times—added rhetorical weight to gun-rights discourse. References to "God-given," "natural," and "constitutionally protected rights" became commonplace. Wayne LaPierre leveraged this rhetorical interrelationship of guns, security, and natural rights when he said that the constitutional right to bear arms "is not bestowed by man, but granted by God to all Americans as our American birthright."[53] Of course, we know how drawing on natural law or divine decree in this way stands in sharp contrast to the history of gun control in America.[54] Nonetheless, the shift seemed to work. Robert Spitzer cited a study in which gun owners claimed that feeling vulnerable to crime and believing the police to be ineffective were key factors leading to their purchase of firearms.[55] Another study found that the most frequently cited reason for handgun ownership is self-protection.[56] A 2017 Pew survey found that 74 percent of gun owners thought of the right to own guns as essential to their own personal sense of freedom.[57] The 2017 data can be traced back to the upheaval of the 1960s, when many white people began to feel like the state could not protect them; thus, for those attracted to such gun-rights arguments, the state should be replaced by one's own ability to use guns for self-defense.

INDIVIDUAL RIGHTS AND THE LINCHPIN OF DEMOCRACY

The individual-rights interpretation of the Second Amendment provided systematic legitimacy for this shift to self-defense by leveraging the rhetorical potency of the Constitution. In a departure from historical precedent, the individual-rights interpretation suggested the Second Amendment protected a personal right to self-defense. The argument faced an uphill legal battle. American courts had long rejected the individual-rights interpretation. As Peter Brown and Daniel Abel wrote in *Outgunned*, decades of judicial interpretation asserted that the Second Amendment only protected gun ownership for members of government militias.[58] Even retired Supreme Court Chief Justice Warren Burger, a Richard Nixon appointee, dismissed as a "fraud" the idea that the Second Amendment protected an individual's right to bear arms.[59] The 2008 Supreme Court decision in *District of Columbia v. Heller* is often held up as the inflection point. However, the *Heller* decision did not so much *shift* public opinion as *follow* it.[60]

In the 1980s an explosion of academic research supporting an individual-rights theory of the Second Amendment began appearing in legal magazines and law journals. Don Kates published one of the first articles, in the *Michigan Law Review* in 1983. He argued the Second Amendment included an individual's right to use guns for self-protection.[61] Gun makers and their allies were the first to notice the political implications of Kates's argument. A trove of individual-rights scholarship from lawyers working for or representing the NRA took the baton from Kates and ran with it. And they ran far. Kates's interpretation would become the touchstone the NRA and its allies would use to develop the necessary systematicity for their preferred legal standing. The interpretation was so effective that it became known as the "standard model"—so well proven that no credible expert disagreed with it.

It is understandable why the NRA and its lawyers and lobbyists were pushing this individual-rights interpretation: it would sell more guns. The NRA is the primary political representative for the interests of Beretta USA, Mossberg, Sig Sauer, Springfield Armory, Sturm Ruger, and Smith & Wesson—*companies that make money selling weapons*. As Spitzer put it, this relationship makes sense on a practical level: the NRA's political work helps generate and sustain the market for the gun industry and their products.[62] The individual-rights interpretation laid the groundwork for the legal sanctioning of a profitable product sold legally to millions of American customers.[63]

The more interesting question is this: why did the wider public—and later the courts—accept such an interpretation, especially when its primary effect was to make gun companies more profitable and gun owners less safe?

Scholars from a variety of academic disciplines have explored that question. Political scientist Robert Spitzer argued, "The desire to treat the Second Amendment as a constitutional touchstone by gun control opponents is understandable, given the 'rights talk' that pervades American political discourse and the enormous political legitimacy that accompanies anything dubbed 'constitutional.'"[64] Journalist Osha Gray Davidson argued that the NRA successfully portrayed their interpretation of the Second Amendment as the "linchpin of democracy . . . Pull it out and the rest of the Bill of Rights unravels." This is because only an armed citizenry could keep a tyrannical government from disregarding the fundamental rights spelled out in the Constitution.[65] Sociologist Jennifer Carlson located the wider acceptance of this interpretation in both socioeconomic factors and the "moral practice" developed in NRA training courses.[66] Constitutional law professor Adam Winkler also noted contextual factors, arguing that rising crime rates in the 1960s correlated with increased NRA memberships and the proportion of its members buying guns for self-protection.[67]

These explanations are not wrong, but they are incomplete.

As the empirical data make clear, fear of gun violence should not lead anyone to buy a gun. Buying a gun to prevent gun violence is akin to smoking cigarettes to prevent lung cancer. To focus on NRA training courses as a site of moral practice, as Carlson suggests, seems like an exogenous explanation for an endogenous attitude. Left unexplained is *why* frightened or angry people would think that guns are the solution to their insecurity. Why not get a dog? Better door locks? Window bars? A home security system? A neighborhood watch? Further, the self-serving dimension of an NRA training course promoting guns as the solution to gun violence should not go unnoticed. Taking a gun training class sponsored by the NRA is akin trying to lose weight by taking a cooking class sponsored by Cuisinart.

Too often, the extant literature assumes a referential gun-rights community. It can seem as if these true believers are all waiting in a room for the prophetic voices of Charlton Heston and Wayne LaPierre to tell them why they need to buy more guns. Recall also how white American men once admonished the state to implement gun-control laws that kept weapons out of the hands of Catholics, Native Americans, slaves, women, and, more recently, Black Panthers. As recently as the 1960s, gun-control laws were supported as a necessary means of preventing threatening groups from outgunning the police. What changed? Or more appropriately, what describes the shifting relationship between systematic gun-rights arguments and the worldview of so many white American men?

A gun-rights community is constituted through discourse. The individual-rights interpretation brought a community of gun advocates together, and then circulated and operationalized a unifying ideology.[68] Further, the systematicity of gun rights not only called a pro-gun constituency into being; it also urged the formation of an identity in relation to a specific set of political demands. Maybe most American gun owners don't understand all the legal details of the individual-rights interpretation, or—recalling the Nancy Jameses of the world—support the idea of their neighbor with the pit bulls stocking machine guns in the basement. But if "gun control" is associated with government actors infringing on a natural, God-given right, the prophetic perversions of Heston and LaPierre do not look so irrational. The political relationship with the Second Amendment urged individuals to defend a fragile and threatened document, and to see gun-control laws as the means by which that document would be destroyed, taking the liberty of the people along with it.[69] As the perception of marginalization expanded to white American men and a legitimate legal foundation of individual rights was laid, prophetic warnings of jackbooted thugs and machine guns become more palatable for this audience. Let me now try to explain *why*.

Government Enmity

In the morning hours of December 4, 1969, FBI agents kicked in Fred Hampton's door and killed him while he lay sleeping, unarmed, next to his pregnant fiancée. For many black Americans, Fred Hampton's death fit a familiar narrative: the institution mandated to protect them had no qualms about kicking in their doors and killing them. What's more, when the Black Panthers took up arms to defend themselves, the state changed the law to keep them from doing so. Understandably, Black Panther discourse reflected a fear of state-sanctioned oppression. But what allowed that fear to spread to white American men?

The answer may have little to do with guns. After the activism and unrest of the 1960s, the Great Society's redistribution policies, and the judicial activism of the Warren Court, "government" was increasingly viewed as an enemy rather than an ally.[70] Especially for white American men, the acceptance of the individual-rights interpretation emerged as the once-revered state was being reframed as a source of insecurity, disorder, and marginalization. The data support this reading. Many Americans now see the federal government as a threat to their freedom and liberty.[71] Today, if the catastrophic homology draws strength from a single political subjectivity this is it: government is the primary cause of society's problems.

Despite the incongruities, the individual-rights interpretation of the Second Amendment aligned with a rhetorical reservoir that could equip white America men with the discursive techniques to respond to a changing world. Guns emerged as one more site of struggle in a larger cultural war. In turn, many Americans, most of them white men, began to understand gun ownership as a form of resistance against government tyranny.

Each Individual Is Accountable for His Actions

Ronald Reagan's portrayal of government as the problem rather than the solution functioned like an exclamation point on this reorientation toward government enmity. Few individuals were as effective in aligning their messaging and their political aspirations with this shifting worldview. Reagan famously said, "The nine most terrifying words in the English language are 'I'm from the government and I'm here to help.'" He also suggested, "We must reject the idea that every time a law's broken, society is guilty rather than the lawbreaker. It is time to restore the American precept that each individual is accountable for his actions."[72] Reagan's messaging reflected a generational shift away from the Eisenhower Republicanism of the previous decades, including attitudes toward gun control.[73]

Reagan's personal experience with the Black Panthers during his governorship of California, and later his two-term presidency, illuminates the impact of this wider acceptance of institutional suspicion. Reagan was willing to use the state's police power to enforce gun-control laws on the Black Panthers in the 1960s, but as the American president, his enthusiastic defense of the individual-rights interpretation aligned with the conditions of this New Right.[74] Adam Winkler even suggested that Reagan's campaign messaging gave "voice to a sentiment that was already strong in the gun rights community."[75] Again, we should challenge Winkler's argument. Consumers of public discourse rarely come to a message as a part of pre-existing community. Instead, through the dynamic oscillation of text and context, new public identities are constructed and affirmed.[76] Here is an important point of rhetorical intervention, and a specific instance where the catastrophic homology can illuminate what a constitutional law professor like Winkler might overlook. There is no "gun rights community"—as Winkler described it—apart from Reagan's messaging. Accordingly, there is no Reagan (or Charlton Heston or Wayne LaPierre) apart from shifting social conditions. Guns can shoot elk and defend against a home invasion; they can also shape flailing subjectivities into stable communities. The legal systematicity offered by the individual-rights interpretation helped redefine what it meant to be an upright American citizen, and in so doing affirmed a strict division between those who were willing to bear arms in defense of liberty—and those who were not. Ultimately, this dynamic oscillation produced a new subjectivity equipped with a coherent legal explanation for responding to a changing world.

As the name indicates, the individual-rights theory of the Second Amendment aligned with the individualism of the historical moment. A target audience of white American men found a coherent subjectivity grounded in a willingness to bear arms against a chaotic world. As I show in the next section, organizations such as the NRA, individuals such Ronald Reagan, and political institutions such as the Republican Party emerged as rich sites for rhetorical invention.[77]

GUNS DON'T KILL PEOPLE

Proclaimed from convention keynote addresses, pasted on bumper stickers, and circulated on internet memes, the most ubiquitous and durable pro-gun messaging reflects militant individualism.[78]

"Guns don't kill people, people kill people."

"When guns are outlawed, only outlaws will have guns."

"Gun control means using both hands."

"The only thing that stops a bad guy with a gun is a good guy with a gun."

These individualistic messages also reflect familiar catastrophic themes. First, militant individualism establishes clear boundaries between gun owners and the proponents of gun control. While the barrier between hunters and nonhunters can seem to operate much like the barriers between race, religion, gender, and socioeconomic status, NRA messaging works hard to align hunters and nonhunters alike into a community united more by attitudes of individualistic aversion to government intervention than by the act of hunting.[79]

And these barriers are never neutral categorizing mechanisms. In a community constituted by militant individualism, those who cannot see the threat of a weakened and compromised state, or who are unwilling to respond to it, must be in on it. Outsiders are not just mistaken. They are evil. Therefore, a blanket unwillingness to consider alternative views, including those informed by evidence connecting guns to gun violence, is the price of admission for gaining entrance into this community.

Second, the NRA does not focus much on persuading its opponents. Instead, it devotes most of its resources to internal communication designed to fire up existing NRA members and to rally support for sympathetic political candidates.[80] Reflecting Christian fundamentalist and anti-environmentalist discourse, the NRA is not concerned with persuading outsiders; instead, its chief function is the continual reconstitution of an internal community.

Furthermore, within the NRA, such militancy is logical, and even necessary. Wayne LaPierre is proud of his extremism, once saying, "To me, 'hardliner' just means protecting the right of Americans to own firearms in this country."[81] Marion Hammer, a former NRA president, is militant in her belief that even the slightest compromise with gun-control advocates is a slippery slope that leads to total government confiscation of firearms.[82] More broadly, Davidson described the NRA in familiar terms: "The group had built its reputation on a refusal to compromise and that inflexibility had become institutionalized. A kinder, gentler NRA was out of the question."[83] Finally, such individualistic messaging can seem harmless enough on a meme or a bumper sticker, but these slogans suggest the existence of a deeper rhetorical reservoir that portrays outsiders as existential threats. And when outsiders are Othered in this way, rhetorical violence is justifiable.[84] Here is where cartoonish individualistic slogans—"gun control means using both hands"—portend troubling political implications. The rhetoric following mass shootings in America reflects the militant individualism illustrated in gun-rights discourse.

Mass Shootings and More Guns

Although far from the main source of gun violence, mass shootings (and the discourse that follows) offer a rich site of rhetorical analysis because these tragic events bring to the surface deeper discursive struggles about guns, gun control, and the communities involved.[85] Mass shootings in America prompt a peculiar ritual: after a gunman murders innocent people, many express outrage, horror, and sympathy for the victims and their families; but soon after, as we all look at the same horrific gun violence, we quickly settle on different explanations for who is at fault and what should be done to keep it from happening again.[86] The Left tends to offer stricter gun laws in response.[87] The Right tends to first offer "thoughts and prayers," and then to swat away gun-control legislation by suggesting that such talk is inappropriate during a time of mourning. But more durably, gun-rights discourse coheres around the militant individualism feeding into the catastrophic homology.

For example, after the 1999 mass shooting at Columbine High School in Colorado, Kristen Hoerl noted descriptions of Eric Harris and Dylan Klebold as "monstrous youth" rather than recognizing the structural conditions motivating the shootings, such as suburban alienation or mental health challenges.[88] In 2011, after a mass shooting in Arizona that included Congressperson Gabriel Giffords, Francesca Marie Smith and Thomas Hollihan noted that the solitary killer, Jared Loughner, was blamed with "surgical isolation."[89] In these narratives, Loughner was depicted as solely responsible for his crimes; and this portrait of a deranged-yet-culpable killer was deployed to counter those searching for the deeper societal causes of gun violence. Not only was Loughner responsible, but because he was deranged we cannot (and should not) try to understand his motives. Jeremy Engels, studying Arizona shooting discourse, noted that Sarah Palin was especially enthusiastic about minimizing the context in which the shooting occurred.[90] According to Palin, Loughner was crazy—plain and simple. In minimizing the social context for the violence, Palin positioned her response in alignment with the larger individualistic urges. Palin, extending Reagan's famous quote about "each individual" being responsible for his actions, suggested, "Acts of monstrous criminality stand on their own. They begin and end with the criminals who commit them."[91] Palin's explanation also foreshadowed an emphasis on the individual mental health of mass shooters by gun-rights rhetors as a rebuttal to calls for stricter gun-control laws.

In 2012, after the mass shooting at Sandy Hook Elementary School in Newtown, Connecticut, Justin Eckstein and Sarah Lefevre, along with Michael Hogan and Craig Rood, detailed how Wayne LaPierre explained away Adam Lanza's killing as another example of one person responsible for violence.[92] LaPierre said, "The truth is, that our society is populated by an unknown number of genuine monsters. People that are so deranged, so evil, so possessed by voices and driven by demons, that no sane person can ever possibly comprehend them." LaPierre later explained that the AR-15-style rifle Lanza wielded was not to blame because "guns don't kill people. Video games, the media and Obama's budget kill people."[93]

Such messaging has an impact on legislative options for redressing gun violence, as laws are reverse-engineered based on the individualistic attitudes induced by this discourse. We cannot hope to understand the shooter's motives—after all, evil cannot be reasoned with. Thus, the state has no grounds to intervene and regulate the military-style assault weapons amplifying the death tolls in mass shootings. The only appropriate response is more guns.

Especially after school and church shootings, gun-rights discourse urges more armed security guards and even armed teachers as a logical legislative response well aligned with militant individualism. As Charlton Heston said two days after the Columbine shootings, "The tragedy was a result of not too many guns, but too few. If there had been one armed guard in the school he could have saved a lot of lives and perhaps ended the whole thing instantly."[94] The NRA's Chris Cox noted after the Parkland, Florida, school shooting in 2018, "We protect our banks, our sports stadiums and our government buildings better than we protect our schools. That must change."[95] In October 2018 President Trump said our gun laws had "little to do" with the mass shooting at a synagogue in Pittsburgh that left eleven dead; rather, Trump said, "If they had protection inside, the results would have been far better."[96]

Because militant individualism forecloses structural solutions, more armed guards and armed teachers seems like a logical response that would limit the violence when the next shooting happens. Blame is cast on violent video games, rock songs, abortion rates, school security measures, and even trench coats—anything but the guns.

Sand in the Gears

These individualistic responses downplay key facts about gun violence. In most school districts, liability issues would limit arming teachers. As Hogan and Rood noted, individualistic appeals about "good guys with guns" are nothing more than cartoonish clichés more appropriate for a bumper sticker than for informing public policy.[97] There is also little evidence that arming teachers would redress the violence. There were armed guards at the Columbine, Parkland, and Santa Fe high school shootings. *The Onion,* a satirical news magazine, lampoons individualistic responses after each shooting by running an updated version of the headline "'No way to prevent this,' says only nation where this regularly happens." The incongruity provides the dark humor: we know how to reduce gun violence. Evidence-based public policies enforced by active state intervention have made other countries safer. The US has already taken similar steps in our regulation of automobiles. And we have saved millions of lives because of it.[98]

We can be sure of one thing: a country with more guns is better for the gun makers Heston, LaPierre, and Cox represent than for most everyone else.[99] The NRA's response to gun violence is as callous as it is predictable. *But it is not irrational.* NRA membership spikes after mass shootings, but not merely because of its militant individualistic messaging; more deeply, the NRA's logic aligns guns with a larger rhetorical reservoir producing a catastrophic community defined by the acceptance of violence.

Those sickened by gun violence in the US cannot help but wonder why the NRA's individualistic messaging is so potent. Why does Chris Cox get to dine at the White House? Why does the NRA have more clout than the PTA or the AARP? Many may also wonder why such impractical messaging resonates with so many Americans. How can the NRA be such a political force when it spouts such foolish messaging after such tragic shootings? Why is it not more obvious that the NRA's messaging enhances the profitability of gun makers but does little to prevent children from being killed in schools? Hogan and Rood suggested that such militant individualistic messaging could be a deliberate red herring meant to distract the public from considering more serious policy responses: when the discussion shifts to arming kindergarten teachers, then discussing background checks and banning assault weapons fades away.[100] These red-herring arguments are rooted in inertia, and as the analysis of anti-environmentalism revealed, there is rhetorical value in maintaining a (profitable) status quo by just trying to *stop stuff*. Blocking gun-control policies is easier than designing them.[101] Red herrings, like arming teachers, throw sand in the gears of the public policy machinery, allowing public anger to subside and NRA lobbyists time to ply their trade. Gumming up gun-control legislation is much easier once the news vans roll out of Newtown and Parkland.[102]

The militant messaging of gun-rights discourse affirms the iterative potency of the larger catastrophic homology. First, individualistic messaging aligns with a worldview marked by institutional betrayal. Also, strong public institutions reduce violence by penalizing aggressors, eliminating criminal incentives, defusing anxieties about pre-emptive attacks, and reducing the need to retaliate.[103] More directly, when institutions like the ATF, the CDC, the FBI, and police departments are supported, violence is reduced. In short, if people believe they cannot trust the police, then the world will seem more dangerous, and many will conclude that they must assume responsibility for their own defense. As Jennifer Carlson put it, guns fit within a larger centripetal force where public disinvestment in institutions amplifies perceptions of disorder; disorder leads to anxiety about crime and violence; and this increased anxiety forecloses structural responses. Only one concrete solution is left: more guns.[104]

White American men are oriented toward this individualistic solution. White men make up the largest percentage of gun owners—ahead of women and people of color by double digits.[105] The divergence is even sharper within NRA membership, where white men are overrepresented by a factor of two (relative to their share of the US population). Here is part of the reason why: when white men *feel* threatened, they are expected to reassert their dominance through violence.[106] Thus, gun culture offers an attractive means of reclaiming a fragile white masculinity. Guns are a cheap, ubiquitous, and socially sanctioned way to exercise dominance.[107]

The actual gun is less consequential. I know this is a cynical conclusion, but it is not unsupported by the evidence: gun owners and their families end up less safe, Wayne LaPierre and Chris Cox take a limo to lunch at the White House, and the private equity firm that owns Remington gets a larger dividend check at the end of the year.

Militant Half-Wish

Thus far, I have argued that gun-rights discourse encourages a vicious cycle oriented toward a catastrophic homology. More specifically, individualistic messaging in gun-rights discourse offers another example of how a missing warrant contributes to deliberative dysfunction. Recall how gun-control supporters connect the empirical data from Harvard professors and CDC researchers to legislation that would reduce gun violence. But also note how the warrant bridging data to claim is missing: not everyone resonates with identities and communities that want to reduce violence. Without acknowledging this overlooked warrant, the public cannot understand American gun-rights discourse, including questionable policies like putting more guns in schools to limit gun violence in schools. Heston, LaPierre, and Cox's foolish messaging looks less fallacious when we acknowledge a formal pattern organized in opposition to reducing violence. In contrast, the goal is to be ready for violence so the weak and unprepared can be separated from the strong and well armed.

Such a troubling conclusion deserves to be tempered. Consider the divergent objectives of the perverted prophets—such as Riley and Falwell, as well as Heston and LaPierre—and the rank-and-file community members. Heston, LaPierre, Palin, and Cox have a material interest in perverting rational argumentation and its ability to inform competent governance. Further, on a conscious level, these prophets and their allies may not long for violence. They may simply enjoy the power and prestige this messaging affords them.

However, we should also not fetishize the rhetor. Heston, LaPierre, Palin, and Cox should be understood as nodes through which discourse is articulated.¹⁰⁸ Recall Charles Strozier's use of *half-wish* and its value for understanding rhetorical invention. Strozier argued that Christian fundamentalists often pull back when confronted with the logical consequences of their apocalyptic formal appeals.¹⁰⁹ They only *half-wish* to see their unbelieving neighbors tormented in a lake of fire. Following Strozier's lead, rhetorical invention in gun-rights discourse should remind us that most gun owners are not nuts. Most would recoil when faced with the logical implications of such militant gun-rights messaging. Public opinion polls illustrate the gap between pro-gun rhetors and most gun-owning Americans; even most NRA members support a range of gun-control measures that NRA leadership rejects. One survey found that 74 percent of NRA members support universal background-check laws that the NRA leadership opposes.¹¹⁰

With those qualifications in mind, I want to close this section by reconsidering the continued viability of such militant messaging. Such an exploration does not so much concern guns or the rationality of the arguments offered in their defense. If the American public's collective goal is the widespread reduction of gun violence, such fallacious messaging about a "good guy with a gun" is not a red herring meant to distract from more serious gun-control legislation that would reduce gun sales. Catastrophe operates on a deeper level. The content of gun-rights discourse is secondary to the formal patterns of the demands and affect it organizes.¹¹¹ In this way, the militant individualistic messaging of gun rights and its troubling formal underpinnings are not aimed at guns or gun-control laws. Instead, as the catastrophic homology suggests, militant individualistic gun-rights messaging seeks to "specify a subject position" in relation to a threatening world. Gun-rights discourse is not merely shouting "Hey, you!" to aggrieved white men; it is creating the cultural conditions allowing them to respond "Yes, me!"¹¹²

THE INEVITABILITY OF EVIL

Gun-rights discourse calls individuals into a community marked by perpetual disorder, chaos, and violence—each symbolic of the forward march of history to a telic destination. Recall the attitude induced by telic temporality: a state of anomie and disorder is identified, which existing authorities cannot explain; a community is then defined by a compelling interpretation of that disorder as the reflection of an advancing underlying system; in the end, a political subjectivity is produced that yearns for disorder as a mechanism to accelerate forward progress and restore order to disordered hierarchies of power.

Order assumes a unique rhetorical weight in gun-rights discourse relevant to these telic urgings. In gun-rights discourse, *order* does not signify a state of collective peace, security, and safety. That is not the world Heston and LaPierre seem to be living in; nor is it the world they seem to desire. *Order* and *disorder* are not antonyms in gun-rights discourse; they are symbiotic. To acknowledge, accept, and prepare for disorder offers those called to this community a thrilling sense of orientational purpose.

In February 2018 Donald Trump articulated the symbiotic relationship between order and disorder. Responding to the Parkland, Florida, shooting, he told an audience at the White House, "You know I really believe, you don't know until you're tested, but I really believe I'd run in there even if I didn't have a weapon and I think most of the people in this room would've done that too."[113] Set aside Trump's intent for a moment. It does not matter whether an unarmed Trump would have run into Marjory Stoneman Douglas High School while Nikolas Cruz was firing his Smith & Wesson M&P15. What is relevant is the *subjectivity* produced when an overweight, out-of-shape, seventy-one-year-old man with bone spurs articulates such a fantasy to the world. Reflecting the same messaging found on the Reddit "progun" message board, or the heroic stories of self-defense in *American Rifleman* magazine, Trump is not just telling the world who he is—*he is telling the world who he wants to be*.[114]

More broadly, Trump's fantasy connects the inevitability of Parkland-style violence with the cultural conditions of the gun-rights community. Barack Obama never could have fantasized about running into Stoneman Douglas High School. Nor could Hillary Clinton. Such a statement from Obama or Clinton would not have made sense. A unique prophetic subjectivity informs why certain rhetors are better positioned to deliver a particular message. For instance, Obama talked about being followed in department stores and drivers locking their car doors when he walked by. By contrast, Trump tells the world a fantasy about facing down an assault-style rifle unarmed. That difference between the rhetorical subjectivity of Obama and Trump is revealing. Trump seemed thrilled by the opportunity to fantasize about running into the school—or more precisely, *telling the world about his willingness to run into the school*. Without Nikolas Cruz and his semiautomatic rifle, Trump does not have the opportunity to perform such a coherent identity.

Trump's articulation also reflects the consistent references to the *inevitability of evil* in gun-rights discourse. For example, after the Columbine shootings, Wayne LaPierre said to Bill Clinton, "Mr. President, you could pass 50 new laws but the problem is bad people still do bad things."[115] LaPierre's description of evil actors, in response to the Sandy Hook shooting, deserves to be quoted at length:

> They walk among us every day. And does anybody really believe that the next Adam Lanza isn't planning his attack on a school he's already identified

at this very moment? How many more copycats are waiting in the wings for their moment of fame—from a national media machine that rewards them with the wall-to-wall attention and sense of identity that they crave—while provoking others to try to make their mark? A dozen more killers? A hundred? More? How can we possibly even guess how many, given our nation's refusal to create an active national database of the mentally ill? And the fact is, that wouldn't even begin to address the much larger and more lethal criminal class: Killers, robbers, rapists and drug gang members who have spread like cancer in every community in this country.[116]

Both gun violence and mass shootings represent ever-present threats that we cannot predict, prevent, or even understand.[117]

The telic temporality of gun-rights discourse portrays school shooters such as Klebold, Harris, Lanza, Loughner, and Cruz as part of a larger cosmological pattern that illuminates disturbing truths about human nature. Guns seem to be neutral, almost inconsequential instruments. For example, in an analysis of Charlton Heston's messaging, Christopher Duerringer and Z. S. Justus note how futile it would seem to be to confiscate guns because evil people would still commit violent acts with other instruments.[118] Donald Trump updated that assertion at the 2018 NRA convention in Dallas when he recounted a story he heard about knife attacks in London. Despite "unbelievably tough gun laws," a prestigious London hospital has been turned into a "war zone for horrible stabbing wounds," according to Trump. "Knives, knives, knives," Trump said, as he mimicked a stabbing motion at a cheering crowd.[119]

Yearning for Catastrophe

The NRA magnifies its constitutive capacity by synthesizing disorder-amplifying rhetoric with its telic urgings. Spitzer described this as a Chicken Little rhetorical style full of prophesies of imminent doom.[120] The NRA thrives when its members feel like the sky is falling. Political scientist Charlotte Hill added texture. After every incident of gun violence that attracts national attention, the NRA sends out mass mailings and emails.[121] Hill recounted that a little more than a week after the Parkland, Florida, shooting, former NRA president Marion Hammer sent out an email to NRA members that read:

> Gun control action is out in full force determined to use the senseless murder of the students and adults at Marjory Stoneman Douglas High School as an excuse to promote their gun ban agenda . . . PLEASE EMAIL THE

FOLLOWING MEMBERS OF THE LEGISLATURE IMMEDIATELY AND TELL THEM NO GUN CONTROL.[122]

Another political scientist and scholar of NRA discourse, Matt Lacombe, put it this way: "The NRA recognizes that its power base is its dedicated, intense membership, which sees guns as a way of life and feels a communal bond with other gun owners." Such an intense bond is based on the shared recognition that community members see the world as it really is and are prepared for the inevitability of evil.

These telic urgings facilitate a yearning for catastrophic conditions. Both the anecdotal and the empirical evidence suggest that legal and political success has an adverse effect on NRA membership, fundraising, and gun sales.[123] The demise of Remington Outdoor—one of the oldest firearm makers in the country—is revealing. The company was acquired in 2007 by Cerberus Capital Management, a private equity firm hoping that Remington's reputation among gun owners could still produce a profit. Cerberus's hopes turned out to be correct in the short term. After the Sandy Hook shooting, in which Adam Lanza used a Remington-made AR-15 to kill twenty children and six adults, Remington gun sales increased by 36 percent. Cerberus was expecting a similar boost after Hillary Clinton won the presidency in 2016. But she lost, fear of gun control dissipated, and sales declined 27 percent. Remington filed for bankruptcy in 2018 after accumulating hundreds of millions of dollars in debt.[124]

The empirical evidence also illustrates the pro-gun paradox. Trent Steidley and Martin Kosla found a strong correlation between demand for firearms, status anxiety, Democratic Party strength, and NRA membership (note what is missing from that list: *actual crime risk* had no impact on gun sales).[125] This led Steidley and Kosla to conclude that crime risk doesn't affect "self-defense motivations."[126] A perspicacious reader may note here that Steidley and Kosla may be drawing their definitional boundaries a bit too tight: "self-defense" and "motivation" do not merely connote physical and material safety. The prospect of a Hillary Clinton presidency, for instance, increased status anxiety unrelated to "actual crime risk." NRA memberships are renewed, and gun shops do a brisk trade in AR-15s, not from fear of crime but from fear of an incoherent subjectivity.

Subjectivity for Sale

The relationship between anxiety, disorder, and consumption aligns with the catastrophic homology's individualistic urgings because the attitudes induced by the pleasures of consumption construct an identity independent of empirical rationality. In other words, the pleasure of consumption and the subjectivity produced matter far more than the instrumental value of the item purchased. It matters little if an AR-15 makes gun owners and their families unsafe. That is not why that gun is bought. This version of what Joshua Gunn and David Beard called the "cry and buy" is not unique to gun-rights discourse.[127] After the terrorist attacks of September 11, 2001, we were urged to respond to the disorder and trauma of the attacks—to "Keep America rolling"—by maintaining our spending habits. But what is relevant in gun-rights discourse is the pragmatic political impact of such pleasure: consumption of firearms is not aimed at creating a more peaceful world. Gun-control discourse from the Left, at times, seems to long for a telic destination free of guns and the violent conditions that necessitate them in the first place. Gun-rights discourse sees that longing as totally unfit for a chaotic world. Here is where the telic messaging intersects with the economic purpose of gun-rights discourse: every gun manufacturer—not just Remington, but all of them—would quickly go bankrupt if guns were purchased for their instrumental value, such as hunting or crime protection. This unstable economic model is further undercut by the physical durability of firearms; unlike cars, cell phones, or blue jeans, guns do not wear out in a way that would require them to be repurchased at predictable intervals.[128] And aside from action movies, guns can only be fired one at a time. Nonetheless, the telic temporality of gun-rights discourse maintains consistent consumption patterns far beyond an instrumental function. The gun sales data make clear that although fewer Americans are buying guns, those who do are buying more of them.[129] Although the prospect of safety is not enhanced with each purchase, subjectivity is. In other words, gun manufacturers are not selling items of practical utility; they are selling an identity. The more guns one acquires, the more coherent that identity becomes. Thus, gun consumption is the means to an important end—progress toward the transformation of a world where the fearful and marginalized are equipped and empowered to respond to the threats posed by criminals . . . *and* out-of-touch, secular liberals.

From My Cold Dead Hands

The telic temporality of gun-rights discourse reveals several important implications. NRA messaging produces a reaffirmation of identity and a sense of belonging in the face of disorder.[130] But consider the clear impediments to forward progress: both individual and institutional enemies are ripe for destruction and disposal, especially those seeking to limit the march of history by reducing gun violence. From this worldview, gun control is pointless: there are too many monsters walking among us. Violence is inevitable. If not guns, they will use other instruments: in 2017 knives were used in a London terrorist attack; a van was used in Barcelona, and a truck in New York City. Gun control merely prevents the law-abiding from being able to defend themselves and their families: When guns are outlawed only outlaws will have guns. Charlton Heston's crowd-pleasing and bumper-sticker-worthy "From my cold, dead hands" and the more recent emergence of the defiant slogan "Come and Take It" inform a political subjectivity defined by a readiness to combat evil in all its forms.

It is worth noting how often self-proclaimed law-abiding gun advocates fantasize about becoming treasonous criminals when faced with the prospect of gun confiscation by the state. Smith & Wesson CEO Ed Schultz said, "My guns will never be confiscated in my lifetime, because the last thing I would do is have a shoot-out. I believe that it's an absolute right for me to have them, and if they [government forces] went that far, I would be willing to give up my life, as I wouldn't want to live here anyway."[131] The real threat—and the true source of disorder—is being unprepared to thwart evil when it presents itself. Who would you be if you were not prepared? Who are you if you cannot defend yourself or your family from the evil monsters walking among us? This preparedness, displayed in the public declaration of one's willingness to use violence, is what separates the insiders from the outsiders, the strong from the weak, and the living from the dead.

A clear set of enemies emerges, and it is not limited to deranged school shooters. Anyone trying to incapacitate the gun owner's ability to respond to this inevitable violence assumes a strange alliance with the actual perpetrators of evil. According to the worldview advanced by gun-rights discourse, the Adam Lanzas and Nicholas Cruzes of the world can't really help it. They are pure evil. Hillary Clinton and Nancy Pelosi can. Thus, the individuals and institutions that slow the march of progress much be opposed, destroyed, and discarded.

Broadly, if the CDC, the ATF, and the FBI support gun-control laws, these institutions must also be thwarted.[132] Consider two ways in which the NRA has acted on these urgings. First, the NRA has adopted a rhetorical strategy of opposing these agencies and their allies. For instance, Davidson has described a favorite NRA tactic of bombarding institutions with negative publicity to reduce their effectiveness.[133] Specifically, the gun lobby and its Republican allies have fought for decades to defund and weaken the Bureau of Alcohol, Tobacco, and Firearms.[134] The catastrophic homology helps explain why: four million gun transactions occur each year; and 40 percent of gun sales occur without a background check. Buying guns at a flea market, gun show, or through a private buyer is not difficult. Unregulated gun sales offer the NRA an ever-present rhetorical escape hatch. When gun violence occurs, and the instruments of that violence are traced back to these unregulated purchases, the NRA can oppose new, stricter gun-control laws by suggesting that the US does not need new gun laws; law enforcement only needs to enforce the laws already on the books. But of course this is an impossible task when the mechanisms to enforce the laws are weakened.[135] Such a political outcome should sound familiar: institutional ineffectiveness promotes distrust; distrust promotes defunding; defunding promotes further ineffectiveness, still more distrust, and even less funding. Apply, lather, rinse, and repeat.

Stifling gun violence research is a second example of telic temporality's political impact. Because it threatens the community's rhetorical construction of the march of history, research identifying a connection between rising levels of gun ownership and the risk of violence must be thwarted. In the 1990s, after a landmark study backed by the Centers for Disease Control and Prevention found that bringing a gun into the home increased the risk of homicide, the NRA led a push for what became known as the Dickey Amendment, which defunded the CDC's support for gun research.[136] The Dickey Amendment stifled the research that would have informed effective legislation aimed at reducing gun violence. Ineffectual legislation resulted, including the 1994 federal assault weapons ban. Instead of crafting laws from evidence-based solutions, the assault weapons ban focused on restricting cosmetic features such as bayonet mounts and threaded gun barrels.[137] The law failed miserably. Such uninformed legislation produces ineffective laws; gun violence is not redressed by such laws, and those failures are held up as another example of institutional ineffectiveness.[138] One can imagine if such logic were applied to all legislation. More troublingly, this notion of telic temporality informs many of our public conversations. Gun-rights discourse has produced a set of formal appeals oriented toward disorder and violence. While few would admit to this, the toxic cynicism of the entire catastrophic homology is reflected in these telic urgings. It is not merely that insufficient information limits the likelihood of new gun laws passing, as Dylan Scott argued.[139] The greater issue is that even when such laws do pass, a lack of information means they are unlikely to be effective. And when one uninformed law does not work, it can seem like all legislative efforts to reduce gun violence are pointless.

After each recent mass shooting, *New York Times* columnist Nicholas Kristof publishes a graphic illustrating the dearth of research on gun violence caused by the NRA's efforts to cut funding. Between 1973 and 2012 the National Institutes of Health awarded 89 research grants for 65 cases of rabies; 120 grants for 266 cases of polio; 212 grants for 400 cases of cholera; 56 grants for 1,337 of diphtheria; and *three grants for four million cases of firearm injury*.[140] We end up spending almost nothing on gun violence and thirty-three thousand Americans die each year. Telic temporality, as it is reflected in the gun-rights discourse examined in the preceding section, helps explain why the American public is willing to put up with such a baffling allocation of public resources.

CONCLUSION

I hope the reflections of the catastrophic homology in this chapter lend insight into public conversations about gun violence in America. Ultimately, gun-rights discourse promotes a deep suspicion of outsider elites meddling in cherished cultures and traditions. Gun-control discourse from the Left too often aligns with those fears. But the NRA's role as defender of American values is little more than a rhetorical fig leaf covering a sophisticated lobbying effort on behalf of the gun industry. The NRA, along with its Institute for Legislative Action, and its PR firm, Ackerman McQueen, are first and foremost political tools for enhancing the profitability of gun makers—an industry that goes bankrupt when people feel safe and secure. The NRA appears to represent an aggrieved community combatting the authoritarian aims of a shadowy network of elites. LaPierre said as much when he called academic, political, and media elites "America's greatest domestic threats."[141] What LaPierre left unacknowledged is his own association with the elite authoritarianism most feared by his target audience. Heston, LaPierre, and Cox are precisely the elites this audience should be most suspicious of. LaPierre looks less like the humble folks whom he claims to represent and more like the millionaire corporate lobbyist that he actually is.[142] Before the NRA, LaPierre managed political campaigns for five different politicians, and he served for years as a board member of the American Association of Political Consultants.[143] The NRA's lobbying efforts on behalf of a company like Remington Outdoor are more aligned with the investment returns of private equity firms in New York City than with rural Americans who want to keep their families safe.

These contradictory allegiances illuminate the divergence between the NRA's political advocacy and the attitudes of most of its own members. The NRA has a long history of opposing gun-control measures that enjoy broad support from its rank-and-file members. These measures include strengthening criminal and mental health background checks; and banning firearms purchases by those on terror watch lists, the severely mentally ill, and violent criminals.[144] A catastrophic homology is informed by that divergence: the NRA does not prioritize reducing gun violence. Rather, the NRA prioritizes the special interests of Cerberus Capital Management and Ackerman McQueen over all else.

Worse, the NRA seems to support the interests of criminals over law enforcement. America has a gun culture, as the NRA emphasizes; but it also has a *gun-control culture* that emerged for a specific reason: without strong gun-control laws, police officers will be outgunned by criminals.[145] Adam Winkler traced our modern gun-control laws as far back as the 1920s and 1930s. More specifically, Winkler cited the Saint Valentine's Day Massacre in 1929, and the political response to it, as a point of inflection.[146] On Valentine's Day in 1929, Al Capone directed his henchmen to execute seven men in a Chicago warehouse. When newspapers published gory images of the massacre, the public was shocked: how could a criminal gang possess more firepower than the police? The subsequent gun-control proposals fit the demands of the New Deal moment. By 1934 the National Firearms Act was passed. It did not confiscate or ban guns. Rather, it imposed onerous taxes on machine guns and sawed-off shotguns and forced the owners of those guns to register them and submit to fingerprinting. Few law-abiding people were impacted: most didn't have machine guns, and those that did didn't mind registering them. Criminals still used guns, but the most lethal weaponry was harder to get and riskier to keep. Law-abiding citizens couldn't have cared less. They could still use guns for hunting or protection. But the police were much less worried about being outgunned. The legislation was so successful that in 1938 Congress passed a similar law, the Federal Firearms Act. During this era, the public supported government and police efforts to restrict access to certain firearms to support law enforcement combatting criminals, pimps, and thieves.

The messaging of the modern gun-rights movement is misaligned with this history of public support for sensible gun control. More specifically, the modern NRA—which portrays virtually any gun-control law as the first step onto a slippery slope toward tyranny and totalitarianism—is a relatively new rhetorical invention that cannot be understood (or challenged) without understanding the homological underpinnings from which it draws much of its strength.

CHAPTER 4

Political Catastrophe and the Rhetoric of Donald Trump

WHILE SIXTY-THREE MILLION Americans voted for Donald J. Trump in 2016, very few did so because he conformed to traditional standards of political experience, competence, or acumen. Instead, a common explanation for the most shocking political upset in recent memory went something like this: Trump's economic populism resonated with a particular subset of American voters; he articulated their economic grievances and social anxieties; he said what they were all thinking, but could not say themselves; he affirmed their fears in a way that other political elites didn't notice or understand; and he promised to leverage his deal-making ability and outsider's status to return this aggrieved community to their empowered positions. Images of grizzled, out-of-work coal miners uniting at Trump rallies to don red MAGA hats and chant "Build the wall!" made for compelling campaign television; more importantly, these images seemed to reinforce the popular explanation for Trump's victory. For example, E. J. Dionne, Norman Ornstein, and Thomas Mann, in their book *One Nation After Trump,* cited a study suggesting that "social and economic forces have isolated the white working class as a political constituency, to the extent that many in this demographic feel like a peripheral afterthought in a country they once defined."[1] Naomi Klein also described white men "losing economic security" as a reason for paying more attention to the real economic concerns of Trump's base.[2] And Nitsuh Abebe connected Trump's emergence to a version of "economic anxiety" propped up by "vivid pictures of families in Ohio or Indiana fretting over mortgage payments in a haze of factory closures, bad backs, and shuttered diners."³ Given the critical tools developed in this book so far, I hope it is clear why the explanation for Trump's victory offered by Dionne, Klein, and Abebe needs to be met with suspicion. A set of incongruities remain. Little evidence suggests Trump voters were motivated by economic anxiety. Exit polls found that voters who prioritized the economy were more likely to support Hillary Clinton than Donald Trump. Another poll found that those whose economic standing was in "fair or poor shape" were almost twice as likely to support Clinton than those who felt more economically stable. Trump supporters were simply not as poor as the economic-anxiety explanation made them out to be.⁴

If one is careful with the data and precise with the variables, a more accurate description emerges of the audience Trump's messaging attracted. Disproportionately white, rural, older, civically disengaged, and nominally Christian men were most responsible for Trump's election.⁵ Joshua Green showed in his book *Devil's Bargain* how Trump's message resonated with this subset of the electorate in key swing states; consequently, these voters supported Trump in numbers no one anticipated. More broadly, this description of Trump's primary audience offers a rich opportunity to explore how empowered individuals are united together into constitutive communities oriented toward the catastrophic homology. For this audience, Trump's election was the culmination of a complex confluence of social, economic, political, and cultural upheavals, sparked by decades of increasing economic stratification, declining American manufacturing, shifting immigration patterns, the rising visibility of alternative gender and sexual identities, and more black and brown faces in positions of power—including the White House.⁶

Trump's messaging resonated. He ran a campaign that appealed to an aggrieved, white, masculine identity that resented feeling out of place in a society (seemingly) overrun by people of color, women, immigrants, and other members of minority groups. Arlie Hochschild's *line cutting* metaphor offers a useful point of comparison: Trump's audience thought they were waiting in line, working hard, playing by the rules, and paying their taxes—only to have a contingent of Others cut in front of them.⁷ Those who remained at the back of the line were left feeling insulted, overlooked, and forgotten. Trump's messaging was well suited to these individuals.

The threat of radical Islamic terrorists attacking American suburbs, along with drug-dealing, rapist Mexican immigrants teeming over the border, activated these fears. Trump was aware of this appeal. After the election, he claimed that he won New Hampshire because it was "a drug-infested den."⁸ For all his unpredictability, Trump stayed on message when he invoked chaos as a primary organizing principle. Given his audience's worldview then, drawing from the well of catastrophe proved advantageous for Trump.

Given how well Trump's rhetoric resonated with his aggrieved audience, the methodological quandary underpinning this book emerges again: because we cannot read the minds of Trump voters, what critical tools are available for illuminating the often-unconscious process of audience constitution?

GUIDING ASSUMPTIONS

I want to begin with four guiding assumptions that further point to how hollow the dominant narrative of Trump's victory is. First, the real-life human that is Donald J. Trump is not especially relevant here. Instead, I conceptualize Trump as a rhetorical construct—a set of symbols that sixty-three million Americans were able to read as constituting a desirable American president. Second, Trump supporters cannot be conceptualized as a referential audience. White, rural, older, civically disengaged, and nominally evangelical men were not all drinking coffee at the local Waffle House waiting for Trump's messaging. Trump's discourse brought into a unified audience individuals who were dispersed and fragmented across experiences and locations. Without the constitutive power of catastrophe, "Trump voters" do not exist. Third, because rhetoric does some of its most important work on reconciliation, I aim to locate a rich site of inquiry in the symbolic resources that smoothed over a glaring set of incongruities. For example, how does a thrice-married casino billionaire with no government experience connect so powerfully with evangelical pig farmers in North Carolina and out-of-work long-haul truck drivers in Ohio? Trump voters were not attracted to his compelling deployment of traditional standards of argumentation. Even during the 2016 campaign, Trump was more Hugh Hefner than Abe Lincoln. And traditional methods of rational argumentation cannot satisfactorily explain why that mattered so little to so many.

Instead, Trump's ability to orient his audience toward the catastrophic homology offers a more compelling explanation for Trump's candidacy and election. Some have argued that although Trump was a political neophyte, he still had his finger on the pulse of American culture at this precise moment. But that does not seem to be the case either. Trump had been running for president since 1988 when he visited crowds that waved "Trump for President" and "Trump in '88" signs. And his message hasn't changed in thirty years. Trump long railed against the corruption of political and economic elites; he decried China's currency manipulation, and later the economic damage of

NAFTA on American workers. As Joshua Green has argued, Trump sounded familiar refrains about our country facing "disaster" because we were "being kicked around" by Japan, Iran, and Saudi Arabia—countries that were "laughing at us" behind our backs.[9] Trump has a history of complaining about immigrants being coddled and refugees being favored over native-born Americans. And references to the threat of black and brown criminals were not new to Trump's 2016 message. In 1989 a group of black and Latino teenagers from Harlem were falsely accused of assaulting and raping a white jogger in Central Park. Trump bought full-page ads in four newspapers calling for their execution.[10] In other words, Trump's message never changed much; the context did. Consequently, Trump's cultural resonance reflects larger shifts in American politics that have been under way since the late 1970s—shifts involving the decaying of institutions vital to representative democracy, including basic norms of governance politics, media, decorum, and civility.

I explore those shifts next. I then attempt to synthesize and integrate those shifts within Trump's orientation toward a catastrophic homology so that, ultimately, I can show how Trump's discourse aligned with this disparate rhetorical reservoir in a way that offers a more complete account of his victory and a richer understanding of his rhetorical appeal.[11]

A WORLD OUT OF CHAOS

Americans have a history of expressing political discontent by flirting with firebrand demagogues, especially during political primaries. Normally, we end up settling down and supporting more moderate candidates. In 2015 and 2016 many scholars and journalists assumed that pattern would hold: Republicans would come to their senses, end their flirtation with Trump, and settle on a candidate who would keep the nation intact and avoid World War III. But Trump won, and not simply because of his red hats or his promise to build a big wall. Trump reflected a decades-long disintegration of postwar order and institutional trust. Understanding Trump's election first requires understanding that disintegration.

After World War II, the US took the lead in developing the institutional mechanisms responsible for binding the world together and spreading liberal democracy. As Dean Acheson, secretary of state under President Truman and one of the principal architects of the postwar order later wrote, "The enormity of the task . . . was to create a world out of chaos."[12] Disagreements over the pragmatic implementation of complex global policies were to be expected, but many were optimistic that the desire to make money and not war, to preserve order through institutional strength, and to promote global cohesion would ameliorate disagreements without bloodshed.

And it did just that.

Acheson's grand ambitions were fulfilled. These prosperous and peaceful decades also offer a more specific reminder: Donald Trump's catastrophic appeals would have failed to resonate under these social conditions. But, in the late 1970s, as the postwar order began to show signs of cracking, and cynicism replaced trust—especially for a subset of empowered Americans— conditions began to shift in a direction that amplified the persuasiveness of Trump's rhetoric.

Looking back, it seems far too many Americans assumed the nation's postwar growth was the result of a unique combination of providence, exceptionalism, and bootstrapping gumption. More precisely, Americans didn't realize that much of our prosperity resulted from the complete devastation of the rest of the industrialized world. This overconfidence turned out to be especially relevant for the millions of working-class Americans now able to attain a lifestyle that included a modest home, two cars, health care, and a pension—all without advanced education or specialized training.[13] Eventually, Asian and European economies rebounded from the devastation of World War II to challenge American global economic supremacy. Billions of new Chinese and Indian workers entered the labor market, and corporations soon realized how much money could be saved by shifting manufacturing sites from Detroit to Dong Nai. Those least prepared for the twin shocks of a shifting manufacturing economy and the competition posed by billions of new workers began to experience the first pangs of declining trust in the postwar institutional order.[14]

As I detailed in a previous book, *Economic Injustice and the Rhetoric of the American Dream*, many corporations took advantage of the cheap labor abroad and outsourced productive capacity.[15] Many working-class Americans were shunted into a contingent labor market just as the cost of food and gasoline began to rise. Concurrently, the welfare state shrank, good jobs with benefits became scarce, and corporations further cut labor costs by turning to temporary and part-time workers. Declining economic prosperity infected once-trustworthy institutions with toxic cynicism: religiously, the shift toward nondenominational fundamentalism encouraged the rise of Pat Robertson and Jerry Falwell's brand of fanaticism; technologically, a fragmented media environment created space for fringe voices to retread tired plotlines about job-taking, undeserving people of color laying siege to what is not theirs; politically, Americans grew more partisan and isolated; and geographically, Americans moved to more segregated churches and neighborhoods that affirmed their narrowing perspectives.[16] Under these conditions, the faltering of shared agreements about empirical validity, institutional strength, and social order revealed the cracks that would soon be split open by Donald Trump's rhetoric of catastrophe.

THE POLITICS OF DISINTEGRATION AND DISTRUST

I concede that aspiring politicians have long emphasized the disorder and chaos that they promise to address if elected. Very few elected representatives win by proclaiming "Things are swell, and let's keep it that way." But usually, aspiring politicians couch their political remedies within an existing institutional order. For instance, politicians often promise to improve the institutions of public education, market capitalism, the military, and even liberal democracy itself. However, declining institutional trust and shifting standards of rationality carved out increased space for an alternative worldview. Politically, it became less important to anchor a candidate's platform and politics to rational argumentation, empirical evidence, and institutional remedies. Concurrently, it became more acceptable for politicians such as Ronald Reagan and Newt Gingrich to attract audiences by appealing to their distrust and cynicism: anything—including complete institutional dysfunction—seemed preferable to the status quo.[17] Strange as it may seem now, Republicans of the middle twentieth century not only tolerated robust government, they directly embraced the idea that it could play an important role by counterbalancing corporate power.[18] That government embrace would soon be broken.

Fear and Trembling in Gingrich and Bush

The rise of Newt Gingrich in the 1990s illustrated what could be accomplished when politicians aligned their messaging with this cynical turn. After a stint teaching history in Georgia, Gingrich ascended the Republican ranks by aligning his rhetoric with this shifting context to directly attack "the corrupt welfare state."[19] He sought to kick over the entire traditional political establishment, toppling both Democrats and Republicans who failed to notice and respond to the fear and trembling Gingrich articulated. He went after opponents with red-faced rage. Employing a familiar technique, Gingrich turned his guns on the internal enemies within his own party: the moderates so comfortable with their power that they could be portrayed as adulterated sell-outs to the corrupt DC establishment. And he portrayed Democrats not as worthy adversaries, but as corrupt enemies that must be eliminated. Gingrich cited Mao's "war without blood" as he encouraged colleagues to win arguments by describing opponents with terms such as *betray, cheat, corrupt, crisis, cynicism, decay, destroy, disgrace, incompetent, lie, radical, sick, status quo, steal, threaten,* and *traitors*.[20] For Gingrich, it was not enough to disagree on policy matters with your opponent: contrarians had to be crushed.

Gingrich peaked in 1994 when his "Contract with America" was announced in front of the US Capitol. In a prescient turn-of-phrase, he called it "a first step towards renewing American civilization."[21] Although Gingrich flamed out in a firestorm of hypocrisy, scandal, and corruption, his discourse illuminated the changing conditions of American politics, marked by hyperpartisanship and a spreading distrust.

The George W. Bush presidency accelerated institutional cynicism. Initially, the Bush administration set out to portray itself as a sober, moderate alternative to the scandal, immorality, and disgrace of the Gingrich-Clinton 1990s. The Bush administration pushed bipartisan immigration reform, support for faith-based social programs, and a softened, compassionate conservatism to restore the belief that government, religious institutions, and the free market could work together to improve people's lives, especially those marginalized by a changing economy.

The terrorist attacks of September 11, 2001, changed all that. For the next seven years, the Bush administration fulfilled the most cynical caricature of institutional incompetence, beginning with the global war on terror and ending with the collapse of the global economy. For an audience whose worldviews were already marked by suspicion, political remedies to their daily challenges seemed unpalatable. In the ashes of the Bush presidency, an audience was united by anger, cynicism, and frustration toward any institution's ability to redress the challenges of their own lives. Republicans ridiculed then candidate Obama for noting how this alienation encouraged the formation of communities unified by "cling[ing] to guns or religion or antipathy to people who aren't like them or anti-immigrant sentiment or anti-trade sentiment as a way to explain their frustrations."[22] But in that statement, Obama illuminated how the failures of George W. Bush accelerated institutional cynicism in a way the Republican political establishment never noticed (but would soon come to rue).

Fire Up the Base

After Obama's 2008 election, the Tea Party capitalized on this spreading cynicism. A decentralized movement that decried ineffective government while fueling white male resentment, paranoia, and racist conspiracy theories emerged. The Republican establishment was comfortable riding the Tea Party wave of institutional distrust while Democrats controlled Congress and the White House in 2009 and 2010. Republican politicians like Paul Ryan and John Boehner were happy to allow Sarah Palin, Sean Hannity, Kid Rock, and Ted Nugent to fire up the base in the hopes that the adults in the room would then use that momentum to cut taxes and welfare spending.[23] But riding Tea Party popularity to electoral success in 2010 would create challenges for the Republican establishment when it came time to govern. Tea Party cynicism was misinterpreted and underappreciated. For a time, this deep cynicism allowed Republican leaders to blame the alienation felt by their base on the Obama presidency; but Republican leaders were blind to the deeper, institutional grievances the George W. Bush presidency should have exposed. This was evidenced in 2012 by the nomination of an out-of-touch elitist—Mitt Romney—who had no chance of connecting with such distrust and alienation. Romney's message could not align with the Tea Party's cry to "take our country back." *It was already his country.* Instead, space was carved out for the constitution of an older, whiter, rural, and nominally religious audience fed up with tone-deaf party elites.[24]

This demographic should sound familiar. A fringe community composed of an insurgency-minded band of outsiders and lapsed conservatives would soon be gathered together by Andrew Breitbart, Steve Bannon, and Donald Trump.

STORMING THE GATES

Andrew Breitbart first rose to prominence by arguing on behalf of an early version of Trump's audience: Americans who felt marginalized by the social, political, and economic upheavals of the early twenty-first century. Breitbart built on Gingrich's foundation. He noticed that most people do not need more data; they need drama, inspiration, heroes, and villains.[25] Breitbart also seemed to understand the importance of context; he cared little about influencing legislation in Washington, DC, and instead—because, as he put it, "politics is downstream from culture"—he sought to influence gut-level emotions.[26]

After Andrew Breitbart died in 2012 of heart failure, an accomplished but quirky former investment banker and entertainment mogul named Steve Bannon took up the baton. Bannon's messaging continued to attract zealous, uncompromising outsiders keen on storming the gates of the political and economic establishment.

Bannon was a true believer. He thought of himself as a courageous defender of Western civilization. He was passionate and dogmatic, quick to the throw the first punch, both literally, in his confrontations with rich prep school rivals, and metaphorically, in his classroom debates at Harvard Business School.[27] While intelligent and accomplished, he was never comfortable within the constraints of traditional institutions. Religiously, he maintained an uneasy relationship with the Catholic Church, ultimately separating from his home parish to join another that offered his preferred Tridentine Mass. Athletically, his confidence fueled a shoot-first basketball style that led to an enduring nickname from his teammates: "coast-to-coast." Later in life, Bannon was drawn to the Honey Badger: a viral sensation reflecting autonomy, power, and not-giving-a-hoot; Bannon adopted this spirit animal, proclaiming his Honey Badger allegiance whenever a controversial decision had to be made. In prep school, and then in the Navy, Harvard, Goldman Sachs, Hollywood, and the video game industry, Bannon was unique in his ability to combine carnage, chaos, and accomplishment. He would have made a fine fundamentalist minister.

Bannon would have never entered politics were it not for a keen awareness of the shifting conditions made manifest in the post-Bush, Tea Party climate. Bannon's message resonated with the institutional cynicism prevalent among certain conservatives. The terrorist attacks of 9/11 were a tragedy, not just for the lost lives, but because they aligned with a deeper cultural worry about Islam's broader attack on Western civilization. Bannon saw in 9/11 evidence of a larger collapsing order. Bannon thought intergovernmental organizations like the European Union, NATO, and the United Nations, and elite leaders like Barack Obama, Angela Merkel, and François Holland, were incapable of defending Western civilization; they were all too ready to accede to political correctness and cultural sensitivities, and to trade in their borders, sovereignty, national identity to appease the elites.[28] The 2008 financial crash was also understood in relation to this condition. Liberals and conservatives alike found fault in political and financial elites in the midst of the collapse, but Bannon took his attribution in an unexpected direction: he did not see the collapse as a mere financial problem; he saw it as a deeper, systemic reflection of selfishness, greed, civic abdication, and cultural rot embedded in our political and financial institutions. In other words, Bannon reflected an orientation toward catastrophe.

For Bannon, the only viable remedy was to expose the rot. The emerging social and cultural conditions of Breitbart and fringe internet culture resonated with Bannon. He was not William F. Buckley or Mitt Romney. He thrived on chaos and did all he could to spread it. As one of Bannon's Breitbart employees said, "If there's an explosion or a fire somewhere, Steve is probably nearby with some matches." Joshua Green compared Bannon to "a human hand grenade, an Internet-era update of the Slim Pickens character in Dr. Strangelove who rides the bomb like a rodeo bull, whoopin' and hollerin' all the way to nuclear annihilation."²⁹ Bannon also reflected the unique conception of hierarchical justice oriented toward a catastrophic homology. Like that of a fundamentalist minister, Bannon's career success fueled his arrogance and ambition. He was not bothered that his community's conspiracy theories and controversial views relegated him to the fringes of DC's elite circles. Because Bannon's previous accomplishments allowed him a measure of security, he did not feel the need to hide his convictions. The world would one day come around. If he could remake existing institutions to conform to his own catastrophic preferences, great; but if not, he would be happy lobbing grenades from the fringes.

THE BLUNT INSTRUMENT

Donald Trump cannot be understood apart from Steve Bannon. But for Bannon, Trump was merely a means to an end—a "blunt instrument"—in Bannon's words.³⁰ Sarah Palin or Michele Bachmann could have served the same purpose. Although confident in his preordained destination, Bannon was surprised that Trump's messaging resonated as well as it did. Reflecting his telic confidence, Bannon said of Trump, "He's taken this nationalist movement and moved it up twenty years. If France, Germany, England, or any of these places had the equivalent of a Donald Trump, they would be in power. They don't."³¹

Together, Bannon and Trump offer a vivid illustration of the dynamic oscillation between text and context required for massive social change. Primed by Newt Gingrich, the Tea Party, Breitbart, and Bannon, Trump's messaging aligned with the condition of a particular audience in a particular moment. Trump skillfully deployed "birtherism," articulated the disaffections of many older, white, American men feeling cut-in-line, and sneered at the never-ending bounds of "political correctness." All this allowed his critique to include the Republican establishment and economic elites in a way the Tea Party resonance demanded but few other Republicans could articulate. In the process, his discourse offered a rich opportunity to understand the most shocking political upset in American history.

Make America Great Again

Although far from a disciplined rhetor, Trump did stay on message by emphasizing the feelings of marginalization, fear, and insecurity facing his target audience.[32] Trump's aggrieved audience was animated by a familiar cultural fiction. They had to fight back to retain their way of life. In an October 2016 speech, Trump referred to the "corrupt political establishment" as a "machine" with "no soul."[33] He warned his audience,

> There is nothing the political establishment will not do—no lie that they won't tell, to hold their prestige and power at your expense. And that's what's been happening. The Washington establishment and the financial and media corporations that fund it exist for only one reason: to protect and enrich itself.

He encouraged his audience by describing his movement as way to replace a "failed [and] totally corrupt political establishment." He continued, "For those who control the levers of power in Washington, and for the global special interests, they partner with these people that don't have your good in mind. Our campaign represents a true existential threat like they haven't seen before." While not unprecedented, Trump's appeals to the feelings of marginalization in his audience extended the political efficacy of what sociologist Nathan Glazer called "defensive offensives," in which formerly empowered individuals are called together and turned into potent political actors to defend what (they think) is rightfully theirs.[34] Further, Trump was able to turn perceived marginalization into prophetic utterances as he offered a return to power for his aggrieved audience by separating and punishing the malevolent threat to status.[35]

The perception of marginalization is especially relevant for white evangelical Christians. Trump's messaging lends insight into why so many pious midwestern conservatives would support with such enthusiasm an impious boor who didn't know how to pronounce Second Corinthians.[36] American evangelical Christians are marked by a worldview sympathetic to Trump's rhetoric of marginalization. Many think they are under attack. Trump's January 2016 speech at Liberty University illustrated this resonance.[37] He promised to "protect Christianity." Against what, he did not make clear; in one reference, it was "bad things." He went on, "And we've got to protect because bad things are happening, very bad things are happening, and we don't—I don't know what it is." He did mention the Syrian civil war as an example of why Christians need protecting: "And if you look what's going on throughout the world, you look at Syria where if you're Christian, they're chopping off heads. You look at the different places, and Christianity, it's under siege." Trump employed a common rhetorical tactic, encouraging the religious audience to circle their wagons against attacks from nebulous outsiders.[38]

When he was three years old, Trump was earning $200,000 a year (in 2018 dollars); by age eight, he was a millionaire.[39] Despite Trump's material advantages, his discourse aligned his own story with the same marginalization of his audience. Trump's *Make America Great Again* slogan was appropriate. *Again* was the operative term—it was a not-so-subtle pledge to return empowered individuals to a privileged status they felt was slipping away. Trump would often devote time in his speeches to describing how *they* were laughing at *us*.[40] In announcing his presidential candidacy in June 2015, Trump complained that Mexico was "laughing at us, at our stupidity."[41] At Liberty University in January 2016, Trump used the phrase *nobody respects us* to describe the US military, and he continued, "They're laughing at us. We don't know what we're doing."[42] In justifying the US withdrawal from the Paris climate accord, Trump asked,

> At what point does America get demeaned? At what point do they start laughing at us as a country? We want fair treatment for its citizens, and we want fair treatment for our taxpayers. We don't want other leaders and other countries laughing at us anymore. And they won't be. They won't be.[43]

Scholars and journalists have argued that while Trump long flirted with running for president to boost his brand and his TV ratings, he ran in 2016 because he was humiliated at the White House Correspondents' dinner in 2013 by comedian Seth Meyers and President Obama.[44]

The appeals to marginalization continued after Trump was elected. Trump's inaugural address was exceptional for its foreboding imagery. Rather than use the speech to bring the country together and heal the wounds of a bitter campaign, Trump doubled down on the cleavage and carnage. Early on Trump said, "Today's ceremony, however, has very special meaning. Because today we are not *merely* transferring power from one Administration to another, or from one party to another—but we are transferring power from Washington, D.C. and giving it back to you, the American People."[45] Note the key modifier *merely* in the second sentence. Unlike all previous transfers of power, Trump is making it clear that this one is different: an outsider has upset the established political order. The physical setting is telling; Trump made this statement while standing in front of prominent members of Congress, as well as former presidents and their families—the exact individuals responsible for withholding power from the American people.

Trump's memorable reference to "American carnage" also reflects perceptions of marginalization:

But for too many of our citizens, a different reality exists: Mothers and children trapped in poverty in our inner cities; rusted-out factories scattered like tombstones across the landscape of our nation; an education system, flush with cash, but which leaves our young and beautiful students deprived of knowledge; and the crime and gangs and drugs that have stolen too many lives and robbed our country of so much unrealized potential. *This American carnage stops right here and stops right now.*

Trump's inaugural address—like much of his campaign—was unconventional. This was not an inaugural address as much as a campaign speech more appropriate for a rally at an airplane hangar in Alabama than a ceremony conducted in front of the Capitol before an audience of dignitaries, former presidents, politicians, and their families.[46]

Overall, Trump's discourse made clear who was to blame for his audience's perceived marginalization: people of color, immigrants, and secular elites functioned as clear-and-present enemies. More specifically, Trump's discourse often held up President Obama as a foil. In his speech accepting the Republican nomination, Trump said, "President Obama has doubled our national debt to more than $19 trillion, and growing. Yet, what do we have to show for it? Our roads and bridges are falling apart, our airports are in Third World condition, and forty-three million Americans are on food stamps."[47] In the same speech, and throughout the campaign, Trump's discourse leveraged stereotypes of black and brown criminality as the cause of fear and loathing for his audience. In the same RNC acceptance speech, Trump said, "The number of new illegal immigrant families who have crossed the border so far this year already exceeds the entire total from 2015. They are being released by the tens of thousands into our communities with no regard for the impact on public safety or resources." Trump's discourse made these fears vivid through consistent references to immigrant crime. In the same speech, he described the murder of a young woman by a released "border crosser" who made his way to Nebraska and "ended the life of an innocent young girl named Sarah Root." Activating all the worst fears of his audience he went on, "She was 21 years-old, and was killed the day after graduating from college with a 4.0 Grade Point Average. Her killer was then released a second time, and he is now a fugitive from the law." Confronted with that message, who wouldn't be anxious? Who wouldn't be attracted to an unconventional candidate who—even though he lacked experience and tweeted a bit too much—articulate their feelings of marginalization and promised to do something about them?

Voting with the Middle Finger

Trump's rhetoric of marginalization was a common and compelling explanation for his stunning victory. And there is ample empirical evidence that Trump's audience did *feel* marginalized. Ninety-one percent of Trump supporters felt that they were "under attack" and that their lives were worse now than ten years ago; this despite the fact that there was little material difference in Donald Trump and Hillary Clinton supporters.[48] Rather, "anxiety about cultural change" was one of the key reasons Trump's rhetoric resonated. Sixty-eight percent of white, working-class voters said the American way of life needed to be protected against foreign influence. Seventy-nine percent of respondents who claimed to often "feel like a stranger in my own country" also voted for Trump.[49] However, there is less evidence to support the claim that Trump supporters were marginalized in any material ways. For instance, Trump voters may have *thought* they lived in a crime-ridden world. However, crime has dropped precipitously in the last twenty-five years.[50] Specifically, many Trump voters *thought* immigrants were crossing the border and committing crimes. But Trump's immigrant bogeyman also does not align with reality. Several studies confirm that immigrants are less likely to commit crimes than native-born Americans, and there is no evidence than undocumented immigrants commit more crimes than any other group.[51] Trump voters *thought* globalized trade took away American jobs.[52] It doesn't. As a share of GDP, global trade increases rather than decreases equality.[53] Trump voters *thought* the police were under attack. They are not. Compared with the 1970s, about half as many officers are murdered each year, and the number of assaults on police officers has also fallen.[54] And many white Trump voters *thought* that black and brown Americans were making economic gains at their expense. They were not, and they are not. There is no serious evidence to support the argument that white Americans are more economically insecure than other racial or ethnic groups.[55] For working-class whites, more specifically, it is nonsense to assume that black and Hispanic Americans have challenged their economic standing. The income gap between white working-class Americans and black and Hispanic Americans is just as large as it was five decades ago.[56]

Trump's economic messaging was starting from a fictional premise. While the *felt cultural marginalization* might have been very real, Americans were living in the safest, healthiest, and wealthiest moment in human history.[57] Consider the possibility that this lack of empirical validity may not have been lost on Trump's audience. Many Trump supporters may have been aware of the tension between the marginalization Trump described and the material comfort of their lives. Further, many Trump supporters may have liked feeling marginalized, leveraging powerlessness as a sign of agency, as Paul Johnson suggested.[58] If so, that tension needed to be reconciled. The analysis in previous chapters located similar tensions in fundamentalist inerrancy, a warming planet, and ubiquitous gun violence. But we also know that audiences cannot coalesce around fiction—at least not for long.[59] Recall also from previous case studies that the language deployed to reconcile tensions need not be grounded in empirical validity, falsifiability, and the standards of rational argumentation. In this case, Trump's messaging circulated tired, well worn, and demonstrably false stories about brown people stealing all the jobs, black people killing the police, and women infringing on men's status. For a worldview marked by marginalization, it seemed the *appearance* of a systematic hermeneutic was primary.

THE SYSTEMIC COHERENCE OF CONSPIRACY

While Trump's speeches and interviews are fraught with contradictions, a closer look reveals a formal pattern to the incoherence. Trump's discourse was deeply systematic. He activated the core dimensions of a conspiratorial worldview aligned with an audience marked by perceptions of marginalization.

Much of Trump's messaging fit the textbook definition of conspiratorial thinking: he seemed sure a secret cabal was plotting to commit illegal, immoral, and harmful acts against the audience.[60] Trump argued that he possessed unique prophetic knowledge that would aid him in exposing this conspiracy. At the RNC convention, Trump described "big business, elite media and major donors" who "are lining up behind the campaign of my opponent because they know she will keep our rigged system in place. They are throwing money at her because they have total control over everything she does. She is their puppet, and they pull the strings."[61] Later, in a television commercial his campaign saved for November 3, Trump warned, "It's a global power structure that is responsible for the economic decisions that have robbed our working class, stripped our country of its wealth, and put that money into the pockets of a handful of large corporations and political entities."[62] The visual representations accompanying these words are revealing. Trump dredged up familiar anti-Semitic conspiratorial touchstones: images of philanthropist George Soros, Federal Reserve chair Janet Yellen, and Goldman Sachs CEO Lloyd Blankfein, spliced together with footage of Hillary Clinton, made it obvious who the corrupt elites were.[63] Conspiratorial references also abounded in Trump's genre-shattering inaugural address:

> For too long, a small group in our nation's Capital has reaped the rewards of government while the people have borne the cost. Washington flourished—but the people did not share in its wealth. Politicians prospered—but the jobs left, and the factories closed. The establishment protected itself, but not the citizens of our country. Their victories have not been your victories; their triumphs have not been your triumphs; and while they celebrated in our nation's Capital, there was little to celebrate for struggling families all across our land.[64]

Trump positioned Hillary Clinton within the secret cabal.[65] In an October 2016 speech in Florida, Trump claimed, "The Clinton machine is at the center of this power structure." He cited examples such as "the WikiLeaks documents, in which Hillary Clinton meets in secret with international banks to plot the destruction of U.S. sovereignty in order to enrich these global financial powers, her special interest friends and her donors."[66] Just as the November 3 TV ad illustrated, the dog whistles contained in "meets in secret with international banks" and "global financial powers" may resonate with an audience wary of Jewish conspirators exerting global influence. Trump described the cabal's agenda as aiming to "elect crooked Hillary Clinton at any cost, at any price, no matter how many lives they destroy. For them it's a war, and for them nothing at all is out of bounds. This is a struggle for the survival of our nation, believe me. And this will be our last chance to save it on Nov. 8, remember that." In the same speech in Florida, Trump said, "And yet, after reading all of these items, where she's so guilty, [James Comey] let her off the hook. While other lives, including General Petraeus and many others, have been destroyed for doing far, far less. This is a conspiracy against you, the American people, and we cannot let this happen or continue."

For scholars, Trump's conspiratorial messaging encourages further consideration of rhetorical plausibility. Put more simply, does it matter that most of this messaging was complete fiction? Michel Foucault argued that the elite could not continuously lie to people and remain in power.[67] Instead, dissembling rhetors must lean on the subtle hegemonic features of genteel consent. If so, does Trump's messaging encourage a fresh look at coercion and consent as an organizing rhetoric in our historical moment? Does it matter that Trump was a shameless liar? Was Foucault naïve?

I hope my findings encourage a unique take on these questions. Rather than dwell on whether Trump told *the truth,* I want to explore the symbolic resources, cultural fictions, and formal plotlines that allow a message to appear both prophetic and systematic. Positioning Trump's messaging in relationship with the extant literature on conspiracy theory offers a chance to do just that.

Challenge Plausibility

Trump's discourse challenges the plausibility of widely circulated explanations. This discursive dimension resonated with individuals already distrustful of the dominant narrative of global change.[68] The worldview of Trump's audience is primed for this iconoclastic messaging. Communities who think they are marginalized tend to see the world in Manichean terms; and this tendency is undergirded by the assumption that "the system" and its stooges are capable of unspeakable evil. Marginalized audiences are primed to think an evil institution is always ready to "do it again."[69] Thus, many are already suspicious of institutional authority. Like all marginalized communities, Trump's audience was receptive to a discourse that pushed back against dominant narratives. Theology, economics, and science are the purview of an elite that, according to Trump's discourse, scorns individuals drawn to his message. Consequently, Trump's constituted audience was likely to be less accepting of the top-down explanation of turmoil, threatening events, actions, and phenomenon.

Trump's prophetic perversion fits with this condition. He cast aspersions on every institution that could be described as *elitist* or *controlling*, including political parties, the courts, the media, the military, and intelligence agencies.[70] In a memorable line from his RNC acceptance speech Trump told his audience,

> Remember: all of the people telling you that you can't have the country you want, are the same people telling you that I wouldn't be standing here tonight. No longer can we rely on those elites in media, and politics, who will say anything to keep a rigged system in place.[71]

Trump's conspiratorial messaging is coherent because it unites the fragmented causes of marginalization into a coherent, underlying plot.[72] Trump's prophecies connected the dots for his audience in a way his Republican primary challengers and Hillary Clinton could not. As the homological points of correspondence cohere, what may—on the surface—seem like baffling rhetorical resonance makes much more sense. Actual or perceived marginalization is usually the cause of a complex confluence of forces, such as shifting scholarly paradigms, scientific technologies, macroeconomic phenomena, and political alignments. Trump's conspiratorial messaging did not dwell much on that; instead, he connected his audience's outlook and the conspiratorial messaging he thundered against. "They're taking our jobs" and "the corrupt machine" are resonant messages that equip individuals with vocabularies to explain the complexity and insecurity of their day-to-day lives.[73] To succeed, the prophetic perversion must both undermine the existing institutional explanation and offer a more vivid, coherent linkage between his or her messaging and the audience's worldview. Trump does so. Once trust is eroded, the floodgates open for the post-truth messaging without regard for traditional standards of evidence.

Trump's use of conspiratorial discourse serves four rhetoric functions. First, conspiracy reflects the felt institutional betrayal of those marginalized by the institutions they once trusted, such as the FBI, but also the State Department, the executive branch, and the mainstream media. Second, conspiracy primes a community to decipher for themselves additional secret plots in Hillary Clinton's health, foreign contributions to the Clinton Foundation, and Clinton's role in the 2012 terrorist attacks on a US diplomatic compound in Benghazi, Libya. Third, Trump's use of conspiracy affirms a larger genealogical thread aligning his messaging with iconic figures on the political Right, including Irving Kristol, David Horowitz, Ann Coulter, Rush Limbaugh, and, closer to the Oval Office, Steve Bannon.[74] Fourth, Trump's conspiratorial messaging fortified his systematic parameters. Consider the subtle but powerful stigma attached to the act of interrogating the logic of Trumpian conspiracies: anyone who asks questions is no longer welcome in his audience. Anyone articulating disbelief, or even hesitancy, must be either ignorant or evil. Community members are required to keep quiet, to keep kayfabe.

Conspiratorial Constitution

While new examples will have emerged by the time you read this, I want to explore three illustrations of the constitutive capacity of Trump's discourse relevant now. First, before officially running for president, Trump drew on the ignorant/evil constitutive entrance point in his promotion of Trump University. Trump said in a promotional video, "At Trump University, we teach success. That's what it's all about, success. It's going to happen to you." He continued:

> We're going to have professors and adjunct professors that are absolutely terrific—terrific people, terrific brains, successful, we are going to have the best of the best. And honestly, if you don't learn from them, if you don't learn from me, if you don't learn from the people that we're going to be putting forward—and these are all people that are handpicked by me—then you're just not going to make it in terms of the world of success.[75]

Consider the implied insult aimed at the thousands who did not go on to successful real estate careers after attending Trump University: they were simply not cut out for success.

As a politician, Trump also set up his constitutive parameters to exclude and diminish his opponents. For example, Trump said at his RNC acceptance speech,

> Our Convention occurs at a moment of crisis for our nation. The attacks on our police, and the terrorism in our cities, threaten our very way of life. *Any politician who does not grasp this danger is not fit to lead our country.* Americans watching this address tonight have seen the recent images of violence in our streets and the chaos in our communities. Many have witnessed this violence personally, some have even been its victims. (my emphasis)[76]

Again, consider the indictment cast on an opposing candidate analyzing crime data and not seeing the carnage that Trump is describing. In Trump's formulation, anyone using evidence to inform judgment is "not fit to lead our country."

Trump's relationship with Secretary of State Rex Tillerson also revealed the constitutive parameters of his messaging. As part of an article on Tillerson's trouble with Donald Trump, Jason Zengerle provided the White House a detailed list of questions about their relationship. The White House responded with an official statement:

> The president has assembled the most talented cabinet in history and everyone continues to be dedicated towards advancing the president's America First agenda. Anything to the contrary is simply false and comes from unnamed sources who are either out of the loop or unwilling to turn the country around.[77]

Thus, all the evidence suggesting a troubled relationship between Trump and Tillerson is debunked, as anyone who sees that evidence for what it is must be either ignorant or evil.

These constitutive parameters had tremendous rhetorical advantages during the 2016 presidential campaign because they prevented Hillary Clinton from running on the continuation of Barack Obama's successes. Her experience, wonkiness, and promise to "Make America Whole Again" were no match for the dark, conspiratorial messaging of Trump.

Trump's conspiratorial systematicity also built in a rhetorical escape hatch. Paradoxically, a lack of evidence for Trump's conspiratorial assertions only serves to strengthen them: the corrupt institutions control the flow of information, so naturally they will not allow the truth about immigrant criminals and inauguration crowd sizes to be known. Trump's failure to present empirical evidence according to the standards of rational argumentation did not damage his standing with his audience. Rather, lack of evidence affirmed that elite authorities were conspiring against his audience. In his October 2016 Florida speech, Trump warned his audience of the cabal's reach:

> They will attack you, they will slander you, they will seek to destroy your career and your family, they will seek to destroy everything about you, including your reputation. They will lie, lie, lie, and then again they will do worse than that, they will do whatever is necessary. The Clintons are criminals, remember that. They're criminals. This is well documented, and the establishment that protects them has engaged in a massive cover-up of widespread criminal activity at the State Department and the Clinton Foundation in order to keep the Clintons in power.[78]

By casting the Clintons as criminals, Trump insulated himself from the standards of rational argumentation. If evidence cannot be found for the Clintons' criminality, it is only because "the establishment" protects them. Counterarguments can all be dismissed with the same retort: *They got to you, too, huh? What a shame.*[79]

Trump's messaging generates a unique political advantage made manifest during the first year of his presidency: he could not fail. To lose is to win, as Trump's failures functioned as more "evidence" of the deep-state conspiracy against him. Many of those horrified by Trump's presidency long for the day when the political pendulum will swing back in the direction of strong support for venerable institutions. Unfortunately, that hope fails to appreciate the rhetorical power of Trump's messaging. Charges of corruption, treason, or incompetence only confirm the worldview of his supporters.[80] Following this logic, Trump's audience is led to conclude that the system is deeply corrupt; therefore, it becomes necessary for virtuous individuals to root out that corruption—no matter the chaotic consequences.

I ALONE CAN FIX IT

Because the system is so rotten, the charge for aspiring presidential candidates is clear: in contrast to the organizational demands of governance in a liberal democracy, an acute version of militant individualism is needed that is capable of covering institutional privilege and deriding government interventions. The most revealing example in Trump's messaging came in his acceptance speech at the Republican National Convention when he said, "Nobody knows the system better than me, which is why I alone can fix it."[81] No presidential candidate has ever said anything like this in a formal address. Most have aimed to unify the party by connecting their candidacy to their party's platform. While Americans generally accept that tactical and technical necessity require the consolidation of power by one winning candidate, no one ever says out loud that they "alone" are the solution to the country's challenges. Instead, most political candidates acknowledge the nation's firm foundations outlined in our sacred documents, but suggest that our principles have been betrayed.[82] Democratic presidential candidates often point to betrayals caused by corporate greed; Republicans since Nixon have had a more challenging task because most are forced during the primary season to portray the entire federal government as a wasteful enterprise. As Reagan's "government is the problem" messaging became the central organizing rhetoric of the party, aspiring Republican presidential candidates have had to balance this distrust of the system with their own vision and aspiration for running it. After all, if Washington is so corrupt, why soil yourself trying to fix it? As a corrective, Republicans have pointed the finger at mooching welfare cheats, overreaching IRS agents, radical college professors, and enabling government bureaucrats who betrayed the public trust. Even for Reagan, the government was not totally corrupt; it was just misguided.[83] Consequently, Republicans' corrective involves targeting the size of government. Pre-Trump, few national politicians were willing to argue that the entire political establishment was corrupt (at least not with the enthusiasm and conviction of corporate-funded conservative think tanks and popular right-wing media figures). Rather, with the right corrective action—voting for them—we can be reunified to pursue the noble mission described in our sacred documents.

However, Trump's discourse expanded the critique of government beyond the traditional boundaries. The consolidation of power described by "I alone can fix it" fits better with cult leaders and authoritarian dictators than with American liberal democracy. Trump's individualistic remedy also fit, however, with a worldview that understood "the system" as rotten. The whole institution is corrupt. The game is rigged. And the problem is not just welfare cheats or radical professors. Trump's outsider status in the 2016 presidential race was justified, as experienced politicians like senators Ted Cruz and Marco Rubio, and governors like John Kasich and Jeb Bush, were too close to the decaying system to understand the depth of the crisis.

Trump's individualism also created unique challenges for Hillary Clinton. It is difficult for a career politician to counter Trump's claims of institutional corruption. As Kenneth Burke would suggest, the idea of *falling back in love* with a misguided institution will not resonate with this audience in this moment. Instead, the rhetorical appeal needs to be darker and more tragic to align with an audience worldview that sees the system as broken beyond repair.[84] In turn, dark, authoritarian, hierarchical, and competitive features—whether religious, ecological, cultural, or political—become rich sites of rhetorical invention.

Resonance is found in the individualistic consolidation of power that Trump embodies. In this way, Trump's messaging betrayed a fundamental assumption of postwar liberal democracy in the US: authoritarian dictators and populist demagogues were unnecessary when religious, corporate, and political interests were kept in check by American democracy. For some, Trump's "I alone can fix it" sounded out of place in a formal address for this reason. But for others, Trump's individualistic discourse aligned with their expectations. The "American carnage" Trump referred to in his inaugural address also aligned with the broader institutional cynicism marking this moment. Trump's ability to diagnose this corruption came from his previous experience as an economic and political insider. Following the path of the prophetic pervert who enters (and then betrays) the corrupt institution, Trump admitted that he attended the weddings of the elite, took their phone calls, and donated to their campaigns—but he has now returned to reveal the truth to the people.

Consider Trump's response to the August 6, 2015, Republican presidential debate, in which he was asked about donating money to Democratic politicians, including Hillary Clinton and Nancy Pelosi. Trump said,

> You better believe it . . . I will tell you that our system is broken. I gave to many people. Before this, before two months ago, I was a businessman. I give to everybody. When they call, I give. And you know what? When I need something from them, two years later, three years later, I call them. They are there for me. And that's a broken system.[85]

Trump effectively played the reluctant prophet.[86] In another example, he told a Florida crowd that he knew the insider elites "would throw every lie they could at me and my family and my loved ones" and "stop at nothing to try to stop me." But, Trump said, "I never knew as bad as it would be. I never knew it would be this vile, that it would be this bad, that it would be this vicious. Nevertheless, I take all of these slings and arrows gladly for you. I take them for our movement so that we can have our country back."[87] Rather than remain on the inside, Trump betrayed the institutions of a corrupt status quo and returned to tell the people the truth.

Ignorance Is Strength

Trump's militant individualism offered his candidacy both opportunities and challenges. As an opportunity, Trump's individualism functioned as gaffe insurance. Trump proved to be impervious to the types of missteps that derail aspiring political candidates, such as boasting about grabbing women's genitals, calling Mexicans rapists, and mocking a reporter with a disability. Supporters voiced displeasure with some of Trump's antics, but many—from rural Iowa to the halls of Congress—excused his actions as the mistakes of an outsider. For example, in reference to Trump's firing of FBI Director James Comey, Paul Ryan said, "The president's new at this. He's new to government. And so he probably wasn't steeped in the long-running protocols that establish the relationships between the DOJ, FBI, and White House."[88] And after Trump accused former president Obama of wiretapping Trump Tower, Devin Nunes, then House Intelligence Committee chair, defended him: "The president is a neophyte to politics. He's been doing this a little over a year. And I think a lot of the things that he says, you guys sometimes take literally."[89] Trump didn't need to worry about appearing polished and articulate. Of course he couldn't debate as well as Ted Cruz—a former Princeton debate champion—and he wouldn't be as informed as Hillary Clinton on global trade policies.[90] Reflecting an Orwellian version of *Ignorance is Strength,* Trump's discourse aligned with an outlook that equated competence with incompetence and arrogance with expertise.

Further, some of Trump's most unseemly behavior was forgiven because his audience had a particular appreciation for wealthy, dominant men who exert their authority, even in crass and indecorous ways.[91] This tolerance of hierarchy offers more grace to the community's prophets, so that "locker room talk" and casual racism do not become the political liabilities that they otherwise would.[92] Indeed, in accordance with this alignment, calling an entire ethnic group "rapists" or bragging about sexual assault does not even qualify as a gaffe. People like Trump get to grab whatever they want and "say what we are all thinking."

Trump's first year in elected office revealed a set of governing challenges inherent in his preference for militant individualism. First, on the campaign trail, Trump drew praise for ridiculing institutional corruption, even within his own party. Individualism worked well for candidate Trump, especially in attracting an audience marked by suspicion of traditional institutions; however, individualism was a limited governing rhetoric, especially for a democracy characterized by a system of checks and balances. Consequently, Trump's White House was marked by internecine infighting during his first year in office. The more moderate voices in Trump's administration, including Jared Kushner, Dina Powell, Gary Cohn, and Ivanka Trump, were described by the alt-right elements of the president's coalition as "globalists" and "swamp creatures" who spend too much time partying with the fake-news media at Martha's Vineyard.[93] Steve Bannon hated working with Paul Ryan and Mitch McConnell, whom he described to Trump as "backstabbers who would inevitably sell him out."[94] Trump and Bannon had a meaningful alliance for a time, but Trump had to fire Bannon shortly into his presidency, not for policy disagreements but because Bannon began to attract the public attention Trump craved.[95] Militant individualism causes its adherents to become paranoid—ever on guard against the emergence of someone more pure, more committed, and more radical coming up from behind. As the militancy fundamentalism suggests, there is a reason certain personalities are comfortable on the fringes. The wilderness is often populated by strong egos and irascible characters who do not always appreciate the compromises required for democratic governance.

These findings also lend insight into a governing challenge for Trump concerning the treatment of his former rivals in the Republican Party. While party squabbles are common during presidential primaries, they usually end at the convention as the losers unite around the nominee. But with Trump's candidacy, many remained opposed to Trump even after he secured the nomination. Prominent neoconservatives, GOP national security experts, and Chamber-of-Commerce Republicans signed open letters declaring their opposition to Trump, with some declaring him unfit for office.[96] Would the president treat these Republican Never Trumpers more charitably than he did during the campaign?

Trump's response to his Republican critics affirmed the rhetorical orientation of the catastrophic homology. Thousands of positions in Trump's administration remained unfulfilled. Three hundred days into the presidency, there were roughly 256 key posts for which Trump had not even nominated anyone, including someone to head the Patent Office, the Federal Emergency Management Agency, the Transportation Security Administration, or the Centers for Disease Control and Prevention.[97] Potential hires were rejected for minor sins. Jason Zengerle cited a senior Trump administration official who said, "The hiring pool is very different from your normal hiring pool. The people the Senate would expect to confirm have all been taken off the table."⁹⁸ The homology is oriented toward a perspective that would rather let the institution wither and die than hire former adversaries with the expertise to run it effectively.

Third, Trump's militant individualism reflects a divergence from the agonistic demands of governance in a liberal democracy. Elected officials do not threaten to lock up the opposition. Liberal democracy demands opponents be accepted as legitimate adversaries.⁹⁹ Trump's messaging departed from those demands. Trump's discourse was antagonistic: those who disagreed with him were enemies to be crushed and humiliated, not representatives of alternative ideas that ought to be considered in a healthy, pluralistic democracy. If Trump "alone can fix it," then those who did not identify with his discourse risked being lumped together as adversarial enemies, unworthy of being taken seriously.¹⁰⁰

Finally, Trump's messaging reflects an inability to redress interconnected and complex challenges once elected. Robert Ivie argued that a Trump administration would never be able to offer a governing corrective beyond "empty gestures to recovered greatness."¹⁰¹ Militant individualism and its urging to divide the world into good and evil explain why. Good/evil dichotomization affects Trump's ability to govern. Climate change or global trade imbalances, for example, are understood primarily as individual struggles for dominance. To redress unfair trade agreements, Trump promised in his RNC speech to "turn our bad trade agreements into great ones." He promised to "get a much better deal for America" by deploying a negotiation tactic familiar to a third-grader: "We'll walk away if we don't get the deal that we want."¹⁰² Trump didn't need to plan for a presidential transition because, as he told Chris Christie, "Chris, you and I are so smart that we can leave the victory party two hours early and do the transition ourselves."¹⁰³ Trump told Laura Ingraham of *Fox News* that low morale was not a concern because the State Department doesn't actually "need all the people that they want."¹⁰⁴ He continued, "You know, don't forget, I'm a businessperson. I tell my people, 'Where you don't need to fill slots, don't fill them.'" After all, he reassured Ingraham, "The one that matters is me. I'm the only one that matters, because when it comes to it, that's what the policy is going to be. You've seen that, you've seen it strongly." To redress immigration challenges, Trump argued forcefully that world peace and respect for our nation's laws will result from building his big wall.

One of the most pernicious policy outcomes encouraged by militant individualism aligned Trump's discourse with the willingness to shut down the government to get what he wants. In the first year of the Trump presidency, Steve Bannon was a primary supporter of this militant individualism.

His parting advice to Trump in August of 2017 reflects this philosophy; even as he was being dismissed from the White House, Bannon urged Trump not to sign any funding agreement that did not include payment for the border wall; if Congress called his bluff, he should veto the bill, even if that caused a government shutdown.[105] Trump has voiced support for a "good government shutdown" on several occasions.[106] For instance, in January 2018 Trump said, "I would love to be able to bring back our country into a great form of unity." But, he continued, "Without a major event where people pull together, that's hard to do. But I would like to do it without that major event because usually that major event is not a good thing."[107] The consequences for his own party that were sure to come, given that they controlled both chambers of Congress and the White House, could be disastrous—but not necessarily to be avoided. It should not be surprising that Trump would later come to "take the mantle"—in his words—for the longest government shutdown in history.

Militant Individualism and the American South

For an example of what militant individualism produces, consider the American South. Militant individualistic discourse resonates well in southern states marked by suspicion of government institutions. This lends predictive insight into the consequences of four (or eight) years of a Trump presidency. The South was the first part of the country to abandon the collectivism of post–World War II society in exchange for the militant individualism that came to define both Republican Party politics and conservative ideologies.[108] The naked pursuit of selfish material interests, always cloaked in the individualistic vocabulary of freedom and liberty, became a defining discursive touchstone. Michael Lind described this process in the South as a counterrevolutionary impulse to the New Deal and postwar liberal political formations. Militant individualism in the South worked to undermine the collective solidarity and social responsibility that animated the golden age of American capitalism.[109] A counterrevolution crushed labor, accelerated economic stratification, limited the welfare state, and harmed the environment. Energy interests, military elites, and giant agribusinesses first took advantage of this civic withdrawal; traditional manufacturing corporations like Toyota and Boeing soon followed. Corporations squeezed politicians for preferential tax conditions, depriving the state of funding for social services; as a result, citizens lacked high-quality schools and hospitals, opportunities for those who relied most on social services evaporated, government atrophied, citizens became less engaged, and power was further concentrated in the hands of the elite.[110] A vicious cycle began in the South that has since accelerated.

The rest of the nation once looked on the South with scorn. Southern conservatives failed to grasp the central truth of postwar American prosperity, preferring individual competition to collectively meeting political challenges. Instead of relegating this version of militant individualism to the dustbin of history, in the early twenty-first century, the rest of the country has begun to look more like Mississippi; it has spread into states such as Wisconsin and Kansas, encouraging the politics of institutional catastrophe. Large parts of the country now resemble the South: weak unions, low wages, environmental degradation, terrible public schools, phony appeals to militaristic patriotism, religious zealotry, dog-whistle xenophobia, casual racism, and decreasing longevity.

DRASTIC ACTION FOR A RIGGED GAME

Given Trump's success in appealing to a marginalized audience, it might be reasonable to expect his discourse to reflect a regressive temporality. Promising to go back in time may align with the troubling fantasy of a past where women and people of color knew their place, everyone was allowed to say "Merry Christmas," and no one questioned rich, white, straight, native-born, male privilege.

There is some evidence for that position. In his RNC speech, Trump said, "Together, we will lead our party back to the White House, and we will lead our country back to safety, prosperity, and peace."[111] The warm-up music at Trump campaign rallies reflected such sentiments, including Elton John, the Beatles, and the Rolling Stones. *Make America Great Again* can also be understood in conjunction with this regressive temporality.

Do these appeals to the past mean that Trump's temporality reflects an exception to the forward-leaning orientation of the homology? Given Trump's opponent, his target audience, and his Republican Party affiliation, it is reasonable to concede that regressive temporal references are likely present in his discourse.[112] No homology is absolute. However, I want to argue that regressive temporality was not the dominant temporal feature—Trump never would have been elected if it were. Instead, it was Trump's telic temporality that offered the vocabulary to reconcile the paradoxical tensions within catastrophe's final destination and the demands of American democracy.

Surmounting Democracy

Trump did not run for president as a traditional conservative. But his supporters did not take issue with his loose party affiliation. Compared with most Republican voters, Trump's audience was less concerned with traditional Republican issues: they were less hawkish on foreign policy, less excited about free trade, and not as interested in cutting marginal tax rates for the wealthy.[113] In turn, Trump did not dwell on those issues during the campaign. Especially on the campaign trail, Trump didn't promise to merely reverse or unwind a century of tax law, essentially returning the US to the Gilded Age. Trump's audience had heard that stale messaging before. More drastic action was needed for a rigged game. Rather than seek to go back in time, Trump encouraged upheaval, disintegration, chaos, and the destruction of political and economic institutions. For this audience, in this historical moment, the institutions were so corrupt that going back in time was an unsatisfying solution.

Further, regressive temporality cannot get this audience to their telic destination. Catastrophe is scandalous in a representative democracy. While the final destination is paradise, this discourse is clear-eyed and transparent about the carnage that will be suffered en route. Venerable institutions will have to be attacked and torn down; natural disasters, global conflicts, and financial crises will have to be passively accepted (and even manufactured). The catastrophic journey will also produce a massive concentration of power and wealth in the hands of a select few. That concentration will be justified, of course, but the democratic arithmetic is still not in catastrophe's favor, as it aims to produce few winners and many losers. Further complicating Trump's position, elected officials are compelled by the Constitution to uphold the law. Steve Bannon can holler from the wilderness about launching "furious attacks" to "shock the system"—the American president cannot be as direct.[114] In turn, telic catastrophe contradicts a democratic worldview. Representative democracy is a hurdle that catastrophe must surmount. A regressive temporality cannot reconcile these tensions; nor can it explain Trump's unique appeal, especially in the 2016 Republican primary. If Republican voters wanted regressive temporality, they would have supported Rick Santorum. How, then, did Trump's messaging manage to reconcile the telic challenges of American electoral politics?

I want to answer that question in two related ways. First, I argue that the distinguishing feature of Trump's telic temporality—what set him apart from Republican primary challengers and Hillary Clinton alike—was his promise to run government like a business. During his RNC acceptance speech, Trump made the connection explicit: "I have made billions of dollars in business making deals—now I'm going to make our country rich again."[115] But second, I want to show that Trump's first year of *running the government like a business* aligned with the underlying expectations of an audience that yearns for a reconciliation they are not permitted to say aloud. More specifically, by analyzing the formal points of correspondence woven throughout Trump's various executive-level departments, I locate an unarticulated but consistent approach to governance that does indeed run government like a business—a business that its managers seek to run into the ground.

Running Government into the Ground

In its first year, the Trump administration hired and supported incompetent and inexperienced people, in a way that has discredited or disassembled the agencies they represented. Many Trump hires were direct adversaries of the agencies they were hired to lead, including Betsy DeVos at the Department of Education, Scott Pruitt at the Environmental Protection Agency, Jeff Sessions at the Department of Justice, and Rick Perry at the Department of Energy.[116] Further, the White House had to rescind several federal district court nominees, and other nominees withdrew because they were unqualified, unable to answer basic legal questions during the confirmation process, ignorant of federal trial rules, and never having prosecuted or defended a case.[117]

Michael Lewis's reporting on the USDA illuminates the pattern of Trump's telic aspirations. For high-level USDA positions, the Trump team hired a country-club cabana attendant, a long-haul truck driver, a gas-company meter reader, and the owner of a scented-candle company (who listed skills like a "pleasant demeanor" on her résumé).[118] Many new USDA hires, Lewis revealed, had no federal policy experience, much less expertise in agriculture; many even lacked basic credentials, such as a college degree. These personnel decisions could be examples of garden-variety nepotism, or of Trump being loyal to the select few who joined his campaign early on. But I maintain that hiring incompetent people is a practical reflection of the catastrophic homology in action. Given Trump's apparent disdain for certain basic functions of government, what's to stop him from hiring a country-club cabana boy with no experience for a high-level position at the USDA? Why not hire a talk-radio host to lead the scientific mission of an agency tasked with protecting the nation's food supply? What's the worst that could happen?

Second, a preference for telic catastrophe is illuminated by the Trump administration's attitude toward resource allocation. Consider the messaging surrounding Rex Tillerson's short stint at the State Department as an example.

In a speech to State Department employees soon after becoming secretary, Tillerson said, "The most important thing I can do is to enable this organization to be more effective, more efficient and for all of you to take greater satisfaction in what you do day in and day out."[119] Aides told reporters that Tillerson loved discussing the navigation of bureaucratic hurdles and reformulating decision trees for maximum efficiency. Tillerson's aims, on the surface, aligned with conservative orthodoxy. Accordingly, shortly after arriving at State, Tillerson announced a plan to eliminate two thousand jobs from the department payroll. Following Trump's orders, he also sought to slash the budget by 30 percent, including deep cuts to economic development and humanitarian aid.[120] Referring to the State Department's new look, spokesperson Heather Nauert said, "The secretary firmly believes coming out of the private sector that we all need to be good stewards of taxpayer dollars."[121] Deploying a phrase with familiar religious connotations, Nauert positioned her department's *stewardship* in accordance with the expectations of a fundamentalist community. But, as I discussed in chapter 2, stewardship is never as neutral as it may appear on the surface.

Trump's telic aspirations were also revealed in his approach to health care. Trump slashed Obamacare's budget for advertising and enrollment, in what looked like a clear attempt to undermine the law.[122] The advertising budget for the open-enrollment period was cut from $100 million to $10 million. Grants to nonprofit groups that helped people enroll in the insurance marketplaces were cut from $63 million to $36 million.[123] The administration also cut the enrollment period in half; and they planned to take down the Healthcare.gov website for several days during the enrollment period—both steps that would surely reduce enrollment.[124] The Department of Health and Human Services removed information from the Affordable Care Act website that contained information about obtaining coverage. In fact, much of that information was deleted the day of Trump's inauguration.[125] None of these actions would make sense if sound governance was the goal. Department of Energy chief of staff Kevin Knobloch articulated such confusion when—after Trump officials showed no interest in learning about the DOE during the transition period before the inauguration—he said, "[The DOE] is a thirty-billion-dollar-a-year organization with about a hundred ten thousand employees. Industrial sites across the country. Very serious stuff. If you're going to run it, why wouldn't you want to know something about it?"[126]

The catastrophic homology offers a compelling response to Knobloch's question: confusing customers, hiding information about your services, and broadcasting the flaws of your product make little sense if the goal is to "run government like a business"—unless, of course, the goal is to run the business into the ground.

The Death Spiral

The ultimate endpoint for the Trump administration on health care, for instance, seems to be a death spiral: fewer people sign up for care, which leads to higher premiums pushing many off the health care exchanges; younger, healthy people are first to drop out, leaving a sicker population which in turn increases costs for everyone, perpetuating the downward spiral.[127] Likewise, Tillerson's behavior at the State Department does not reflect competent management practices in any sector, public or private. Tillerson would have never walked into ExxonMobil without any knowledge of the organization and made major decisions—he would have been fired if he had.

Tillerson crushed the morale at the State Department. Tom Malinowski, an assistant secretary of state in the Obama administration, described the State Department this way: "There's furniture stacked up in the hallways, a lot of empty offices. The place empties out at 4 p.m. The morale is completely broken."[128] Departing employees are not being replaced. One year in, forty-eight ambassadorships and twenty-one of the twenty-three assistant secretary positions were still unfilled, and the most senior stations in diplomatic service were covered by temporary employees or left vacant. Tillerson probably knew all this would force the most competent and experienced people to leave the State Department. Tarak Shah, an administrator in the DOE said, "People are heading for the doors . . . and that's really sad and destructive. The best and the brightest are the ones being targeted. They will leave fastest. Because they will get the best job offers."[129] Within the State Department, Gardiner Harris noted that employees with the most experience in developing countries—those most familiar with institutional distrust and the conspiracy theories fostered as a result—were the first to notice that Tillerson's decisions didn't look like incompetence or ignorance.[130] More broadly, many of Tillerson and Trump's critics missed what this discourse should have been illuminating. Many have assumed that saving money on hotel rooms at United Nations meetings reflected Tillerson and Trump's efforts at good stewardship of taxpayer money. Critics saw the focus on bureaucratic minutia and stewardship as administrative incompetence: that Tillerson (or Trump) cannot understand the importance of low-level diplomacy, of the face-to-face relationship development that happens at these conventions. John Negroponte, George W.

Bush's ambassador to the United Nations, remarked that if Tillerson really wanted to do his job well, he would leave the tinkering with the department's organization structure to low-level assistants. "It's really unfortunate that that is the secretary's highest priority," Negroponte said.[131]

But Negroponte missed the point. During Tillerson's tenure at State, he was always well within his power to hire a capable team of aides to reorganize the department so he could be "focused on more important affairs," as Mr. Negroponte suggested.[132] That Tillerson did not lends insight into the deeper purpose of this version of "stewardship": Tillerson is a competent institutional manager, as he displayed during his decades running the world's largest corporation.[133] This analysis points to a more sinister explanation. If reform, stewardship, and competence were the desired outcomes, then Tillerson—of all people—would know not to pursue such a chaos-inducing strategy. Indeed, Tillerson's hiring decisions were not attributable to nepotism, incompetence, or mismanagement. When gauging Tillerson's impact, it is instructive to contrast his behavior at State with his behavior at ExxonMobil—between an organization Tillerson wanted to thrive and an organization he wanted to kill. This is catastrophic governance at its most clear and potent: manufacturing incompetence, promoting disrepute, and, thus, shifting public opinion in an advantageous—but catastrophic—direction. For audiences constituted by the rhetoric of catastrophe, Tillerson's lack of diplomatic experience is irrelevant. It doesn't really matter if he knows anything about the State Department, just as it matters not if Scott Pruitt knows anything about the environment, or Betsy DeVos knows anything about public education. The unique functions of each department are inconsequential. What matters is their association with a larger federal apparatus worthy of destruction.

CONCLUSION

Critics of Donald Trump and Rex Tillerson reflect the missing warrant I discussed in the introduction. John Negroponte thought Tillerson's priorities were misaligned, that a team of aides should be doing the reorganizing at State, and that Tillerson should focus on matters of greater concern. But if the pursuit is catastrophe, then there is nothing more important than what Trump and Tillerson were doing. Tillerson may have been well aware that destroying low-level relationships, cutting staff, and slashing the budget would crush the morale of the State Department. But more broadly, criticisms of the Trump administration seem to only resonate with an audience constituted by rational argumentation, shared order, and collective social progress. For Tillerson,

Pruitt, DeVos, and Trump, that is not a worthy set of beliefs or goals: far from it. My assessment offers key insights into the Trump administration's advancement of a particular telic agenda—a belief that the institutions of democracy should be accelerated down a path to catastrophe.

Consider the quote by Sam Rayburn: *Any jackass can tear down a barn, but it takes a skilled carpenter to put one up.* Such a quote could be used to describe the difficulties inherent in building political institutions. However, an analysis of Trump's discourse reveals that Washington, DC, is not Rayburn's farm. In the corridors of power, even a jackass must have a measure of rhetorical skill if he hopes to advance the cause of catastrophe—to create a place in which American citizens distrust the precise institutional mechanisms responsible for the nation's peace and prosperity, where citizens yearn for anything and anyone, including an inexperienced, demagogic carnival barker rather than sobriety, competence, and expertise. And in the end, Trump's discourse illuminates the rhetorical blueprint needed to ensure that government conforms to the most pernicious and ineffectual caricatures of its catastrophe-minded audience.

CONCLUSION

Consequences and Alternatives

RHETORICAL CRITICISM offers the opportunity for ethical commentary on the conditions in which it is produced.[1] When done well, this is the discipline at its best: connecting the concepts of rhetorical theory to practical social, economic, and political consequences. In other words, the catastrophic homology is inconsequential without a rich exploration of its impact on the day-to-day lives of an audience constituted by catastrophe. Therefore, I conclude this dark slog with a short discussion of the political consequences of catastrophic rhetoric, and what—if anything—describes an alternative.

THE CONSEQUENCES OF CATASTROPHE

The catastrophic homology is a reaction not only to rational argumentation but also to a wimpy form of effete liberalism that—to borrow a line from Principal Skinner on *The Simpsons*—urges us to think that "no one is better than anyone else and everyone is the best at everything." Instead, catastrophe allows the strong a chance at unrestrained, full-throated, balls-to-the-wall competition. Catastrophe is emancipating in this way: a breath of fresh air for those thought to be stifled by "political correctness," state interventions to make everyone equal, and tax dollars going to support the losers.

Consequently, a catastrophic audience is drawn to pronounced hierarchies of wealth, status, and power—a hierarchy that is not to be feared or redressed. Quite the opposite: if the terms of competition are just—free men competing in a free market unspoiled by state interference—the hierarchical result is sanctioned. Over-the-top performances of wealth, power, and status result. For prophets and followers alike, the *performance* of one's place on the hierarchy is vital. Donald Trump sued *Forbes* when they did not include him in their 2011 Billionaire list for the same reason that fundamentalist rhetors from Charles Finney to William Riley to Jerry Falwell lean heavily on quantifiable metrics of religious success, including the size of their congregations, the number of books they sell, and the money they can raise.[2] Extractivist industries, gun-rights advocates, and the Trump administration reflect a world where you get everything you can *because* you can: if the North Sea can be drilled, if mass shootings can sell more guns, if you can "grab 'em by the pussy" because you are a star, you do it. The hierarchy sanctions it all. This perception of justice further points to the struggle that Trump Republicans and liberal progressives will have finding common ground: for many Americans, pronounced economic stratification represents a fly in the ointment of American democracy; but for catastrophic audiences, American greatness is defined by such fly ointment.

Convenient Cynicism

The catastrophic audience affirms a political outlook marked by what Henry Giroux called "convenient cynicism."[3] *Convenient,* as the audiences constituted by stratification are perceived to benefit the most from potent (but empty) appeals to "freedom" and "liberty"; *cynical,* as any attempt to redress hierarchy will fail. The case studies under examination here reflect the practical impact of this convenient cynicism. For example, when anti-environmentalism is brought to its political conclusion, audiences are urged to equate ecological calamity with restoration and reorder. A catastrophic audience is encouraged to sit back and let natural disasters separate the strong from the weak, the industrious from the lazy, and the saved from the damned. These dark conclusions are grounded in an accurate assessment of how climate change is already impacting us. The knife blade that is climate change will eventually cut everyone, but in the short term, the first and deepest cuts will be felt by the most physically and economically vulnerable communities suffering from heat waves, floods, pollution, higher food prices, and crop failures.[4] The people with the smallest carbon footprints—those living on remote Pacific Islands, low-lying areas of Bangladesh, and in Houston's Fifth Ward—end up suffering the most from its effects. Gun-rights discourse begins from the cynical premise that violence is a fundamental part of the human condition and that our institutions can do little to redress it. Instead, audiences are urged to be prepared for when violence does occur, to protect yourself and your family. Human efforts to alter telic progress, even for the better, are not only bound to fail but also contrary to the human condition.[5] Donald Trump articulated this cynical outlook when asked who was to blame for the killing and dismemberment of Saudi journalist Jamal Khashoggi in 2018: Trump didn't blame one person (Mohammed bin Salman) or one country (Saudi Arabia). Instead, he said, "Maybe the world should be held accountable, because the world is a vicious place."[6] Trump's answer resembles similar reactions to questions about Vladimir Putin's willingness to kill dissenting Russian journalists. Trump said, "There are a lot of killers. We have a lot of killers. Well, you think our country is so innocent?" While one might assume religious, ecological, cultural, and political catastrophe might encourage political efforts to redress chaos, that outcome may not be aligned with catastrophe's urgings; instead, for audiences constituted by catastrophe's telic temporality, any attempt to ameliorate or even solve these crises smacks of futility and weakness.

Catastrophic messaging may seem harmless enough when it appears as a meme or on a bumper sticker. However, my findings point to the presence of a deeper rhetorical aquifer that portrays outsiders as existential threats. If the metrics for stratification are fair, natural and divine categories of us/them are produced; and the lowly look to be suffering from an irreversible and essential flaw deep in their core—a flaw that requires either conversion or eradication.[7] This is a characteristic of catastrophic rhetoric in action: there is no third option. Jerry Falwell describes this communication style well: "It is not sharing, it is preaching. It is not dialogue, it is preaching . . . It is not coffeehouse, conversational communication, ecumenicity—it is preaching."[8] Falwell and his catastrophic audiences never become vulnerable; any interaction implies conquest, conversion, and if that doesn't work, ridicule, exclusion, and disposal. As Wander put it, "God's word does not invite rebuttal; it terminates debate—a conclusion as obvious to the believer as the unbeliever."[9] Catastrophic vocabularies end up conforming to expectations of aggression, force, and toxic masculinity where enemies are identified and vanquished. And when outsiders are Othered in this way, violence is almost inevitable.[10]

Yearning for Chaos

The catastrophic homology urges a significant number of Americans to not only resist collective efforts to redress calamity but actually yearn for crisis and chaos. It is better to have some suffer than to retard the forward progress of history with misguided state interventions slowing telic progress and limiting human freedom. Suffering also offers motivation for society's losers and lessens the responsibility of the winners to care for them. Consequently, this telic destination discourages public investment in shared institutions and social support programs.[11]

Here, one might be tempted to lump catastrophe's political urgings within traditional American political paradigms. For instance, catastrophe might reflect small-government conservativism, and the assumed political passivity of fundamentalists might reflect calls for a restrained federal government.

Those assumptions would be misguided.

Catastrophe is not passive; nor does it seek a smaller government. It does not want to return to a mythic, idealized past marked by pre-institutional social arrangements. It is not neoliberal. It does not desire to shrink government to a size that could be drowned in a bathtub. Nor is catastrophe apocalyptic in the premillennial sense. Catastrophe does not seek to resist political action. Nor does it respond to chaos with indeterminacy and disengagement; it does not wait for the promises of the next world to dive in, and it does not sit back and wait for God's wrath to smite the secular humanists.[12] Rather, catastrophe seeks to deploy all the symbolic and coercive powers of the state to affirm existing hierarchies and protect them in the future. Catastrophe fuels an oligarchic art of governance marked by selective forms of state intervention to defend the resources of the rich and powerful and to enhance profit maximization wherever possible. Such oligarchic governing rationales may be clear in the Trump administration, but the iterative effect of noticing a shared homology illuminates why catastrophic communities are also more comfortable with antidemocratic concentrations of wealth and power across religious, ecological, and cultural discourses. Anti-environmentalism may seem like it is trying to return power to the working class in Louisiana and the destitute in Mumbai by combatting an environmental cabal of elite scientists; in reality, it is a foolish ruse designed to maximize the extractivist profits of ExxonMobil for as long as possible. Gun-rights discourse may seem like it is returning power to the freedom-loving gun owner by combatting an elite political and intellectual cabal; in reality, it is a foolish ruse designed to maximize the profits of Smith & Wesson and the political power of Wayne LaPierre.

Such dark and cynical conclusions cry out for an alternative vocabulary. As I argued in the introduction, the homology is not inevitable, and neither are the political consequences I just described. And so, in the next section, I try to carve out space for an alternative vocabulary as I pivot from the consequences to the contingency of catastrophe.

THE CONTINGENCY OF CATASTROPHE

The homological dimension of catastrophe should remind us that audience constitution often occurs beyond direct, critical awareness. We also know that rarely does a single speech or other rhetorical act produce immediate changes in public opinion. And we know that audiences cannot be conceptualized as if all members of a community are waiting in a room to be addressed.[13] Instead, the catastrophic audience is a product of dynamic oscillation with a complex set of conditional constraints making possible the emergence of an audience that coheres and responds to conclusions such as these . . . perhaps according to conditions and events that have never occurred before, nor will ever occur again.

One example is especially noteworthy for understanding the contingency of these political conclusions: *Calamity is preventable*. Upheaval and chaos can bring people together. The rhetoric of catastrophe induces an attitude that equates natural disaster, economic turmoil, war, and civil strife with social fragmentation and collective disorder. However, that is not an inevitable equation. The historical record reveals quite the opposite. Enrico Quarantelli dedicated his life's work to detailing prosocial human responses to upheaval.[14] Natural disasters can strengthen community identification, he found; people suffer, but suffering can bring people together. Quarantelli found that hysteria is rare, looting is uncommon, and greedy opportunists are the exception to the rule. Government institutions, often rigid in their initial response, are nudged toward justice by groups of ordinary people who spontaneously unite to respond to challenging conditions. As social animals, we are often at our collective best when we respond to chaos. Quarantelli's work suggests that when we are battered by hurricanes, floods, landslides, wildfires, and earthquakes (or disasters more of our own making), we can achieve a new degree of solidarity—in opposition to catastrophe's hierarchical, individualistic, and circle-the-wagons urgings. Optimistically, it seems that social cohesion and basic human kindness—even in the face of chaos—are more aligned with our human condition than the catastrophic urgings described here.[15]

The contingency of catastrophe affirms the principles of rhetorical invention common to all rhetors. For fundamentalist rhetors, we established that inconsistencies are explained away with references to inerrancy or a premillennial apocalyptic narrative. It may seem like many of these political consequences flow smoothly and naturally from biblical inerrancy or premillennial dispensationalism. Just as Moses parted the Red Sea and Joshua got God to halt the sun, welfare spending is evil and defense spending is divine. But of course, inerrancy evokes the stability of biblical truths, as it also allegorizes, adopts, and rearticulates that truth within the context of changing spiritual, social, and political demands and conditions.[16] Premillennialism has also been shown to be quite malleable, evolving and changing in response to social conditions. Anti-environmentalism has been shown to be a fluid and dynamic genre. George H. W. Bush wanted to fight the greenhouse effect with the White House Effect, and Newt Gingrich sat on a couch next to Nancy Pelosi for a TV spot urging action on climate change.

Deference to science is not the determining factor in such evolutions. Recall how inadequate the scholarly credentials of anti-environmental rhetors were. Calvin Beisner introduced the anti-environmentalist documentary *Where the Grass Is Greener* by saying, "We really have gathered some of the very top minds in the field here."[17] That is total fiction. Beisner tracked down a bunch of hacks and charlatans to repeat stale talking points that have been thoroughly debunked by the actual top minds in the field. But notice how that rebuttal relies on a rational standard of *best minds* that holds little persuasive force for a catastrophe-minded audience. Anti-environmentalist rhetors are experts because of their actions—their adherence to and advocacy for the catastrophic plan. A consistent standard for judging whether sacred texts should be read literally or figuratively is not necessary. The *action* produced by the reading is paramount. This conclusion affirms the arguments of Sharon Crowley and Lisa Vox: anyone can have access to catastrophe's hidden truths, regardless of educational or professional status, as long as their faith and probity allow them to foreclose any alternative reading.

Gun-rights rhetoric has also changed shape. The history of the NRA shows how it evolved from a shooting club to a lobbying organization. More specifically, for most of its history the NRA was focused less on the Second Amendment's defense of the individual right to keep and bear arms and more on organizing target shooting competitions.[18] The Second Amendment, like inerrancy and premillennialism, is the creative infusion of reactionary political aims and creative legal scholarship designed to cover advantageous legislative influence in a wash of timelessness and stability.[19]

Finally, few reflect the contingency of catastrophe as well as Donald J. Trump. Trump is not a loyal Republican, and he was ill equipped to be president. But his supporters were willing to look past his liberal leanings (support for tariffs and Russia, aversion to free trade, waffling claims about abortion, changing his party affiliation five times) and mine others (conservatives on the Supreme Court, tax cuts, selective deregulation) to align his candidacy with their worldview.

The catastrophic homology affirms, complicates, and extends these touchstones. Because speech works within a complicated, diffused process of gradual changes, the catastrophic homology can issue an invitation to meaning—it can reach outward to unite social conditions, messaging, rhetors, and individuals into an audience—to orient fragmented and dispersed identities in the direction of these political conclusions. And by illuminating the iterative, dynamic effect of the homology coming together across such disparate discourses, catastrophic rhetoric deepens our understanding of modern political conversations in fresh and exciting ways. Not a single speech, rhetor, or even genre can account for such implications. Formal pattern detection informs the direction urged by such political orientations through a consistency, transcendence, and permeation across genres and discourses, all united at a shared rhetorical well.

These conclusions are affirmed by ample amounts of discursive evidence across disparate discourses all drawing from the same catastrophic source. The ecological, cultural, and political discourses do not necessarily set out to end here: catastrophe is a product of decades of rhetorical heavy lifting outside the audience's critical awareness. Validity and reliability come from the evidence supplied here, along with formal connections the reader may be able to notice in his or her own life. Note also the dearth of counterexamples to the catastrophic implications drawn from these discourses. The agonism described by Dewey, Mouffe, Asen, and Giroux is nowhere to be found. Fundamentalism, anti-environmentalism, gun-rights rhetoric, and Trumpism do not offer counterevidence for a widely shared, deliberative, agonistic outcome. There is no comic corrective. No humility. No grace. No humor. No levity. It is all chaos. It is all tragedy. It is all catastrophe.

CONCLUSION

I have shown in the preceding case studies how catastrophe sweeps the legs out from underneath appeals to shared human progress. The world is dark. Calamity is unavoidable. Violence is inevitable. But those outcomes are not to be feared; rather, calamity is to be manufactured and leveraged to reorder unjust hierarchies of power. Catastrophic audiences may not always be aware of the rhetorical reservoir they draw from, and they may pull back when faced with the pragmatic political consequences of becoming party to such rhetoric; nonetheless, Donald Trump is president, the world continues to warm, and thirty thousand more Americans were killed by guns last year.

Roderick Hart argued that critics could examine audiences of true believers to understand and even predict social phenomena according to the relationship between doctrinal coherence, social conditions, and political practice.

The catastrophic homology informs, from a unique level of abstraction, why some political roads will be less rocky than others. If rhetoric shapes political practice, and political practice shapes reality, we must continue to analyze why some political consequences seem inevitable and others, like redressing climate change, seem almost unimaginable to so many.

Catastrophe and the Comic Corrective

The comic corrective has the potential—in particular contexts with particular individuals—to push back against catastrophe's tragic urgings. The comic is defined by a posture of humility, of gentle prodding, of optimism for shared progress by way of repairing the social order. In contrast to catastrophe, the comic corrective privileges correction and reinstatement—not punishment, victimization, and mortification.[20] The comic corrects exaggerations and the hubris of tragic catastrophe. It identifies human errors and seeks to correct them. The comic is *conservative* (but not in a way James Dobson would appreciate). It repairs social order. It redresses the divisions of society through rhetoric's compensatory ability to foster identification.[21]

For a useful juxtaposition with this Shakespearian tragedy, consider the common association between humor and the comic corrective. The comic encourages us to laugh at each other and ourselves. But there is no humor in the rhetoric of catastrophe. Donald Trump, for example, rarely ever laughs in public. David Litt referenced *The Sound of Music* when he called Trump the "Captain von Trapp of commanders-in-chief."[22] Litt went on to point out that even corny, throwaway jokes bring people together; even those who did not vote for Trump, and who may even despise him, can appreciate the humility of a self-deprecating joke. We know Trump can insult and mock. But those "jokes" are tragic—they separate the world into losers and winners. This lack of humor is not unique to Trump, of course. And by following the critic's maxim and considering what is not here, it becomes clear that these discourses are united in their lack of humor. There is simply no discursive space for levity in the rhetoric of catastrophe.

For the reader who has accompanied me through this dark slog, I want to emphasize the optimistic potential of the comic corrective. This has been a challenging book to write, in part because it has required so much focus on so many vile discourses. The prevalence and power of the rhetoric of catastrophe makes the human condition look bleak. But Kenneth Burke's comic corrective does equip us with guidance for responding to the William Rileys, Jerry Falwells, James Dobsons, Calvin Beisners, Wayne LaPierres, and Donald Trumps that we confront in our daily lives. As Celeste Michelle Condit wrote,

The comic frame tells us that we are all, inevitably, impure. To the extent that we strive for understanding and a better world, we must forgive each other our failings, for we are each equally the clowns of our own dramas. Rather than a tragic challenge and defense that requires one of us to win and one to lose, one of us to scapegoat and one scapegoater, we step outside the tragic mode.[23]

The comic corrective allows us to do just that. It allows us to understand that the Falwells, Beisners, LaPierres, Trumps of our lives are not evil. They are clowns.

However, the catastrophic homology warns against the naïve assumption that a comic corrective is the proper alternative vocabulary for all drawn to the catastrophic community. Some individuals are unreachable by these comic nudgings. This is unsettling for many rhetorical scholars. We'd rather assume, as David Frank suggests, that reasoning and rationality can correct errors in thought.[24] And we'd like to think that modes of deliberate reasoning could aid in resisting fascism and demagoguery. Following in the tradition of Kenneth Burke, social unification is so often the aim of rhetorical criticism, and, as Schwarze argued, the comic corrective is thought to be well suited for unifying divided individuals.[25] Once we are unified the rhetor can employ the comic frame to acknowledge shared points of social identification. For many, this is the value of the comic corrective: it rejects the divisions at the heart of tragic rhetoric for the unification of a renewed moral order.

November 9, 2016, may have sobered us up from such drunken optimism. Trump's election urged a reconsideration of the scope of the comic—specifically—and rational argumentation—more generally. Would Hillary Clinton have won if she had deployed more deliberate reasoning? More broadly, could gun-rights enthusiasts be swayed by more rationality? Do anti-environmentalists need more scientific evidence—not just to exchange the SUV for the Prius, but to support state interventions that keep carbon emissions in the ground?

Maybe. And scholars should not concede all that terrain. But my findings also affirm an argument proposed by Stephen Schwarze: it is possible that division is not the problem that needs to be remedied.[26] Division may not be a cause for eternal and transcendent rhetorical rehabilitation. Maybe division need not be minimized; instead, division and its consequential marginalization and polarization may be advantageous. In other words, the desire for unification in all cases is misguided. Schwarze showed how promoting division and polarization may be appropriate responses in situations where identification and unification require damaging social conditions, injustice, and oppression. And as the rhetoric of catastrophe demonstrates, unification may come with a high price tag, such as the destruction of the collective institutions required for a functional democracy to manage the challenges of governing 330 million people in a complicated global milieu. Catastrophe seeks to retard the development of institutions capable of facilitating the exchange of goods, services, and ideas that have been fundamental to elevating living standards over the last two centuries.[27] As Steven Pinker wrote, the institutional ability to aid collective action, to regulate the greedy proclivities of unrestrained capitalism, and to leverage its unique wealth-creation capacities through redistributive policies have improved the lives of more people than anything else in human history. Michael Lewis further illustrated the value of institutions, detailing how the US government is the most important institution for redressing complicated, global problems.[28] Schwarze urges caution in our assumption that more deliberation, more communication, and more comic corrective will defend such institutions against the attacks of catastrophic rhetoric and their emboldened and reckless audiences.

Rational argumentation is a superior form of discourse in many contexts, especially when laws need to be made by the institutions charged with maintaining a healthy democracy. But here is the rub: scholars and activists need not seek to convert all catastrophists to the side of rational argumentation. Nor should scholars and activists seek to educate all catastrophists out of their ignorance. The mere *existence* of catastrophe is not the challenge to be redressed. Instead, our goal should be to sharpen the critical tools that can keep catastrophe on the fringes of public discourse. Falwell, Robertson, and Dobson can have massive megachurches and tons of best-selling books; Calvin Beisner can speak to large audiences at the Creation Museum in Petersburg, Kentucky; Wayne LaPierre can do the same each year at the NRA convention. Donald Trump can own casinos and star in reality TV shows; Steve Bannon can operate on the fringes of white supremacist internet cesspools. They just need to be kept away from the White House.

Alternatives Vocabularies

I hope future research can extend these findings by exploring the symbolic resources and discursive formations that marginalize catastrophic messaging and the rhetors who rely on it. However, given my experience with the case studies examined in the preceding chapters, I close with a short discussion of what such an alternative vocabulary could look and sound like.

First, ecological conversations must better align the threat of climate change with our social, economic, cultural, and political constraints. My findings encourage us to reject the information deficit model and to adopt a nonpositivistic and rhetorically nuanced approach to exploring how context and social affiliation influence climate change message reception. In turn, we should focus less on individual perceptions of climate change discourse, and pay more attention to the cultural differences and social institutions that influence pre-existing assumptions. For example, concerned scholars, activists, and citizens alike should position their arguments within the social practices of their target audience.[29] Likewise, climate messaging must be able to adjust information to their audiences' already held values and assumptions. Redressing climate change will require a set of constructive and motivating messages tailored to particular values and beliefs.

The power of the *image* may prove useful in connecting the impact of a warming planet to pre-existing values and assumption. Humans have a well-developed capacity to identify and respond to threats when we can visualize their consequences.[30] For example, in the documentary film *Chasing Ice*, National Geographic photographer James Balog and his crew set up to be the first to capture on camera images of ice sheets *calving*. Balog explains the rationale for his project: "The public doesn't want to hear about more statistical studies, more computer models, more projections; what they need is a believable, understandable piece of visual evidence; something that grabs them in the gut." Watching Manhattan-size chunks of ice break off in real time may remind the viewer of a dystopian Hollywood movie, but such an image also offers a vivid example of what climate change is doing to the planet. The image-work in *Chasing Ice* represents one visual technique that may illustrate how audiences willing to pull back from catastrophe's telic destination may be open to redressing climate change.[31]

The creators of *Chasing Ice* have since leveraged the visual force of the film to engage in direct political action. Launching the "Chasing Ice Ohio Tour" in the spring of 2014, the creators focused on one specific congressional district in Ohio represented by climate change denier Pat Tiberi. At a screening in the district, hundreds of Tiberi's constituents saw the film and were moved enough to contact him directly about his position on climate change. According to the *Chasing Ice* website, "In response, Congressman Tiberi shifted his stance on the issue. The Tour serves as a case study for the level of impact that a film can have to create change on our political system."[32]

Regarding alternatives to catastrophic gun-rights rhetoric, I think we can start by conceding that much of the gun-rights discourse examined here is fallacious and cynical. Worse, if these catastrophic inferences are plausible, gun-rights discourse urges individuals to enact a subject position that is toxic to personal, familial, and societal safety. For those interested in improving public conversations about gun violence, however, I don't think amplifying those findings will help. We also know that most Americans are not motivated to reform our gun-control laws based on what has worked in Australia or Denmark. America seems willing to accept more violence than other industrialized nations if the alternative threatens common perceptions of freedom and liberty.[33] Finally, while it is tempting to use the political climate produced by mass shootings to advance gun-control legislation, the short-term gains in public opinion are not worth the long-term backlash. Especially at schools and churches, and especially when the survivors mobilize like the Parkland, Florida, students did, mass shootings attract public conversation, but they account for only 1.2 percent of gun deaths.[34] Such a strategy leaves gun-control advocates open to charges of political opportunism, even as they are promoting laws that would do little to stop gun violence.[35]

If less gun violence is the goal, then focusing on mass shootings—even at schools and churches—seems misdirected. It is unlikely that the policies proposed after Columbine, Sandy Hook, or Parkland would reduce violence.[36] Banning assault weapons or raising the minimum age to buy a gun are symbolic victories that do little to address a broader epidemic. Tragically, there are few viable legislative options capable of preventing the next Parkland-type shooting. However, there is an alternative point of intervention. Legislation should instead focus on the daily, routine violence facilitated by gun culture in the US, where almost forty people are killed each day because of the criminal misuse of guns.[37] Lowering that number, even a fraction, can prevent the equivalent of a Parkland-a-day.

Finally, identifying an alternative to the political catastrophe of Donald Trump presents some unique challenges. Catastrophe aligns with the primary purpose of mainstream American media: it draws an audience. Trump's ability to influence the news cycle is masterful, and catastrophe explains part of the reason why he can suck up so much oxygen. Further, he was elected president in 2016 when few thought he could win, and he may be serving his second term by the time you read this. Or, he may be defeated in 2020 and his presidency will be a shameful historical blip. We know neither how this will play out nor what discourse will emerge in relation to these potential outcomes. Nonetheless, with the health of American democracy on the line, I ought to consider how catastrophic political rhetoric, in general, might be blunted.

Trump's catastrophic messaging is impervious to rational argumentation. The 2016 election, and Trump's unflinching support among Republicans throughout his first term, reveals that many Americans do not have the time or the energy to engage in political disagreements with much nuance and sophistication. With 2020 in mind, the Democratic candidate should not respond to Trump's catastrophic messaging. This will not be easy: the office of the presidency and all its trappings make it hard to look past the fact that Trump is not a legislative interlocutor. Trump is a carnival barker, and he must be treated like one. Or as Aaron Huertas suggested, Trump's opponents need to treat him the same way a stand-up comedian handles a heckling audience member screaming "Do your old stuff!"[38] A savvy comedian will not reply to a drunken heckler with a rational argument justifying her preference for the new material. She would acknowledge the interruption (it would be distracting not to); she would disarm it ("Wow, you started drinking early, huh?"); and then she would transition back to her set ("This guy reminds me of the ex-boyfriend I was just talking about . . .").

Trump opponents should respond in kind. Avoiding pointing out how far Trump deviates from the standards of rational argumentation. The shock of the presidency divorced from the best obtainable version of the truth has worn off. And not enough people care anyway. *Post-truth* was the 2016 Word of the Year for a reason.

The 2018 midterm elections offered a chance to test this strategy. Democratic candidates generally avoided Trump's catastrophic trolling. When Trump talked about MS-13 in American cities, Democrats talked about preexisting conditions; when Trump talked about "criminals and unknown Middle Easterners" mixed into the migrant caravans, his opponents talked about college debt.

Will such alternative vocabularies remedy the rhetorical potency of the catastrophic homology? We must balance the optimistic potential of these alternative vocabularies with the more sobering reality of a catastrophic homology. My findings indicate that for many the threat of ecological, cultural, and political harm has become a powerful platform for exercising individual achievement, reaffirming hierarchy, and restoring order to a disordered world—rather than a motivating force for collective solidarity and expanding public engagement to take on a massive, global challenge. Going forward, the challenge may be knowing who is receptive to alternative vocabularies and who just needs to be barred from influencing public policy.

ACKNOWLEDGMENTS

I WANT to acknowledge and thank the many people who helped improve and clarify the arguments presented here. Barry Brummett helped sharpen my use of the rhetorical homology. Alec Baker and Sharon Downey were instrumental in honing the original argument that would become this book. Brian Spitzberg improved my discussion of systematicity. Rachel Clancy helped with the discussion of rational argumentation. Karen Winslow helped improve the Christian fundamentalism chapter. Chris Duerringer was a huge help with the gun-rights chapter. Joseph Harris and Becky LaVally improved the clarity and eloquence of the arguments.

I also want to acknowledge and thank Ben Winslow, Shabab Siddiqui, Eli Mangold, Allie Doherty, Josh Hanan, and Lisa Perks for their insight and inspiration.

My editor at The Ohio State University Press, Tara Cyphers, was a joy to work with—a true interlocutor who greatly enhanced the arguments and their presentation. The two anonymous reviewers were wonderful: insightful, stimulating, and encouraging. They made this a much better book than it otherwise would have been.

Many of the arguments presented here were developed and sharpened within a smart, talented, and kind community of scholars, students, friends, and family. More specifically, I want to thank the 2018 *Public Address* graduate seminar at San Diego State and the 2018 Presidential Rhetoric seminar of the Rhetoric Society of America, led by Mary Stuckey and John Murphy. I want to acknowledge a pair of grants from the SDSU University Grant Program that helped with funding for this project. Bill Snavely, Heather Canary, and Kara Bauer also were instrumental in securing the necessary resources to work on this project.

Closer to home, I want to thank my wife, Addie, for providing a warm, supportive climate to work on this project. My sons, William and Benjamin, provided constant inspiration and joy.

I am dedicating this book to my parents, Dale and Karen Winslow: thank you for the years of patience, support, and love. *Truth crushed to earth shall rise again.*

NOTES

NOTES TO INTRODUCTION

1. Pinker, *Enlightenment Now*, 359.
2. Hochschild, *Strangers in Their Own Land*; Jones, *The End of White Christian America*; Klein, *No Is Not Enough*, 89.
3. Oliver and Wood, "Conspiracy Theories." In 1964 Richard Hofstadter famously detailed what he called the "paranoid style of American politics," composed of heated exaggeration and conspiratorial fantasy in response to the threats posed by a changing liberal order. Post-truth vocabularies have never been hard to locate on the fringes of the Know-Nothing party, the John Birch Society, the Tea Party, and Occupy Wall Street, as well as among individual political figures like Barry Goldwater, Pat Buchanan, Ross Perot, and Jesse Ventura (see Hofstadter, *The Paranoid Style*).
4. Klein, *No Is Not Enough*, 17; Pinker, *Enlightenment Now*; 41–50; Thompson, *Enough Said*; Winslow, *Economic Injustice*.
5. Gunn, "On Political Perversion," 177.
6. Asen and Gent, "Reconsidering Symbolic Use," 3; Habermas, *Between Facts and Norms*; Habermas, *The Theory of Communicative Action*, 25; see also Rehg, "Evaluating Complex," 471.
7. Asen and Gent, "Reconsidering Symbolic Ise," 3.
8. Rehg, "Rhetoric, Cogency," 475.
9. Crowley, *Toward a Civil Discourse*, 3; Perelman and Olbrechts-Tyteca, *The New Rhetoric*.
10. Burke, *A Rhetoric of Motives*; Derrida, cited in Mouffe, *The Return of the Political*, 141; Crowley, *Toward a Civil Discourse*, 20; Mouffe, cited in Giroux, *Terror of Neoliberalism*, 132; Miller, "Should We Name the Tools?" 25; Warner, "Publics and Counterpublics," 424.
11. Burke, *A Rhetoric of Motives*, 52; Butterworth, "The Passion of the Tebow," 21.
12. Rehg, "Rhetoric, Cogency," 481. See also Asen, "Imagining in the Public Sphere," 345; Ackerman and Coogan, *The Public Work of Rhetoric*, x.
13. *Oxford English Dictionary*, s.v. "catastrophe." I want to concede early on that I am not the first to theorize upheaval and convulsion. Friedrich Hegel's dialectic valorized conflict and chaos as a way to ward off social petrification and stagnation. Karl Marx assumed that violent class conflicts pushed history forward to its communist utopia. More recently, biologists have examined the upheaval of a natural world where some plants and animals must be destroyed for the good of the ecosystem. Economists have examined the redemptive value of bankruptcy laws as a way to incentivize risk and entrepreneurship. Some software engineers looked forward to the chaotic consequences

of Y2K at the turn of the millennium as a "wake-up call," yearning for "the good that could come out of this event." Foreign policy analysts have examined the way American foreign interventions seek to manufacture and then capitalize on geopolitical turmoil as a way to construct more democratic institutions in the developing world. Health policy scholars have examined how natural disasters provide cover for draconian cuts to medical care. And autocratic dictators have long manufactured crises to justify the consolidation of power and exercise of authoritarian force (see Hegel, in Mueller, *Retreat From Doomsday*; Marx, in Montgomery and Chirot, *The Shape of the New*; see also Pinker, *Enlightenment Now*, 165; Friedman, *Thank You for Being Late*, Kindle edition, loc. 5260; Vox, *Existential Threats*, 166; Klein, *The Shock Doctrine*; Pearson, *No Apparent Distress*).

14. Cloud, "The Null Persona"; McGee, "The 'Ideograph'"; Wander, "The Third Persona."
15. Charland, "Constitutive Rhetoric," 142; See also Brummett, *Rhetorical Homologies*, 174, 219; Warner, "Publics and Counterpublics," 415.
16. Burke, *Counter-Statement*, 42; Brummett, *Rhetorical Homologies*, 15; Jameson, *The Political Unconscious*; Richards, *The Philosophy of Rhetoric*, 30; Ogden and Richards, *The Meaning of Meaning*, 55.
17. Brummett, *Rhetorical Homologies*, 3. Black ("Extending the Rights," 317) and Kathryn Olson's ("Detecting a Common," 218) work also illustrate these distinguishing features of the rhetorical homology from other methods, including formal and genre criticism.
18. Charland, "Constitutive Rhetoric," 137.
19. Richards, *The Philosophy of Rhetoric*, 30.
20. Ogden and Richards, *The Meaning of Meaning*, 55.
21. Burke, *Counter-Statement*, 31.
22. Burke, *Counter-Statement*, 138, 124.
23. Burke, *Counter-Statement*, 124.
24. Goodnight, "The Personal, Technical, and Public Spheres of Argument," 201.
25. Jamieson and Campbell, "Rhetorical Hybrids"; Winslow, "Colonizing Caster Semenya."
26. Hart, *Modern Rhetorical Criticism*, 121–24.
27. Jamieson, "Generic Constraints and the Rhetorical Situation," 165.
28. Gunn, "On Political Perversion," 173–74; Winslow, "Colonizing Caster Semenya."
29. Jamieson, "Generic Constraints," 162–66.
30. Brummett, *Rhetorical Homologies*.
31. Brummett, *Rhetorical Homologies*, 220.
32. Fiske and Hartley, *Reading Television*.
33. Hebdige, *Subculture*; Willis, *Profane Culture*; Winslow, "Rhetorical Homology."
34. Brummett, *Rhetorical Homologies*.
35. Brummett, *Rhetorical Homologies*, 1.
36. Jamieson, "Antecedent Genre as Rhetorical Constraint," 406; Campbell and Jamieson, *Form and Genre*, 21.
37. Brummett, *Rhetorical Homologies*, 6–7, 16, 223.
38. Black, "Extending the Rights," 317.
39. Olson, "Detecting a Common."
40. Winslow, "Rhetorical homology."
41. Winslow, "Rich, Blessed, and Tenured."
42. Coogan and Ackerman, "Introduction."
43. Ackerman and Coogan, *The Public Work of Rhetoric*, 7.
44. Bostdorff, *The Presidency and the Rhetoric of Foreign Crisis*, 9.
45. Edelman, *Constructing the Political Spectacle*; Edelman, *Politics as Symbolic Action*, 66.
46. Bostdorff, *The Presidency*, 1.
47. Bostdorff, *The Presidency*, 14.
48. Edelman, *Constructing the Political Spectacle*.
49. Bostdorff, *The Presidency*, 205.

50. Vox, *Existential Threats.*
51. Asen, "Imagining in the Public Sphere," 352; Gunn, "On Political Perversion."
52. Bostdorff, *The Presidency,* vii, 207.
53. Brummett, *Contemporary Apocalyptic Rhetoric,* 88.
54. Hoyningen-Huene, "Systematicity."
55. Edwards, *Superchurch,* 6.
56. Pigliucci, "The Demarcation Problem," 24.
57. Darsey, *The Prophetic Tradition,* 9.
58. Fuchs, "What Makes Sciences 'Scientific'?"
59. Pigliucci, "The Demarcation Problem," 10–11.
60. Bowler, *Blessed,* 12; Gunn and Cloud, "Agentic Orientation."
61. Anderson, "New Sentences."
62. See Smith, Virginia, *Clean: A History of Personal Hygiene and Purity.* (Oxford: Oxford UP, 2007); Sartwell, Crispin, "How Would You Draw History," *New York Times,* Nov. 19, 2018.
63. Foust and Murphy, "Revealing and Reframing Apocalyptic," 160.
64. Hesford, Licona, and Teston, *Precarious Rhetorics,* Location 131; see also Quarantelli and Dynes, "Community Conflict."
65. Edwin Black made a similar argument when he noted how well the metaphor of communism-as-cancer fits with the Rightist ideology. A similar contemporary fit between catastrophe and conservatism is evident, but not inevitable; rather, surface-level fit is the product of decades of deeper rhetorical work—work performed by the catastrophic homology (Black, "The Second Persona," 119).
66. Lee, "Considering Political Identity"; Safire, *Safire's Political Dictionary.*
67. "Word of the Year 2016 is . . ."
68. Smith, *American Evangelicalism.*
69. Crowley, *Toward a Civil Discourse,* 157; I follow the methodological lead of Barbara Herrnstein Smith (*Belief and Resistance,* xix) and Sharon Crowley (*Toward a Civil Discourse,* x) here to show how it is possible to illuminate this alignment process in fundamentalism in politically urgent and theoretically rich ways without mocking fundamentalist individuals. My methodological imperative includes accurate descriptions of fundamentalist discourse, representative quotations, sober extrapolation, accounting for the best of fundamentalist arguments (not just the most extreme), and offering enough evidence that the plausibility of these patterns becomes clear in the minds of the reader.

NOTES TO CHAPTER 1

1. Marsden, *Understanding Fundamentalism and Evangelicalism,* 4–5; see also FitzGerald, *The Evangelicals,* Kindle edition, loc. 77.
2. Balmer, *Mine Eyes Have Seen the Glory,* 336; Crowley, *Toward a Civil Discourse,* 14; Marsden, *Understanding Fundamentalism and Evangelicalism,* 57.
3. Falwell, *Strength for the Journey,* 360.
4. FitzGerald, *The Evangelicals,* Kindle edition, loc. 4976.
5. Marsden, *Fundamentalism and American Culture,* 159; see also FitzGerald, *The Evangelicals,* Kindle edition, loc. 1247; Jones, *The End of White Christian America.*
6. Balmer, *Mine Eyes,* 43; FitzGerald, *The Evangelicals,* Kindle edition, loc. 2581.
7. Although many immigrants were Catholics, for whom, presumably, myth, miracle, and tradition served important rhetorical functions, Molly Worthen described why this emerging form of fundamentalist inerrancy was unique: "Catholics obeyed the authority (and ambiguities) of church tradition and Vatican decree, and Mormons accepted an equally powerful magisterium while expecting changing and continuing revelation through their prophet, the president of the church. Neither church entertained the fic-

tion that Christians might understand scripture without guidance or interpretive frameworks" (*Apostles of Reason*, 73).
8. Olson, "Performing Embodiable Topoi," 302–3.
9. Mouffe, *The Democratic Paradox*, 104.
10. FitzGerald, *The Evangelicals*, Kindle edition, loc. 111.
11. Moody, *The New Sermons*, 535.
12. Moody, *The New Sermons*, 534.
13. Moody, cited in Rossing, *The Rapture Exposed*, 13.
14. FitzGerald, *The Evangelicals*, Kindle edition, loc. 65.
15. Hunter, *American Evangelicalism*.
16. FitzGerald, *The Evangelicals*, Kindle edition, loc. 1013.
17. Hunter, *American Evangelicalism*.
18. Bostdorff, *The Presidency*, 205.
19. FitzGerald, *The Evangelicals*, Kindle edition, loc. 999.
20. FitzGerald, *The Evangelicals*, Kindle edition, loc. 1013.
21. Moody, *Short Talks*, 94.
22. McLoughlin, *Modern Revivalism*, 213.
23. Balmer, *Mine Eyes*, 32; FitzGerald, *The Evangelicals*, Kindle edition, loc. 111; Vox, *Existential Threats*, 13. "Premillennial" refers to Christ returning *before* the thousand-year reign (compared with postmillennial, meaning Christ will return *after* an age of peace); "dispensation" refers to the stages of time in which the future of the planet is predicted in the books of Daniel and Revelation.
24. Brummett, *Contemporary Apocalyptic Rhetoric*, 66; Crowley, *Toward a Civil Discourse*, 103; FitzGerald, *The Evangelicals*, Kindle edition, loc. 1156.
25. Balmer, *Mine Eyes*, 33–34.
26. Crowley, *Toward a Civil Discourse*, 131–32.
27. FitzGerald, *The Evangelicals*, Kindle edition, loc. 1546.
28. Riley, "Report of World Conference on the Fundamentals of the Faith," *School and Church*, July–September 1919, cited in Edwards, *Superchurch*, 68.
29. FitzGerald, *The Evangelicals*, Kindle edition, loc. 2066; Marsden, *Fundamentalism and American Culture*, 159.
30. Balmer, *Mine Eyes*, xv; Edwards, *Superchurch*, 64; FitzGerald, *The Evangelicals*, Kindle edition, loc. 1687; Marsden, *Fundamentalism and American Culture*, 215.
31. Edwards, *Superchurch*, 64–65; FitzGerald, *The Evangelicals*, Kindle edition, loc. 1710; Marsden, *Fundamentalism and American Culture*, 121.
32. Hague, "History of the Higher Criticism," 87–122.
33. Marsden, *Understanding Fundamentalism and Evangelicalism*, 57.
34. Balmer, *Mine Eyes*, 336; Brummett, *Contemporary Apocalyptic Rhetoric*, 63; FitzGerald, *The Evangelicals*, Kindle edition, loc. 1239.
35. Balmer, *Mine Eyes*, xv; FitzGerald, *The Evangelicals*, Kindle edition, loc. 1524.
36. Edwards, *Superchurch*, 51.
37. Edwards, *Superchurch*, 8, 72; Fraser, "Rethinking the Public Sphere"; Pezzullo, "Resisting 'National Breast Cancer Awareness Month,'" 347. Carolyn R. Miller describes this methodological challenge as an exploration into the rhetoric of concealment. Miller, "Should We," 31.
38. For a useful example of the fluidity of appropriation, see Black, "Extending the Rights," 313. The term *counterpublic* has become a contested concept in rhetorical studies, and so I should make clear that my use of the term to describe Christian fundamentalism affirms the term's relationship to discursive responses based on the exclusion of communities from dominant spheres a fair description of how many conservative Protestants felt in this moment. At the same time, my use of counterpublic also affirms the contributions of Robert Asen and Catherine Helen Palczewski in illustrating the dangers of

assuming that counterpublic conceptualization depends on the actual exclusion of persons from mechanisms of power. In other words, *counterpublic* may describe the public speech used to develop oppositional identities in second-wave feminist groups *and* Christian fundamentalists (see Pason, Foust, and Rogness, "Introduction").

39. Edwards, *Superchurch*, 7–8.
40. Balmer, *Mine Eyes*, xiv; FitzGerald, *The Evangelicals*, Kindle edition, loc. 106.
41. Brummett, *Contemporary Apocalyptic Rhetoric*, 25, 44.
42. Balmer, *Mine Eyes*, 43.
43. Edwards, *Superchurch*, xi.
44. Popp, "Visual Culture," 505.
45. Jones, *The End of White Christian America*; Frykholm, *Rapture Culture*, 107; Vox, *Existential Threats*, 130–31.
46. Warner, *Publics and Counterpublics*, 119–21.
47. Kaplan, *The Most Dangerous Branch*, 321.
48. "LGBTstats: Quiz: Poverty and the LGBT Community"; McDermott, "The Myth of Gay Affluence."
49. McDermott, "The Myth of Gay Affluence."
50. FitzGerald, *The Evangelicals*, Kindle edition, loc. 2957, 3066; Vox, *Existential Threats*, 78–79.
51. FitzGerald, *The Evangelicals*, Kindle edition, loc. 3034.
52. McLoughlin, *Billy Graham*, 139.
53. Chávez, "Focus on the Family."
54. Kurt Bruner, cited in Klemp, *The Morality of Spin*, 120; see also Chávez, "Focus on the Family."
55. Popp, "Visual Culture," 501, 509.
56. Edwards, *Superchurch*, 6.
57. Wilkens and Thorsen, *Everything You Know about Evangelicals Is Wrong*, 85.
58. Edwards, *Superchurch*, 52.
59. Riley, "The Great Divide or Christ and the Present Crisis," *School and Church*, July–September 1919, cited in *Superchurch*, 70–71.
60. Riley, "Dr. W. B. Riley Endorses the Fort Wayne Gospel Temple, Its Pastor, and Tabernacle Movement," *Fort Wayne Gospel Temple*, May 24, 1940, cited in Edwards, *Superchurch*, 75.
61. FitzGerald, *The Evangelicals*, Kindle edition, loc. 503; Vox, *Existential Threats*, 168.
62. Edwards, *Superchurch*, 124–25.
63. Wilkens and Thorsen, *Everything You Know*, 85.
64. Frank Newport, "One-Third of Americans Believe the Bible Is Literally True," *Gallup News* Service, May 25, 2007.
65. Marsden, *Fundamentalism and American Culture*, 159; FitzGerald, *The Evangelicals*, Kindle edition, loc. 7821.
66. Vox, *Existential Threats*, 43.
67. FitzGerald, *The Evangelicals*, Kindle edition, loc. 7821.
68. Worthen, *Apostles of Reason*, 110.
69. Falwell, *Listen, America!*
70. Worthen, *Apostles of Reason*, 31.
71. Machen, "What Fundamentalism Stands for Now, Defined by a Leading Exponent."
72. FitzGerald, *The Evangelicals*, Kindle edition, loc. 1628.
73. Torrey, "The Certainty and Importance," 104.
74. Marsden, *Fundamentalism and American Culture*, 112; Worthen, *Apostles of Reason*, 21.
75. Vox, *Existential Threats*, 46.
76. Vox, *Existential Threats*, 134.

77. Edwards, *Superchurch*, 64–65; FitzGerald, *The Evangelicals*, Kindle edition, loc. 1710; Marsden, *Fundamentalism and American Culture*, 119.
78. Thomas, "Old Testament Criticism and New Testament Christianity," 6.
79. Reeve, "My Experience with the Higher Criticism," 102–3.
80. Machen, "What Fundamentalism Stands for Now."
81. Oshatz, *Slavery and Sin*.
82. Vox, *Existential Threats*, 17; for a vivid example, see LaHaye, *Revelation Unveiled*, 17.
83. FitzGerald, *The Evangelicals*, Kindle edition, loc. 1299; Vox, *Existential Threats*, 15.
84. Reid, *The Works of Thomas Reid*, 97, 129.
85. Barron, *Heaven on Earth?* 30; FitzGerald, *The Evangelicals*, Kindle edition, loc. 1299.
86. Crowley, *Toward a Civil Discourse*, 144; Vox, *Existential Threats*, 193; Worthen, *Apostles of Reason*, 30.
87. Edwards, *Superchurch*, 83.
88. Standaert, *Skipping Towards Armageddon*, 34; Wilkens and Thorsen, *Everything You Know*, 46; Worthen, *Apostles of Reason*, 10.
89. Marsden, *Fundamentalism and American Culture*, 57–58.
90. FitzGerald, *The Evangelicals*, Kindle edition, loc. 1070, 2458; Worthen, *Apostles of Reason*, 199.
91. FitzGerald, *The Evangelicals*, Kindle edition, loc. 4575; Wilkens and Thorsen, *Everything You Know*, 92; Worthen, *Apostles of Reason*, 200.
92. Crowley, *Toward a Civil Discourse*, 147.
93. FitzGerald, *The Evangelicals*, Kindle edition, loc. 6518.
94. Connolly, *The Ethos of Pluralization*, 105.
95. Edwards, *Superchurch*, 88.
96. Balmer, *Mine Eyes*, 24; Vox, *Existential Threats*, 14.
97. Edwards, *Superchurch*, 12.
98. Crowley, *Toward a Civil Discourse*, 122.
99. Wall text, *What do we teach?* Creation Museum, Petersburg, KY.
100. Darsey, *The Prophetic Tradition*, 31–32.
101. Machen, "What Fundamentalism Stands for Now."
102. FitzGerald, *The Evangelicals*, Kindle edition, loc. 2364.
103. Harding, *The Book of Jerry Falwell*, 70.
104. Edwards, *Superchurch*, 13; FitzGerald, *The Evangelicals*, Kindle edition, loc. 2424; Vox, *Existential Threats*, 49; Worthen, *Apostles of Reason*, 31.
105. Marsden, *Fundamentalism and American Culture*, 188.
106. Johnson, *The Scopes "Monkey Trial,"* 81.
107. Marsden, *Fundamentalism and American Culture*, 186–87.
108. Grebstein, *Monkey Trial*, 164–66.
109. Harding, *The Book of Jerry Falwell*, 67–72.
110. Moran, *The Scopes Monkey Trial*, 166.
111. Johnson, *The Scopes "Monkey Trial,"* 85.
112. Harding, *The Book of Jerry Falwell*, 73.
113. Marsden, *Fundamentalism and American Culture*, 122; Vox, *Existential Threats*, 43; Wilkens and Thorsen, *Everything You Know*, 90; Worthen, *Apostles of Reason*, 223.
114. Grebstein, *Monkey Trial*, 158–67; Marsden, *Fundamentalism and American Culture*, 186–87.
115. Johnson, *The Scopes "Monkey Trial,"* 81.
116. Harding, *The Book of Jerry Falwell*, 71.
117. Johnson, *The Scopes "Monkey Trial,"* 90.
118. Harding, *The Book of Jerry Falwell*, 73.
119. Fitzgerald, *The Scopes Trial*, 73.
120. Fitzgerald, *The Scopes Trial*, 73; Moran, *The Scopes Monkey Trial*, 162.

121. Moran, *The Scopes Monkey Trial*, 163.
122. Harding, *The Book of Jerry Falwell*, 72–73.
123. Crowley, *Toward a Civil Discourse*, 74.
124. Carpenter, *Revive Us Again*; Crowley, *Toward a Civil Discourse*, 136; FitzGerald, *The Evangelicals*, Kindle edition, loc. 2476, 2500; Harding, *The Book of Jerry Falwell*.
125. FitzGerald, *The Evangelicals*, Kindle edition, loc. 2530; see also Worthen, *Apostles of Reason*, 19.
126. Balmer, *Mine Eyes*, 95; Edwards, *Superchurch*, 79.
127. FitzGerald, *The Evangelicals*, Kindle edition, loc. 1637.
128. Balmer, *Mine Eyes*, 133; Worthen, *Apostles of Reason*, 46.
129. FitzGerald, *The Evangelicals*, Kindle edition, loc. 2585.
130. FitzGerald, *The Evangelicals*, Kindle edition, loc. 953.
131. Popp, "Visual Culture," 502.
132. Dobson, "The Future of the Family."
133. Dobson, "A Historic Occasion."
134. Dobson, "A Historic Occasion."
135. Dobson, cited in Becker, "Dr. James C. Dobson's Jeremiad: The Proverbial Father."
136. Black, "The Second Persona," 119.
137. FitzGerald, *Cities on a Hill*, 164; see also Worthen, *Apostles of Reason*, 170.
138. Schaeffer, *The Complete Works of Francis Schaeffer*, 477.
139. Schaeffer, *The Complete Works of Francis Schaeffer*, 489; see also Worthen, *Apostles of Reason*, 216.
140. FitzGerald, *The Evangelicals*, Kindle edition, loc. 7532.
141. Dobson and Bauer, *Children at Risk*.
142. Dobson and Bauer, *Children at Risk*, 294–25.
143. Popp, "Visual Culture," 512.
144. Falwell, *Strength for the Journey*.
145. Vox, *Existential Threats*, 81.
146. FitzGerald, *The Evangelicals*, Kindle edition, loc. 5884; Vox, *Existential Threats*, 75–76.
147. FitzGerald, *The Evangelicals*, Kindle edition, loc. 161.
148. Dobson, cited in Becker, "Dr. James C. Dobson's Jeremiad."
149. Stanton, "Are Same-Sex Families Good for Children?"; see Platt, "Focusing the Family," 603.
150. Dobson, "A Historic Occasion."
151. Popp, "Visual Culture," 511.
152. Foust and Murphy, "Revealing and Reframing," 154; Worthen, *Apostles of Reason*, 77.
153. Premillennial dispensation offers a vivid example of telic temporality. John Nelson Darby divided time into seven *dispensations*, starting with Adam in the Garden of Eden and concluding with the rapture of true believers and the thousand-year reign of Christ on earth (Carpenter, *Revive Us Again*, 248–49). Darby had a profound influence on the acceptance of telic temporality for fundamentalists. Ranging as far back as Increase Mather in the seventeenth century, up through Jerry Falwell and Tim LaHaye in the twenty-first, premillennialism assumes that because society is descending into such a state of chaos and sin, the only remedy is divine, cataclysmic intervention (FitzGerald, *The Evangelicals*, Kindle edition, loc. 283).
154. Standaert, *Skipping Towards Armageddon*, 8.
155. *Thief in the Night*.
156. Hagee, *Daniel to Doomsday*.
157. Crowley, *Toward a Civil Discourse*, 114.
158. Crowley, *Toward a Civil Discourse*, 115.
159. FitzGerald, *The Evangelicals*, Kindle edition, loc. 5464.
160. Vox, *Existential Threats*, xiii.

161. Falwell, *American Can Be Saved*, 29.
162. Examples abound. Jerry Falwell "opposed almost all forms of assistance to the poor, including food stamps, on the grounds that welfare programs sap the biblically mandated work ethic," and he urged believers to oppose welfare as an example of "government to take resources from some and bestow them on others." James Dobson wanted to gut welfare programs and shift aid to churches and families. Pat Robertson conceded that some welfare programs were useful after the Great Depression but that after the economic turmoil of the 1970s a "profound moral revival" was needed to get the size of the government under control. He said, "Those who love God must get involved in the election of strong leaders," and they should choose men and women who "pledged to reduce the size of government, eliminate federal deficits, free our productive capacity, ensure sound currency" (see Brummett, *Contemporary Apocalyptic Rhetoric*, 137; Edwards, *Superchurch*, 138; FitzGerald, *The Evangelicals*, Kindle edition, loc. 5396, 7986; Phillips-Fein, *Invisible Hands*, Kindle edition, loc. 4061). More cynically, historian Randall Balmer described a sermon by H. E. Schmul from Salem, Ohio, who said, "One thing that is happening is good, even though it's bad. I'm talking about AIDS. The real answer is a change in the hearts of men. God's way of all purity, of all chastity is the way. God's plan is the *only* way! Amen." Balmer pointed to the salutary effect of the AIDS epidemic in Schmul's mind. Schmul continued, "Some people are backing up on this homosexual thing. Some of the gays that had to have sex the homosexual way are changing their minds after seeing their buddies drop off or fall over like flies. When they're sure that a person has AIDS is going to go down the tubes and go out into eternity—they're really beginning to change their minds a little." Schmul seemed pleased with that result (Balmer, *Mine Eyes*, 239). More recently, Michael Lewis's book *The Fifth Risk* makes the general political implications of this discourse clear: "No one will say they want kids to go hungry to punish lazy parents, or gay men to die of AIDS to punish sexual deviants, but they can run social support programs so ineptly that they 1) Lose political support (or never emerge); and 2) Let kids go hungry, gay men to die, and the earth to burn" (Kindle edition, loc. 928). The Trump administration's response to asylum seekers at the US–Mexico border also illuminates the political consequences of a catastrophic governing rationale. Harsh immigration policies, including separating children from their parents, seem to be designed to make life so miserable for asylum seekers that they will not want to make the journey north.
163. Boone, *The Bible Tells Them So*, 53. Such telic urgings presented challenges for political participation, as Pat Robertson discovered when he ran for president in 1988. Randall Balmer relayed a retort to Robertson's political promises made to a pastors' luncheon in Concord: "'Wait a minute,' one of the ministers replied to Robertson's lofty political proposals. 'The next event on the eschatological clock is the return of Christ. Things in society should get worse rather than better. If Christians worked to turn our nation around, that would be a humanistic effort and delay Christ's return'" (Balmer, *Mine Eyes*, 173).
164. FitzGerald, *The Evangelicals*, Kindle edition, loc, 1799, 8472, 8560, 8571; Hart, "The Rhetoric of the True Believer"; Vox, *Existential Threats*, 75–76, 81.
165. Edwards, *Superchurch*, 76.
166. Crowley, *Toward a Civil Discourse*, 126; Edwards, *Superchurch*, 66, 77.
167. Crowley, *Toward a Civil Discourse*, 10.
168. Wall text, *The Lake of Fire*, Creation Museum, Petersburg, KY.
169. Edwards, *Superchurch*, 175.
170. FitzGerald, *The Evangelicals*, Kindle edition, loc. 8300.
171. Edwards, *Superchurch*, 134; FitzGerald, *The Evangelicals*, Kindle edition, loc. 8300.
172. The rhetorical homology is especially useful for illustrating this vital methodological distinction. Following Olson and Black, stranger rapists and deer hunters should not be lumped together—they do not seek the same ends. However, they may employ for-

mally consistent patterns of discourse that, consequently, reveal larger societal truths far beyond rapists and hunters. Put more simply, the rhetorical homology allows the critic to focus on consequences, not mind reading.

173. Mouffe, *The Democratic Paradox*, 102–3.
174. Edwards, *Superchurch*, xv–xvi.
175. Edwards, *Superchurch*, 17.
176. Chávez, "Focus on the Family."
177. Minnery, "Our Father Knows Best."
178. Dobson, "Was a Good Family Life Easier to Achieve in Earlier Days?"
179. Chávez, "Focus on the Family."
180. Platt, "Focus on the Past," 9.
181. Popp, "Visual Culture," 508.
182. Dobson, "The Future of the Family."
183. Coontz, *The Way We Never Were*; Reid, *Families in Jeopardy*; Platt, "Focus on the Past," 5.
184. Fraser, *By the People*, 773; Levitt and Dubner, *Superfreakonomics*.
185. Coontz, *The Way We Never Were*; Dreman, *The Family on the Threshold of the 21st Century*.
186. Cloud, "The Rhetoric of 'Family Values,'" 387.
187. Harding, *The Book of Jerry Falwell*, 230.
188. FitzGerald, *The Evangelicals*, Kindle edition, loc. 1826; Guyatt, *Have a Nice Doomsday*, 156; Standaert, *Skipping Towards Armageddon*, 33; Vox, *Existential Threats*, 41; Worthen, *Apostles of Reason*, 178.
189. Harding, *Book of Falwell*, 19–20.
190. FitzGerald, *The Evangelicals*, Kindle edition, loc. 5624.
191. FitzGerald, *The Evangelicals*, Kindle edition, loc. 9055.
192. Brummett, *Contemporary Apocalyptic Rhetoric*, 174.

NOTES TO CHAPTER 2

1. Ceccarelli, "Manufactured Scientific Controversy," 204–5; Friedrichs, *The Future*, 23–24.
2. Antonio and Brulle, "Climate Change Denial," 200; Good, "The Framing of Climate Change," 234.
3. Friedrichs, *The Future*, 163–64; Nerlich, Koteyko, and Brown, "Theory and Language of Climate Change Communication."
4. Elsasser and Dunlap, "Leading Voices," 761; Pew Research Center, "Increasing Partisan Divide on Energy Policies" ; McCright and Dunlap, "Cool Dudes"; McCright and Dunlap, "Anti-reflexivity," 107.
5. Leiserowitz, "Communicating the Risks of Global Warming."
6. Norgaard, *Living in Denial*, 187.
7. Perkowitz, "Praxis Forum," 67–69.
8. Choi, "The Competition between Frames and Counterframes in the U.S. Media's Social Construction of Global Warming"; Saad, "Americans as Concerned."
9. Norgaard, *Living in Denial*, 178–79.
10. Norgaard, *Living in Denial*, 180–87.
11. Newport, "Little Increase in Americans' Global Warming Worries."
12. Donald J. Trump, Tweet, November 6, 2012.
13. "Mulvaney Says Climate Change Research Is 'A Waste of Your Money.'"
14. Foust, Bradley, Ben-Hamoo, and Polonitza, "The Relationship between Political Ideology and Climate Change"; Moser and Dilling, "Communicating Climate Change," 168–69.
15. Norgaard, *Living in Denial*, 179.
16. Moser and Dilling, "Communicating Climate Change," 164.
17. Foust and Murphy, "Revealing and Reframing Apocalyptic Tragedy," 151.

18. Kellstedt, Zahran, and Vedlitz, "Personal Efficacy, the Information Environment, and Attitudes toward Global Warming and Climate Change in the United States." See also Friedrichs, *The Future*, 165.
19. Krosnick, Holbrook, Lowe, and Visser, "The Origins and Consequences of Democratic Citizens' Policy Agendas"; Norgaard, *Living in Denial*, 2; Pinker, *Enlightenment Now*, 139.
20. Goodnight, "The Personal, Technical," 202.
21. Regarding my range of discourses, I locate catastrophic points of correspondence throughout the messaging of the Cornwall Alliance—a Christian public policy organization that targets conservative evangelicals, including their book *Resisting the Green Dragon*, documentary *Where the Grass Is Greener*, and website wegetit.org; the Heartland Institute—a public policy think tank based in Illinois known for rejecting the scientific consensus on global warming; anti-environmentalist Senator James Inhofe's book *The Greatest Hoax: How the Global Warming Conspiracy Threatens Your Future*; and material from the Creation Museum in Petersburg, Kentucky, including a DVD and booklet called *Global Warming*, along with my own experience visiting the museum.
22. Mayer, *Dark Money*.
23. *Where the Grass Is Greener*.
24. Beisner, "Resisting the Green Dragon of Environmentalism."
25. Wanliss, *Resisting the Green Dragon*, back dust jacket.
26. "Resisting the Green Dragon."
27. Ball, "Global Warming: A Scientific," 80.
28. Taylor, James M., "Global Warming," (Creation Museum DVD).
29. Land, Richard, "Global Warming," (Creation Museum DVD).
30. Ball, "Global Warming: A Scientific," 80.
31. Chilton, "Global Warming: A Scientific," 80.
32. Vox, *Existential Threats*, 172.
33. Lindsey, *Apocalypse Code*, 112, 146.
34. Vox, *Existential Threats*, 160.
35. *Where the Grass Is Greener*.
36. Land, Richard, "Global Warming," (Creation Museum DVD).
37. Christy, "Global Warming: A Scientific," 85.
38. Christy, "Global Warming: A Scientific," 85.
39. Graham, *Storm Warning*, cited in Vox, *Existential Threats*, 161.
40. Vox, *Existential Threats*, 163.
41. *Where the Grass Is Greener*.
42. *Where the Grass Is Greener*.
43. Beisner, "Resisting the Green Dragon of Environmentalism,"
44. Mayer, *Dark Money*; Romm, "Front Group for Polluting Billionaires Wastes $140K."
45. "Global Warming," (Creation Museum DVD); see also "Global Warming: A Scientific," 83.
46. "We Get It."
47. *Where the Grass Is Greener*.
48. Vardiman, "Global Warming: A Scientific," 82.
49. O'Connor, "How Fossil Fuel Money Made Climate Change Denial the Word of God."
50. *Where the Grass Is Greener*.
51. Brummett, *A Rhetoric of Style*; Winslow, "Promise Keepers and the Rhetoric of the Stylized Other."
52. "We Get It."
53. Wile, "Global Warming: A Scientific," 88.
54. Oard, "Global Warming: A Scientific," 89.
55. Beisner, "Resisting the Green Dragon of Environmentalism."

56. Beisner, "Global Warming," (Creation Museum DVD).
57. "We Get It."
58. *Where the Grass Is Greener.*
59. Ceccarelli, "Manufactured Scientific Controversy," 196; see also Giddens, *The Politics of Climate Change,* 25.
60. Mayer, *Dark Money,* chapter 8: "The Fossils."
61. Lewandowsky, Oreskes, Risbey, Newell, and Smithson, "Seepage," 9.
62. Mayer, *Dark Money.*
63. Lewandowsky et al., "Seepage."
64. Beisner, "Resisting the Green Dragon of Environmentalism."
65. Vox, *Existential Threats,* 150.
66. Vox, *Existential Threats,* 150.
67. *Where the Grass Is Greener.*
68. *Where the Grass Is Greener.*
69. Ball, "Global Warming," (Creation Museum DVD).
70. *Where the Grass Is Greener.*
71. Beisner, "Global Warming: A Scientific," 87.
72. Vox, *Existential Threats,* 163.
73. *Where the Grass Is Greener* (all citations in this paragraph).
74. *Where the Grass Is Greener.*
75. Vox, *Existential Threats,* 139.
76. Beisner, "Resisting the Green Dragon of Environmentalism."
77. O'Connor, "How Fossil Fuel."
78. O'Connor, "How Fossil Fuel."
79. "We Get It." Accessed July 1, 2017. http://www.we-get-it.org/.
80. O'Connor, "How Fossil Fuel."
81. Creation Museum timeline.
82. Vox, *Existential Threats,* 146.
83. Vox, *Existential Threats,* 181.
84. *Where the Grass Is Greener.*
85. O'Connor, "How Fossil Fuel."
86. O'Connor, "How Fossil Fuel."
87. Wile, Jay, "Global Warming," (Creation Museum DVD).
88. "We Get It." Accessed July 1, 2017. http://www.we-get-it.org/.
89. O'Connor, "How Fossil Fuel."
90. O'Connor, "How Fossil Fuel."
91. Wall text. "7 C's in God's Eternal Plan." Creation Museum, Petersburg, Kentucky.
92. Horn, *Rancher, Farmer, Fisherman,* 42.
93. Land, "Global Warming: A Scientific," 73.
94. O'Connor, "How Fossil Fuel."
95. Lisle, "Global Warming: A Scientific," 89.
96. Spadaro and Figueroa, "Evangelical Fundamentalism and Catholic Integralism."
97. O'Connor, "How Fossil Fuel."
98. "We Get It."
99. Corbett and Durfee, "Testing Public (Un)Certainty of Science," 132.
100. Friedrichs, *The Future,* 108.
101. Moser and Dilling, "Communicating Climate Change," 163–66; Ockwell, Whitmarsh, and O'Neill, "Reorienting Climate Change"; Mike Hulme, cited in Corry and Jørgensen, "Beyond 'Deniers' and 'Believers,'" 166.
102. Lakoff, "Praxis Forum," 74; Robelia and Murphy, "What Do People Know about Key Environmental Issues?" 317.

103. Russill, "Tipping Point Forewarnings," 149–50.
104. Norgaard, *Living in Denial*, 203.
105. Ceccarelli, *Shaping Science with Rhetoric*, x.
106. Ceccarelli, *Shaping Science with Rhetoric*, 3; see also Moser and Dilling, "Communicating Climate Change: Closing the Science-Action Gap," 166; Goodnight, "The Personal, Technical," 202; Peeples, Bsumek, Schwarze, and Schneider, "Industrial Apocalyptic," 242.
107. Corry and Jørgensen, "Beyond 'Deniers' and 'Believers,'" 166; Hakkinen and Akrami, "Ideology and Climate Change Denial," 63.
108. Kristof, "Overreacting to Terrorism?"
109. Kristof, "Overreacting to Terrorism?"
110. Foust and Murphy, "Revealing and Reframing Apocalyptic Tragedy," 162–64; Hulme, "Climate Change"; Witte and Allen, "Meta-analysis of Fear Appeals"; Russill, "Tipping Point Forewarnings," 147; Norgaard, *Living in Denial*, 205.
111. Moser and Dilling, "Communicating Climate Change," 161.
112. Leonhardt, "Americans Are Again Getting More Worried about the Climate."
113. Guth and Kellstedt, "How Green Is My Pulpit?" 13; Vox, *Existential Threats*, 159.
114. Strozier, *Apocalypse*, 72.
115. Rossing, *The Rapture Exposed*, 7.
116. Vox, *Existential Threats*, 111.

NOTES TO CHAPTER 3

1. Brady Campaign to Prevent Gun Violence; Kertscher, "Which Is Higher"; Kristof, "Let's Talk About the NRA"; Frankel, "The Government"; Hogan and Rood, "Rhetorical Studies," 360; Lunceford, "Armed Victims," 333.
2. Amsden, "Dimensions of Temporality," 458.
3. Stephen King, cited in Hogan and Rood, "Rhetorical Studies," 367–68.
4. Kahan, Peters, Dawson, and Slovic, "Motivated Numeracy," 54–86; also see Spitzer, *The Politics of Gun Control*, 145.
5. Harpine, "The Illusion of Tradition," 153.
6. See Collins, "The Second Amendment"; Duerringer and Justus, "Tropes"; Hogan and Rood, "Rhetorical Studies and the Gun Debate"; Lunceford, "Armed Victims."
7. Cole, "What Liberals Can Learn From the N.R.A"; Winkler, *Gunfight*.
8. Duerringer and Justus, "Tropes."
9. Foucault, *Discipline and Punish*.
10. Anglemyer, Horvath, and Rutherford, "The Accessibility of Firearms"; Eckstein and Lefevre, "Since Sandy Hook"; Carter, *The Gun Control Movement*, 20; Kaplan, "Congress Quashed Research"; Kellermann, Rivara, Rushforth, Banton, Reay, Francisco, Locci, Prodzinski, Hackman, and Somes, "Gun Ownership as a Risk Factor"; Kristof, "How to Reduce Shootings"; Miller, Azrael, and Hemenway, "State-Level Homicide Victimization Rates"; Lopez, "More Guns Mean More Gun Murders"; Matthews, "11 Facts About Gun Violence"; Miller, Azrael, and Hemenway, "Firearms and Violent Death"; Brown and Abel, *Outgunned*, 4; Spitzer, *The Politics of Gun Control*; Winkler, *Gunfight*, 29.
11. Carter, *The Gun Control Movement*, 50; Eckstein and Lefevre, "Since Sandy Hook," 226; Engels, "The Rhetoric of Violence," 124; Hayden, "Family Metaphors and the Nation," 200; Hepburn and Hemenway, "Firearm Availability and Homicide."
12. Collins, "Rights Talk," 87; Gunn and Beard, "On the Apocalyptic Columbine."
13. Goodnight, "Gabrielle Giffords," 694; Winkler, *Gunfight*, 2.
14. Carter, *The Gun Control Movement*, 66; Davidson, *Under Fire*, 27; Feldman, *Ricochet*, 4; Spitzer, *The Politics of Gun Control*, 75–77.
15. Davidson, *Under Fire*, 29; Winkler, *Gunfight*, 65.
16. Winkler, *Gunfight*, 64–65; see also Spitzer, *The Politics of Gun Control*, 76.
17. Spitzer, *The Politics of Gun Control*, 81.

18. Carter, *The Gun Control Movement*, 67–69.
19. Davidson, *Under Fire*, 19; Winkler, *Gunfight*, 67.
20. Wilson, *Guns, Gun Control, and Elections*, 7; Winkler, *Gunfight*, 21; Pinker, *Better Angels*, 5; Spitzer, *The Politics of Gun Control*, 49.
21. Winkler, *Gunfight*, 116. See also Carter, *The Gun Control Movement*, 25; Ott, Aoki, and Dickinson, "Ways of (Not) Seeing Guns"; Spitzer, *The Politics of Gun Control*, 38; Waldman, *The Second Amendment*; Winkler, *Gunfight*, 13, 116; Wuertenberg, "Gun Rights Are About Keeping White Men on Top."
22. Lunceford, "Armed Victims," 338; Winkler, *Gunfight*, 2.
23. Winkler, *Gunfight*, 65.
24. Medlock, "NRA = No Rational Argument?"
25. Winkler, *Gunfight*, 230, 256.
26. Gatchet and Cloud, "David, Goliath, and the Black Panthers," 5; McCann, "On Whose Ground?"
27. Scott, "Justifying Violence"; see also Winkler, *Gunfight*, 235; Winkler, "MLK and His Guns."
28. McCann, "On Whose Ground?" 482.
29. Winkler, *Gunfight*, 237–43.
30. Collins, "The Second Amendment," 740; Hauser, *Vernacular Voices*; Winkler, *Gunfight*, 13–14, 254.
31. Carlson, "Why So Many American Men Want to Be the 'Good Guy with a Gun.'"
32. Igielnik and Brown, "Key Takeaways on Americans' Views of Guns and Gun Ownership."
33. Carlson, "Why So Many American Men"; Carlson, *Citizen-Protectors*, 263.
34. Carlson, "Why So Many American Men"; Ott, Aoki, and Dickinson, "Ways of (Not) Seeing Guns," 232.
35. Mayer, *Dark Money*; also see Carter, *The Gun Control Movement*, 110–11.
36. Winkler, *Gunfight*, 83, 255.
37. Davidson, *Under Fire*, 175; Harpine, "The Illusion of Tradition," 157.
38. Winkler, *Gunfight*, 85.
39. Cox, "Political Report: Election 2008," "Political Report, The Court Speaks"; see also Pfau, "Bright Lines," 256.
40. LaPierre, cited in Winkler, *Gunfight*, 85.
41. For examples, see LaPierre, "Address to CPAC"; Pfau, "Bright Lines," 257–59.
42. Collins, "Rights Talk and Political Dispositions," 745.
43. Amsden, "Dimensions of Temporality," 458; Engels, "The Politics of Resentment," 304.
44. Collins, "Rights Talk and Political Dispositions," 88.
45. Engels, "The Rhetoric of Violence," 130–31.
46. Lunceford, "Armed Victims," 339; see also Collins, "Rights Talk and Political Dispositions," 87.
47. Brown and Abel, *Outgunned*, 115.
48. Davidson, *Under Fire*, 156.
49. Winkler, *Gunfight*, 71.
50. LaPierre, cited in Lunceford, "Armed Victims," 339; see also Harpine, "The Illusion of Tradition," 157. Michigan Representative John Dingell is credited with first calling ATF agents "jackbooted fascists" (Carter, *The Gun Control Movement*, 74; Davidson, *Under Fire*, 50; Spitzer, *The Politics of Gun Control*, 134).
51. Carlson, "Why So Many American Men"; Davidson, *Under Fire*, 121; Spitzer, *The Politics of Gun Control*, 46; Carter, *The Gun Control Movement*; Winkler, *Gunfight*, 256.
52. Eckstein and Lefevre, "Since Sandy Hook," 226–27; Waldman, *The Second Amendment*.
53. LaPierre, cited in Graham, "Wayne LaPierre's Cynical Exploitation of Outrage"; for other examples, see Lunceford, "Armed Victims," 335.
54. Hogan and Rood, "Rhetorical Studies," 360.

55. Spitzer, *The Politics of Gun Control*, 55.
56. Spitzer, *The Politics of Gun Control*, 151.
57. Igielnik and Brown, "Key Takeaways."
58. Brown and Abel, *Outgunned*, 295; see also Carter, *The Gun Control Movement*, 24; Davidson, *Under Fire*, 135; Spitzer, *The Politics of Gun Control*, 31.
59. Cole, "What Liberals Can Learn from the N.R.A."
60. Cole, "What Liberals Can Learn from the N.R.A."; Winkler, *Gunfight*, 296; see also Eckstein and Lefevre, "Since Sandy Hook," 226; Spitzer, *The Politics of Gun Control*, 17.
61. Kates, "Handgun Prohibition," 204; Winkler, *Gunfight*, 96, 105–11.
62. Spitzer, *The Politics of Gun Control*, 79.
63. For example, NRA efforts during the Trump presidency—championed by Donald Trump, Jr.—to legalize silencers would be a huge boon for the gun makers, by allowing for the sale of both the silencers for the firearms and more guns with threaded barrels needed to accommodate the silencers. Nicholas Kristof said the new laws could amount to more than $1 billion in increased sales. See Kristof, "Let's Talk About the NRA," and Carter, *The Gun Control Movement*, 74.
64. Spitzer, *The Politics of Gun Control*, 40.
65. Davidson, *Under Fire*, 134.
66. Carlson, "Why So Many American Men."
67. Winkler, *Gunfight*, 65.
68. Collins, "Rights Talk and Political Dispositions," 87–88; Warner, *Publics and Counterpublics*, 114.
69. Harpine, "The Illusion of Tradition,"159; Winkler, *Gunfight*, 99.
70. Engels, "The Rhetoric of Violence," 129; Winkler, *Gunfight*, 255.
71. Harpine, "The Illusion of Tradition," 157.
72. Jones and Rowland, "Redefining the Proper Role."
73. Phillips-Fein, *Invisible Hands*, Kindle edition, loc. 1099.
74. Winkler, *Gunfight*, 97.
75. Winkler, *Gunfight*.
76. Collins, "Rights Talk and Political Dispositions," 87–88.
77. Spitzer, *The Politics of Gun Control*, 104–5.
78. Carter, *The Gun Control Movement*, 3; Duerringer and Justus, "Tropes," 182.
79. Tonn, Endress, and Diamond, "Hunting and Heritage on Trial," 178.
80. Spitzer, *The Politics of Gun Control*, 81.
81. Davidson, *Under Fire*, 240–41; Winkler, *Gunfight*, 68.
82. Spitzer, *The Politics of Gun Control*, 91.
83. Davidson, *Under Fire*, 158.
84. Engels, "The Rhetoric of Violence," 128–29.
85. Kristof, "How to Reduce Shootings."
86. Carlson, "Why So Many American Men"; Hogan and Rood, "Rhetorical Studies," 366.
87. Eckstein and Lefevre, "Since Sandy Hook," 226; Engels, "The Rhetoric of Violence," 124; Hayden, "Family Metaphors and the Nation," 200; Rood, "Our Tears Are Not Enough," 47.
88. Hoerl, "Monstrous Youth," 268.
89. Smith and Hollihan, "Out of Chaos," 598.
90. Engels, "The Rhetoric of Violence," 125.
91. Sarah Palin, cited in Smith and Hollihan, "Out of Chaos," 598.
92. Eckstein and Lefevre, "Since Sandy Hook," 231; Hogan and Rood, "Rhetorical Studies," 366.
93. Duerringer and Justus, "Tropes," 188–89.
94. Brown and Abel, *Outgunned*, 106; see also Winkler, *Gunfight*, 76.
95. Willingham, "The NRA's Message for Students Walking Out Today."
96. Rogers and Mays, "Trump Calls for Unity after Synagogue Shooting."

97. Hogan and Rood, "Rhetorical Studies," 367; see also Scott, "We Aren't Having an Evidence-Based Debate About Guns."
98. Spitzer, *The Politics of Gun Control*, 43.
99. Scott, "We Aren't Having an Evidence-Based Debate About Guns." For a concise review of the *more guns equates to more violence* argument, see "Homicide," Harvard Injury Control Research Center.
100. Hogan and Rood, "Rhetorical Studies," 367.
101. Spitzer, *The Politics of Gun Control*, 141.
102. Wills, "Our Moloch"; also see Carter, *The Gun Control Movement*, 108.
103. Pinker, *Better Angels*, Kindle edition, loc. 1032; Pinker, *Enlightenment Now*, 166–69; Spitzer, *The Politics of Gun Control*, 2.
104. Carlson, "Why So Many American Men."
105. Igielnik and Brown, "Key Takeaways"; Wuertenberg, "Gun Rights." And on men and gun rights, see Carter, *The Gun Control Movement*, 52; Spitzer, *The Politics of Gun Control*, 12.
106. Robert Sapolsky articulated this incentive structure well: "In our world riddled with male violence the problem isn't that testosterone can increase levels of aggression. The problem is the frequency with which we reward aggression" (*Behave*, 107).
107. Carter, *The Gun Control Movement*, 52; Spitzer, *The Politics of Gun Control*, 49; Wuertenberg, "Gun Rights."
108. Engels, "The Rhetoric of Violence," 133.
109. Strozier, *Apocalypse*, 72.
110. Davidson, *Under Fire*, 168; Duerringer and Justus, "Tropes," 183; Kristof, "Let's Talk About the NRA"; Graham, "Wayne LaPierre's Cynical Exploitation of Outrage"; Medlock, "NRA = No Rational Argument?"; Scott, "We Aren't Having an Evidence-Based Debate About Guns"; Spitzer, *The Politics of Gun Control*, 99.
111. Collins, "Rights Talk and Political Dispositions," 87.
112. Charland, "Constitutive Rhetoric." Thanks to Christopher Duerringer for making this connection.
113. Ebbs, "Trump Says He Would Have 'Run in There' to Stop Parkland Shooting."
114. Parker, "Live-Streaming the Apocalypse."
115. LaPierre, cited in Brown and Abel, *Outgunned*, 145.
116. LaPierre, "NRA: Full Statement by Wayne LaPierre in Response to Newtown Shootings."
117. Eckstein and Lefevre, "Since Sandy Hook," 235.
118. Duerringer and Justus, "Tropes," 189.
119. Taylor, "Trump's Comments."
120. Spitzer, *The Politics of Gun Control*, 107.
121. Osha Davidson described the "legislative alerts" sent out by the NRA: a four-page letter mailed to members when gun-control bills began to be considered (*Under Fire*, 149); Lacombe, "The Political Weaponization of Gun Owners."
122. "Florida Alert! Help Stop Gratuitous GUN CONTROL"; "How N.R.A. Fundraising Shapes the Political Landscape."
123. Winkler, *Gunfight*, 57.
124. Haag, "Remington, Centuries-Old Gun Maker, Files for Bankruptcy as Sales Slow."
125. Steidley and Kosla, "Toward a Status Anxiety Theory of Macro-level Firearm Demand."
126. Steidley and Kosla, "Toward a Status," 86.
127. Gunn and Beard, "On the Apocalyptic Columbine," 213–14.
128. Brown and Abel, *Outgunned*, 56; Carter, *The Gun Control Movement*, 111.
129. Spitzer, *The Politics of Gun Control*, 79; Wilson, *Guns, Gun Control, and Elections*, 3.
130. Gunn and Beard, "On the Apocalyptic Columbine," 213.
131. Brown and Abel, *Outgunned*, 197.
132. On the NRA's relationship with law enforcement, see Spitzer, *The Politics of Gun Control*, 90.
133. Davidson, *Under Fire*, 50.

134. Carter, *The Gun Control Movement*, 74; Spitzer, *The Politics of Gun Control*, 93.
135. Brown and Abel, *Outgunned*, 145, 247; Stanley, *How Fascism Works*, 161.
136. Davidson, *Under Fire*, 293; Spitzer, *The Politics of Gun Control*, 43; Walker, "Why the U.S. Lacks Gun Violence Research."
137. Brown and Abel, *Outgunned*, 94; Kristof, "How to Reduce Shootings"; Spitzer, *The Politics of Gun Control*, 6.
138. Scott, "We Aren't Having an Evidence-Based Debate about Guns"; Winkler, *Gunfight*, 75.
139. Scott, "We Aren't Having an Evidence-Based Debate about Guns."
140. Kristof, "How to Reduce Shootings"; see also Frankel, "The Government"; Spitzer, *The Politics of Gun Control*, 93.
141. Davidson, *Under Fire*, 164–66.
142. Feldman, *Ricochet*, 11.
143. Davidson, *Under Fire*, 241.
144. Wilson, *Guns*, 11.
145. Swedler, Simmons, Dominici, and Hemenway, "Firearm Prevalence and Homicides of Law Enforcement Officers in the United States"; Carter, *The Gun Control Movement*, 67.
146. Winkler, *Gunfight*, 190.

NOTES TO CHAPTER 4

1. Dionne, Ornstein, and Mann, *One Nation After Trump*, 26.
2. Klein, *No Is Not Enough*, 89.
3. Abebe, "American's New Anxiety Disorder."
4. Carnes and Lupu, "It's Time to Bust the Myth"; Dionne, Ornstein, and Mann, *One Nation After Trump*, 161; Schaffner, MacWilliams, and Nteta, "Explaining White Polarization in the 2016 Vote for President."
5. Dionne, Ornstein, and Mann, *One Nation After Trump*, 164; Filipovic, "The All-Male Photo Op Isn't a Gaffe. It's a Strategy"; Green, *Devil's Bargain*; Tyson and Maniam, "Behind Trump's Victory."
6. Anderson, "Every Woman Is the Wrong Woman"; Bostdorff, "Obama, Trump," 699; Stuckey, "American Elections," 687; Wilz, "Bernie Bros and Woman Cards."
7. Hochschild, *Strangers in Their Own Land*.
8. Merica, "Trump Argues He Won New Hampshire Because It Is a 'Drug-Infested Den.'"
9. Dionne, Ornstein, and Mann, *One Nation After Trump*, 139; Green, *Devil's Bargain*, 37.
10. Burns, "Why Trump Doubled Down on the Central Park Five."
11. Given the dynamic nature of the Trump presidency, I should acknowledge here that I am curtailing my range of "Trump discourse" at the midterm elections of November 2018. Also, as I develop this argument, I do not mean to reduce the complexities of the 2016 US presidential election to one person's messaging. I also acknowledge that the peculiarities of the US Electoral College, Russian meddling, and Hillary Clinton's strategic and tactical errors were among a number of influential factors.
12. Dean Acheson, cited in Filkins, "Rex Tillerson."
13. McCloskey, *The Rhetoric of Economics*, 13; McCloskey, "Growth, Not Forced Equality."
14. Pinker, *Enlightenment Now*, 112.
15. Winslow, *Economic Injustice*; also see Lears, *Something for Nothing*, 21; Zinn, *A People's History of the United States*, 570, 648. The broader impact of economic conditions on institutional trust must be reconciled with the empirical findings I discussed earlier related to Trump's election. In alignment with the first homological touchstone—perceived marginalization—I want to reconcile this contradiction by again emphasizing that I am focusing less on actual material conditions and more on the perceptions of institutional betrayal and feelings of threat and insecurity prompted by evolving social, economic, and political conditions.
16. Packer, *The Unwinding*, 23.

17. Dionne, Ornstein, and Mann, *One Nation After Trump*, 75; Stuckey, "American Elections," 676.
18. MacLean, *Democracy in Chains*, 52; Phillips-Fein, *Invisible Hands*, Kindle edition, loc. 1099.
19. Newt Gingrich, cited in Packer, *The Unwinding*, 21.
20. Packer, *The Unwinding*, 23.
21. Gingrich, cited in Packer, *The Unwinding*, 23.
22. Pilkington, "Obama Angers Midwest Voters with Guns and Religion Remark."
23. Suderman, "The G.O.P. Is a Mess. It's Not All Trump's Fault."
24. Stuckey, "American Elections," 673.
25. Dionne, Ornstein, and Mann, *One Nation After Trump*, 138; Green, *Devil's Bargain*, 143.
26. Green, *Devil's Bargain*, 86
27. Green, *Devil's Bargain*, 50–55, 83, 148.
28. Green, *Devil's Bargain*; Bob Woodward connects Bannon's views to Trump's in his book *Fear*, which quotes Trump saying "I think we could be so rich, if we weren't stupid. We're being played [as] suckers, especially NATO." Woodward then writes, "Collective defense was a sucker play" (*Fear*, Kindle edition, loc. 4240).
29. Green, *Devil's Bargain*, 4, 139–40.
30. Steve Bannon, cited in Green, *Devil's Bargain*, 208.
31. Green, *Devil's Bargain*, 208.
32. Gunn, "On Political Perversion," 171; Stuckey, "American Elections," 682.
33. "Donald Trump's Speech Responding to Assault Accusations."
34. Glazer, "Fundamentalism: A Defensive Offensive," 250–51; see also Jones, *The End of White Christian America*, Kindle edition, loc. 601.
35. Gunn, "On Political Perversion," 171.
36. Bostdorff, "Obama, Trump," 699.
37. "Donald Trump Speech at Liberty University."
38. Smith, "Ronald Reagan's Rhetorical," 53–54.
39. Buettner, Craig, and Barstow, "11 Takeaways."
40. Bostdorff, "Obama, Trump," 696; Lee, "Considering Political Identity."
41. "Donald Trump Announces a Presidential Bid."
42. "Donald Trump Speech at Liberty University."
43. "Statement by President Trump on the Paris Climate Accord."
44. Green, *Devil's Bargain*, 32.
45. "The Inaugural Address."
46. Ivie, "Trump's Unwitting Prophecy."
47. "Donald Trump 2016 RNC."
48. Bostdorff, "Obama, Trump"; Johnson, "The Art of Masculine," 238. As Jason Stanley put it, "There is a crucial distinction between feelings of resentment and oppression and genuine inequality and discrimination" (*How Fascism Works*, 94).
49. Dionne, Ornstein, and Mann, *One Nation After Trump*, 161.
50. Rubin, "Here's Proof That Trump Is Ignorant and Deluded about Crime."
51. Perez-Pena, "Contrary to Trump's Claims, Immigrants Are Less Likely to Commit Crimes."
52. Bostdorff, "Obama, Trump," 699; Dionne, Ornstein, and Mann, *One Nation After Trump*, 152.
53. Rothwell, "Myth of the 1 Percent."
54. Kaste, "Is There a 'War on Police'? The Statistics Say No."
55. Badger, "Whites Have Huge Wealth Edge Over Blacks (But Don't Know It)"; Desmond, "How Homeownership Became the Engine of American Inequality"; "Demographic Trends and Economic Well-Being."
56. Campos, "White Economic Privilege Is Alive and Well."
57. Pinker, *Better Angels*. Joshua Gunn described the rehearsing of the victim identity by Trump supporters as akin to a game they get to choose to play, often at a distance,

unhinged from serious material consequences of marginalization. See Gunn, "On Political Perversion," 178.
58. Johnson, "The Art of Masculine," 39. Johnson put it well when he described such powerlessness as "evidence of authentic political grievance" (247).
59. Cloud, *Reality Bites*, 34; Terry Eagleton, *Ideology*, 13.
60. Ackerman and Coogan, introduction to *The Public Work of Rhetoric*, 10; Brummett, "Burke's Representative Anecdote as a Method in Media Criticism," 171; Stuckey, "American Elections," 682. For a primer on how Trump's conspiratorial *messaging* aligns well with the extant literature on conspiracy theory and rhetoric, see Stewart, Smith, and Denton, *Persuasion and Social Movements*, 285.
61. "Donald Trump 2016 RNC."
62. Green, *Devil's Bargain*, 9.
63. "Donald Trump's Argument for America"; see also Dionne, Ornstein, and Mann, *One Nation After Trump*, 144; Rozsa, "Donald Trump's Argument for America."
64. "The Inaugural Address."
65. Griffin, "The 'Morning/Mourning' After."
66. "Donald Trump's Speech Responding to Assault Accusations."
67. Foucault, *Discipline and Punish*, 36.
68. Stewart, Smith, and Denton, *Persuasion and Social Movements*, 286; For more examples, see Bob Woodward's 2018 book *Fear*, in which he describes in detail several interactions between Trump, Reince Priebus, Steven Mnuchin, and Gary Cohn that illustrated Trump's conspiratorial assumptions (Kindle edition, loc. 1874, 1912, 3116, 3232, and 3779).
69. Stewart, Smith, and Denton, *Persuasion and Social Movements*, 300.
70. Lee and Quealy, "The 425 People, Places and Things Donald Trump Has Insulted on Twitter."
71. "Donald Trump 2016 RNC."
72. Johnson, "The Art of Masculine," 231.
73. Nimmo and Combs, *Mediated Political Realities*; see also Stewart, Allen, and Denton, *Persuasion and Social Movements*, 285.
74. Following the lead of Jamieson and Cappella, I do not mean to suggest that these figures share the exact same DNA as conjoint twins; rather, I note the common homological ancestry fueling a shared commitment to catastrophe (*Echo Chamber*, 42).
75. Trump, cited in Dionne, Ornstein, and Mann, *One Nation After Trump*, 44.
76. "Donald Trump 2016 RNC."
77. Zengerle, "Rex Tillerson."
78. "Donald Trump's Speech Responding to Assault Accusations."
79. Bob Woodward detailed how Trump's rejection of rational argumentation influenced his ability to manage sophisticated domestic and international policy decisions. Domestically, Rex Tillerson, Peter Navarro, Gary Cohn, and Steven Mnuchin each struggled to sway Trump's decision-making based on empirical evidence. Woodward quotes an unnamed official in the administration saying, "There's some things where he's already reached the conclusion and it doesn't matter what you say. It doesn't matter what arguments you offer. He's not listening" (Kindle edition, loc. 3232). Woodward goes on to describe Trump and Bannon's deliberation style in familiar terms: "Their discussions were not designed to persuade but, like their president, to win—to slay, crush and demean" (loc. 3298). Internationally, Woodward offered several vivid examples of how Trump's worldview forecloses sophisticated policy analysis, especially in relation to his inability to make sense of complex American military interventions in the Middle East. On Afghanistan, Trump once asked aides, "When are we going to start winning some wars? We've got these charts. When are we going to win some wars?" (loc. 3090). Trump's advice for his generals included, "You should be killing guys. You don't need a strategy to kill people." On the quagmire caused by the Syrian civil war, Trump told his

national security adviser H. R. McMaster, "We should just declare victory, end the wars and bring our troops home" (loc. 3189).
80. Ivie, "Trump's Unwitting Prophecy," 714.
81. "Donald Trump 2016 RNC." Paul Johnson described how Trump went on in this speech to substitute himself for government by autonomously threatening Ford in a way that forces them to bring plants back from Mexico into the US and by singularly coercing America's competitors to his will ("The Art of Masculine," 245).
82. Burke, *A Rhetoric of Motives*.
83. Jones and Rowland, "Redefining the Proper Role."
84. Burke, *The Philosophy of Literary Form*.
85. "RNC August 6 Debate."
86. As Darsey defined it, prophets claim to speak for another. Donald Trump seems to be called to deliver a message that is not his own, even against his will (see Darsey, *The Prophetic Tradition*, 16).
87. "Donald Trump's Speech Responding to Assault Accusations."
88. McLeod, "Paul Ryan Defends Trump's Interactions with Comey."
89. Sullivan, "House Intel Chair: Media Take Trump Tweets Too Literally."
90. Dow, "Taking Trump Seriously"; Rossing, "No Joke," 549.
91. Klein, *No Is Not Enough*, 258.
92. Benoit, "Image Repair"; Dow, "Taking Trump Seriously," 137. Craig Smith called this feature of Trump's appeal "bar talk" in that Trump could shout to the world what would usually only be heard after a few drinks in the darkened corner of a bar ("Ronald Reagan's Rhetorical Re-Invention of Conservatism," 52). Robert Terrill argued that part of Trump's resonance came from his willingness to plainly articulate what others—shackled by political correctness—could only imply ("The Post-Racial and Post-Ethical Discourse of Donald J. Trump," 498).
93. Peters and Grynbaum, "Steve Bannon, Back in the Outside."
94. Peters and Grynbaum, "Steve Bannon, Back in the Outside."
95. Green, *Devil's Bargain*, 241.
96. Zengerle, "Rex Tillerson."
97. Lewis, *The Fifth Risk*, Kindle edition, loc. 329; Naylor, "Trump Administration Has More Than 250 Unfilled Jobs."
98. Zengerle, "Rex Tillerson."
99. Mouffe, *The Democratic Paradox*, 102.
100. Terrill, "The Post-Racial," 501–3.
101. Ivie, "Trump's Unwitting Prophecy," 713.
102. "Donald Trump 2016 RNC."
103. Lewis, *The Fifth Risk*, Kindle edition, loc. 79.
104. Chappell, "'I'm the Only One That Matters,' Trump Says of State Dept. Job Vacancies."
105. Peters and Grynbaum, "Steve Bannon, Back in the Outside."
106. Wright, "Donald Trump: Our Country Needs a Good 'Shutdown.'"
107. Alcindor, "Trump Says It Will Be Hard to Unify Country Without a 'Major Event.'"
108. Fraser and Gerstle, *Ruling America*, Kindle edition, loc. 279.
109. Lind, "Conservative Elites and the Counterrevolution Against the New Deal."
110. Hochschild, *Strangers in Their Own Land*, Kindle edition, loc. 1403.
111. "Donald Trump 2016 RNC."
112. Stanley, *How Fascism Works*, 3.
113. Green, "Joshua Green on *Devil's Bargain*."
114. Green, *Devil's Bargain*, 237.
115. "Donald Trump 2016 RNC."
116. Dionne, Ornstein, and Mann, *One Nation After Trump*, 114.
117. Savage, "Poor Vetting Sinks Trump's Nominees for Federal Judge."

118. Lewis, "Inside Trump's Cruel Campaign Against the U.S.D.A.'s Scientists."
119. Harris, "With Cost-Cutting Zeal." See also Harris, "Diplomacy?" and Zengerle, "Rex Tillerson."
120. Filkins, "Rex Tillerson."
121. Harris, "With Cost-Cutting Zeal."
122. Goodnough and Pear, "Trump Administration"; Sullivan and Roubein, "Critics See Trump Sabotage on ObamaCare."
123. Goodnough and Pear, "Trump Administration."
124. Sullivan and Roubein, "Critics See Trump sabotage."
125. Carlsen and Park, "The Same Agency That Runs Obamacare."
126. Lewis, *The Fifth Risk*, Kindle edition, loc. 247.
127. Sullivan and Roubein, "Critics See Trump Sabotage."
128. Filkins, "Rex Tillerson."
129. Lewis, *The Fifth Risk*, Kindle edition, loc. 371.
130. Harris, "Diplomacy?"
131. Harris, "Diplomacy?"
132. Harris, "Diplomacy?"
133. Coll, *Private Empire*.

NOTES TO CONCLUSION

1. Blair, "We Are All Just Prisoners Here of Our Own Device," 44; Cloud, *Reality Bites*, 47; Rowland, "Purpose, Evidence," 64.
2. Edwards, *Superchurch*, 114; Jamieson and Cappella, *Echo Chamber*, 64.
3. Giroux, *The Terror of Neoliberalism*, 136.
4. Climate change scholars are already detailing the impact of what has become known as the *climate gap*. Poor communities are the least prepared to anticipate, cope, resist, and recover from the consequences of climate change. Economic underdevelopment will increase exposure and disaster losses for poor countries and amplify the magnitude of cyclones, droughts, and flooding (World Bank, *Acting on Climate Change*, 4). In underdeveloped states without the ability to manage climate crises, food shortages and unpredictable weather produce vulnerable citizens deprived of the necessary supplies to survive. Further, starvation, drought, disease, and other environmental pressures exacerbate underlying ethnic conflicts. Scarcity-driven migration is already provoking violent clashes between migrants and native-born populations. A 2015 US Department of Defense report referred to climate change as a geopolitical "threat multiplier" with the potential to upend "domestic stability all over the world." A 2018 United Nations report on climate change warns of "world of worsening food shortages and wildfires, and a mass die-off of coral reefs as soon as 2040—a period well within the lifetime of much of the global population" (see Bales, *Blood and Earth*; Friedman, *Thank You for Being Late*, Kindle edition, loc. 4489; Mooallem, "Our Climate Future"; Frosch, Pastor, Sadd, and Shonkoff, "The Climate Gap," 5; 25; Smith, "Unfriendly Climate"; World Bank, *Acting on Climate Change*.
5. Boone, *The Bible Tells Them So*, 53.
6. Phillips, "Confronted with the Bloody Behavior of Autocrats."
7. Maddux, *The Faithful Citizen*.
8. Falwell, "The Church at Antioch," in *Capturing a Town for Christ*, cited in Edwards, *Superchurch*, 129.
9. Wander, "The Third Persona."
10. Engels, "The Rhetoric of Violence," 128–29; Zirin, "The Fragile, Toxic Masculinity of Donald Trump."
11. Doherty, *Radicals for Capitalism*, 409.
12. On commonly understood apocalyptic political urgings of passivity, see Brummett, *Contemporary Apocalyptic Rhetoric*; Edwards, *Superchurch*, 80–81.

13. Blair, "We Are All," 45; Rowland, "Purpose, Evidence," 60, 72.
14. Quarantelli and Dynes, "Community Conflict."
15. Mooallem, "Enrico L. Quarantelli."
16. Edwards, *Superchurch*, 83, 88.
17. *Where the Grass Is Greener.*
18. Winkler, *Gunfight*, 64.
19. Kaplan, *The Most Dangerous Branch*, 257.
20. Olson, "The Comic Strategy of 'Deferral to Study.'"
21. Burke, *A Rhetoric of Motives*, 21–22.
22. Litt, "Is Nothing Funny, Mr. President?"; see also Rueckert, *Encounters with Kenneth Burke*, 118.
23. Condit, "Framing Kenneth Burke," 81.
24. Frank, "Rhetoric's Effects," in *The Effects of Rhetoric*, 112–13.
25. Schwarze, "Environmental Melodrama," 241.
26. Schwarze, "Environmental Melodrama," 241.
27. Pinker, *Enlightenment Now*, 83.
28. Lewis, *The Fifth Risk*, Kindle edition, loc. 86.
29. Goodnight, "The Personal, Technical," 198; see also Anthony Leiserowitz, cited in Peeples, Bsumek, Schwarze, and Schneider, "Industrial Apocalyptic," 242; Corry and Jørgensen, "Beyond 'Deniers' and 'Believers,'" 169; Moser and Dilling, "Communicating Climate Change," 161; Fahnestock, "Accommodating Science," 334. For a specific example, see Scott Alexander's brilliant description of environmental messaging that could resonate with the context of anti-environmentalists: "Ethnic Tension and Meaningless Arguments."
30. Asen, "Imagining in the Public Sphere," 358; Finnegan, "Social Engineering."
31. *Chasing Ice.*
32. "Chasing Ice Ohio Tour," http://chasingice.com/ourimpact/.
33. Carter, *The Gun Control Movement*, 49; Spitzer, *The Politics of Gun Control*, 6.
34. Kristof, "How to Reduce Shootings"; see also Davidson, *Under Fire*, 290.
35. See Rood, "Our Tears Are Not Enough," 61.
36. Winkler, *Gunfight*, 10.
37. Winkler, *Gunfight*, 2.
38. Huertas, "Advice for 2020 Candidates."

BIBLIOGRAPHY

Abebe, Nitsuh. "America's New Anxiety Disorder." First Words. *New York Times Magazine*, April 18, 2017. https://www.nytimes.com/2017/04/18/magazine/americas-new-anxiety-disorder.html.

Ackerman, John M., and David J. Coogan, eds. *The Public Work of Rhetoric: Citizen-Scholars and Civic Engagement*. Columbia: University of South Carolina Press, 2010.

Alcindor, Yamiche. "Trump Says It Will Be Hard to Unify Country Without a 'Major Event.'" *PBS NewsHour*, January 30, 2018. https://www.pbs.org/newshour/politics/trump-says-it-will-be-hard-to-unify-country-without-a-major-event/.

Alexander, Scott. "Ethnic Tension and Meaningless Arguments." *Slate Star Codex*, November 4, 2014. http://slatestarcodex.com/2014/11/04/ethnic-tension-and-meaningless-arguments/.

Amsden, Brian. "Dimensions of Temporality in President Obama's Tucson Memorial Address." *Rhetoric & Public Affairs* 17 (2014): 455–76.

Anderson, Karrin Vasby. "Every Woman Is the Wrong Woman: The Female Presidentiality Paradox." *Women's Studies in Communication* 40, no. 2 (2017): 132–35.

Anderson, Sam. "New Sentences." *New York Times Magazine*, December 9, 2018.

Anglemyer, Andrew, Tara Horvath, and George Rutherford. "The Accessibility of Firearms and Risk for Suicide and Homicide Victimization among Household Members: A Systematic Review and Meta-analysis." *Annals of Internal Medicine* 160 (2014): 101–10. https://doi.org/10.7326/M13-1301.

Antonio, Robert J., and Robert J. Brulle. "Climate Change Denial and Political Polarization." *The Sociological Quarterly* 52 (2011): 195–202.

Asen, Robert. "Imagining in the Public Sphere." *Philosophy & Rhetoric* 34, no. 4 (2002): 345–67.

Asen, Robert, and Whitney Gent. "Reconsidering Symbolic Use: A Situational Model of Use of Research Evidence in Polarised Legislative Hearings." *Evidence & Policy* (2018), https://doi.org/10.1332/174426418X15378681033440.

Badger, Emily. "Whites Have Huge Wealth Edge Over Blacks (But Don't Know It)." *New York Times*, September 18, 2017. https://www.nytimes.com/interactive/2017/09/18/upshot/black-white-wealth-gap-perceptions.html.

Bales, Kevin. *Blood and Earth: Modern Slavery, Ecocide, and the Secret to Saving the World*. New York: Random House, 2016. Kindle.

Balmer, Randall. *Mine Eyes Have Seen the Glory: A Journey into the Evangelical Subculture in America*. 4th ed. New York: Oxford University Press, 2006.

Barron, Bruce. *Heaven on Earth? The Social and Political Agendas of Dominion Theology*. Grand Rapids, MI: Zondervan, 1992.

Becker, Robert. "Dr. James C. Dobson's Jeremiad: The Proverbial Father." *Conference Papers—National Communication Association*, January 2008, p. 1.

Beisner, Calvin. "Resisting the Green Dragon of Environmentalism." *YouTube*, May 26, 2011. Accessed July 1, 2017. https://www.youtube.com/watch?v=EOH3aPLjCio.

Benoit, William. "Image Repair on the Donald Trump 'Access Hollywood' Video: 'Grab Them by the P*ssy.'" *Communication Studies* 68, no. 3 (July 2017): 243–59. https://doi.org/10.1080/10510974.2017.1331250.

Black, Edwin. "The Second Persona." *Quarterly Journal of Speech* 56, no. 2 (1970): 109–19. https://doi.org/10.1080/00335637009382992.

Black, Jason Edward. "Extending the Rights of Personhood, Voice, and Life to Sensate Others: A Homology of Right to Life and Animal Rights Rhetoric." *Communication Quarterly* 51, no. 3 (2003): 312–31.

Blair, Carol. "We Are All Just Prisoners Here of Our Own Device." In *The Effects of Rhetoric and the Rhetoric of Effects*, edited by Amos Kiewe and David W. Houck, 31–58. Columbia: University of South Carolina Press, 2015.

Boone, Kathleen. *The Bible Tells Them So: The Discourse of Protestant Fundamentalism*. Albany: State University of New York Press, 1989.

Bostdorff, Denise M. "Obama, Trump, and Reflections on the Rhetoric of Political Change." *Rhetoric & Public Affairs* 20, no. 4 (2017): 695–706.

———. *The Presidency and the Rhetoric of Foreign Crisis*. Columbia: South Carolina University Press, 1994.

Bowler, Kate. *Blessed: A History of the American Prosperity Gospel*. New York: Oxford University Press, 2013.

Brady Campaign to Prevent Gun Violence. "About Gun Violence." 2018. http://www.bradycampaign.org/about-gun-violence.

Brown, Peter Harry, and Daniel G. Abel. *Outgunned: Up Against the NRA*. New York: The Free Press, 2003.

Brummett, Barry. "Burke's Representative Anecdote as a Method in Media Criticism." *Critical Studies in Mass Communication* 1, no. 2 (1984): 161–76. https://doi.org/10.1080/15295038409360027.

———. *Contemporary Apocalyptic Rhetoric*. New York: Praeger, 1991.

———. "Premillennial Apocalyptic." In *Critical Questions: Invention, Creativity, and the Criticism of Discourse and Media*, edited by William L. Nothstine, Carole Blair, and Gary A. Copeland, 157–61. Boston: McGraw-Hill, 2003.

———. "The Homology Hypothesis: Pornography on the VCR." *Critical Studies in Mass Communication* 5 (1988): 203–20.

———. "The Representative Anecdote as a Burkean Method, Applied to Evangelical Rhetoric." *Southern Speech Communication Journal* 50, no. 1 (1984): 1–23.

———. *A Rhetoric of Style*. Carbondale: Southern Illinois University Press, 2008.

———. "Rhetorical Theory as Heuristic and Moral: A Pedagogical Justification." *Communication Education* 33, no. 2 (1984): 97–107.

———. *Rhetorical Homologies: Form, Culture, and Experience*. Tuscaloosa: University of Alabama Press, 2004.

———. *Uncovering Hidden Rhetorics: Social Issues in Disguise*. Los Angeles: SAGE, 2007.

Buettner, Russ, Susanne Craig and David Barstow. "11 Takeaways From The Times's Investigation Into Trump's Wealth." *New York Times*, October 2, 2018. https://www.nytimes.com/2018/10/02/us/politics/donald-trump-wealth-fred-trump.html.

Burke, Kenneth. *Attitudes Toward History*. Berkeley: University of California Press, 1984.

———. *Counter-Statement*. Berkeley: University of California Press, 1968.

———. *Language as Symbolic Action: Essays on Life, Literature, and Method*. Berkeley: University of California Press, 1966.

———. *Permanence and Change: An Anatomy of Purpose*. Berkeley: University of California Press, 1954.

———. *The Philosophy of Literary Form: Studies in Symbolic Action*. 3rd ed. Berkeley: University of California Press, 1973.

———. *A Rhetoric of Motives*. Berkeley: University of California Press, 1950.

Burns, Sarah. "Why Trump Doubled Down on the Central Park Five." *New York Times*, October 27, 2016. https://www.nytimes.com/2016/10/18/opinion/why-trump-doubled-down-on-the-central-park-five.html.

Butterworth, Michael L. "The Passion of the Tebow: Sports Media and Heroic Language in the Tragic Frame." *Critical Studies In Media Communication* 30, no. 1 (2013): 17–33.

Campbell, Karlyn Kohrs, and Kathleen Hall Jamieson. *Form and Genre: Shaping Rhetorical Action*. Falls Church, VA: Speech Communication Association, 1978.

Campos, Paul F. "White Economic Privilege Is Alive and Well." *New York Times*, July 29, 2017. https://www.nytimes.com/2017/07/29/opinion/sunday/black-income-white-privilege.html.

Carlsen, Audrey, and Haeyoun Park. "The Same Agency That Runs Obamacare Is Using Taxpayer Money to Undermine It." *New York Times*, September 4, 2017. https://www.nytimes.com/interactive/2017/09/04/us/hhs-anti-obamacare-campaign.html.

Carlson, Jennifer. *Citizen-Protectors: The Everyday Politics of Guns in an Age of Decline*. Oxford: Oxford University Press, 2015.

———. "Why So Many American Men Want to Be the 'Good Guy with a Gun.'" *Vox*, March 24, 2018. https://www.vox.com/the-big-idea/2018/3/23/17156084/carry-gun-laws-parkland-culture-good-guy-gun-male-identity.

Carnes, Nicholas, and Noam Lupu. "It's Time to Bust the Myth: Most Trump Voters Were Not Working Class." *Washington Post*, June 5, 2017. https://www.washingtonpost.com/news/monkey-cage/wp/2017/06/05/its-time-to-bust-the-myth-most-trump-voters-were-not-working-class/.

Carpenter, Joel. *Revive Us Again: The Reawakening of American Fundamentalism*. New York: Oxford University Press, 1997.

Carter, Gregg Lee. *The Gun Control Movement*. New York: Twayne, 1997.

Ceccarelli, Leah. "Manufactured Scientific Controversy: Science, Rhetoric, and Public Debate." *Rhetoric & Public Affairs* 14 (2011): 195–228.

———. *Shaping Science with Rhetoric: The Cases of Dobzhansky, Schrodinger, and Wilson.* Chicago: University of Chicago Press, 2001.

Chappell, Bill. "'I'm the Only One That Matters,' Trump Says of State Dept. Job Vacancies." *NPR*, November 3, 2017. https://www.npr.org/sections/thetwo-way/2017/11/03/561797675/im-the-only-one-that-matters-trump-says-of-state-dept-job-vacancies.

Charland, Maurice. "Constitutive Rhetoric: The Case of the Peuple Québécois." *Quarterly Journal of Speech* 73 (1987): 133–50.

Chávez, Karma R. "Focus on the Family." In *Culture Wars in America: An Encyclopedia of Issues, Viewpoints, and Voices,* edited by Roger Chapman and James Ciment, 227. New York: Routledge, 2013.

Chasing Ice. Directed by Jeff Orlowski. Exposure, 2012. Film.

Choi, Jihyang. "The Competition between Frames and Counterframes in the U.S. Media's Social Construction of Global Warming." Paper presented at the annual meeting of the International Communication Association, Sheraton Phoenix Downtown, Phoenix, May 5, 2012. http://citation.allacademic.com/meta/p554971_index.html.

Cloud, Dana. *Reality Bites: Rhetoric and the Circulation of Truth Claims in the U.S. Political Culture.* Columbus: The Ohio State University Press, 2018.

———. "The Rhetoric of 'Family Values': Scapegoating, Utopia, and the Privatization of Social Responsibility. *Western Journal of Communication* 62 (1998): 387–419.

Cole, David. "What Liberals Can Learn from the N.R.A." *New York Times*, March 11, 2106. http://www.nytimes.com/2016/03/11/opinion/what-liberals-can-learn-from-the-nra.html.

Coll, Steve. *Private Empire: ExxonMobil and American Power.* New York: Penguin, 2012.

Collins, Laura J. "Rights Talk and Political Dispositions." *Rhetoric & Public Affairs* 19, no. 1 (Spring 2016): 83–90.

———. "The Second Amendment as Demanding Subject: Figuring the Marginalized Subject in Demands for Unbridled Second Amendment." *Rhetoric & Public Affairs* 17 (2014): 737–56.

Condit, Celeste M. "Framing Kenneth Burke: Sad Tragedy or Comic Dance?" *Quarterly Journal of Speech* 80, no. 1 (1994): 77–82.

Connolly, William E. *The Ethos of Pluralization.* Minneapolis: Minnesota University Press, 1995.

Coontz, Stephanie. *The Way We Never Were: American Families and the Nostalgia Trap.* New York: Basic Books, 1992.

Corbett, J., and J. Durfee. "Testing Public (Un)Certainty of Science: Media Representations of Global Warming." *Science Communication* 26, no. 2 (2004): 129–51.

Corry, Olaf, and Dan Jørgensen. "Beyond 'Deniers' and 'Believers': Towards a Map of the Politics of Climate Change." *Global Environmental Change* 32 (2015): 165–74.

Cox, Chris. "Political Report: Election 2008 and the Long Road Ahead." *American Rifleman,* January 2009, p. 62.

———. "Political Report: The Court Speaks, and the Fight Goes On." *American Rifleman,* September 2008, p. 112.

Crowley, Sharon. *Toward a Civil Discourse: Rhetoric and Fundamentalism.* Pittsburgh, PA: University of Pittsburgh Press, 2006.

Darsey, James. *The Prophetic Tradition and Radical Rhetoric in America.* New York: New York University Press, 1997.

Davidson, Osha Gray. *Under Fire: The NRA and the Battle for Gun Control.* Iowa City: University of Iowa Press, 1998.

"Demographic Trends and Economic Well-being." *Pew Research Center: Social and Demographic Trends,* July 27, 2016. http://www.pewsocialtrends.org/2016/06/27/1-demographic-trends-and-economic-well-being/.

Desmond, Matthew. "How Homeownership Became the Engine of American Inequality." *New York Times Magazine,* May 9, 2017. https://www.nytimes.com/2017/05/09/magazine/how-homeownership-became-the-engine-of-american-inequality.html.

Dewey, John. *The Public and Its Problems.* Athens, OH: Swallow Press, 1927/1954.

Dionne, E. J., Norman J. Ornstein, and Thomas E. Mann. *One Nation After Trump: A Guide for the Perplexed, the Disillusioned, the Desperate, and the Not-Yet Deported.* New York: St. Martin's Press, 2017.

Dobson, J. "A Historic Occasion." *Citizen,* 17, November 2003, 22–28.

———. "The Future of the Family: Dr. James Dobson Looks Ahead to the New Millennium." *Focus on the Family.* http://www.focusonthefamily.com/docstudy/newsletters/ A000000794.cfm.

———. "Was a Good Family Life Easier to Achieve in Earlier Days?" *Focus on the Family.* http://www.webcitation.org/5T9p3CZea. Accessed: December 20, 2019.

Dobson, James C., and Gary L. Bauer. *Children at Risk: What You Need to Know to Protect Your Family.* Dallas, TX: Word, 1990.

Doherty, Brian. *Radicals for Capitalism: A Freewheeling History of the Modern American Libertarian Movement.* New York: PublicAffairs, 2007.

"Donald Trump 2016 RNC Draft Speech Transcript." *Politico,* July 21, 2017. https://www.politico.com/story/2016/07/full-transcript-donald-trump-nomination-acceptance-speech-at-rnc-225974.

"Donald Trump Announces a Presidential Bid." *Washington Post,* June 16, 2015. https://www.washingtonpost.com/news/post-politics/wp/2015/06/16/full-text-donald-trump-announces-a-presidential-bid/.

"Donald Trump Speech at Liberty University." *CNN,* January 18, 2016. http://transcripts.cnn.com/TRANSCRIPTS/1601/18/ath.01.html.

"Donald Trump's Argument for America." *YouTube,* November 6, 2016. https://www.youtube.com/watch?v=vST61W4bGm8.

"Donald Trump's Speech Responding to Assault Accusations." *NPR,* October 13, 2016. http://www.npr.org/2016/10/13/497857068/transcript-donald-trumps-speech-responding-to-assault-accusations.

Dow, Bonnie J. "Taking Trump Seriously: Persona and Presidential Politics in 2016." *Women's Studies in Communication* 40, no. 2 (2017): 136–39.

Dreman, Solly. *The Family on the Threshold of the 21st Century: Trends and Implications.* Mahwah, NJ: Lawrence Erlbaum Associates, 1997.

Duerringer, Christopher M., and Z. S. Justus. "Tropes in the Rhetoric of Gun Rights: A Pragma-Dialectic Analysis." *Argumentation & Advocacy* 52, no. 3 (2016): 181–98.

Eagleton, Terry. *Ideology: An Introduction.* London: Verso, 1991.

Ebbs, Stephanie. "Trump Says He Would Have 'Run in There' to Stop Parkland Shooting." *ABC News,* February 26, 2018. https://abcnews.go.com/Politics/trump-bump-stocks-congress-act/story?id=53362605.

Eckstein, Justin, and Sarah T. Partlow Lefevre. "Since Sandy Hook: Strategic Maneuvering in the Gun Control Debate." *Western Journal of Communication* 81, no. 2 (2017): 225–42.

Edelman, Murray. *Constructing the Political Spectacle.* Chicago: University of Chicago Press, 1988.

———. *Politics as Symbolic Action.* Chicago: Markham, 1971.

Edwards, Jonathan J. *Superchurch: The Rhetoric and Politics of American Fundamentalism.* East Lansing: Michigan State University Press, 2015.

Elsasser, Shaun W., and Riley E. Dunlap. "Leading Voices in the Denier Choir: Conservative Columnists' Dismissal of Global Warming and Denigration of Climate Science." *American Behavioral Scientist* 57, no. 6 (2013): 754–76. https://doi.org/10.1177/0002764212469800.

Engels, Jeremy. "The Politics of Resentment and the Tyranny of the Minority: Rethinking Victimage for Resentful Times." *Rhetoric Society Quarterly* 40, no. 4 (2010): 303–25.

———. "The Rhetoric of Violence: Sarah Palin's Response to the Tucson Shooting." *Symploke* 20 (2012): 121–38.

Fahnestock, Jeanne. "Accommodating Science: The Rhetorical Life of Scientific Facts." *Written Communication* 3, no. 3 (1986): 275–96.

Falwell, Jerry. *American Can Be Saved.* Murfreesboro, TN: Sword of the Lord Publishers, 1979.

———. *Listen, America!* Garden City, NY: Doubleday, 1980.

———. *Strength for the Journey: An Autobiography.* New York: Simon & Schuster, 1987.

Feldman, Richard. *Ricochet: Confessions of a Gun Lobbyist.* New York: John Wiley & Sons, 2008.

Filipovic, Jill. "The All-Male Photo Op Isn't a Gaffe. It's a Strategy." *New York Times,* March 27, 2017. https://www.nytimes.com/2017/03/27/opinion/the-all-male-photo-op-isnt-a-gaffe-its-a-strategy.html.

Filkins, Dexter. "Rex Tillerson at the Breaking Point: Will Donald Trump Let the Secretary of State Do His Job?" *New Yorker,* October 16, 2017. https://www.newyorker.com/magazine/2017/10/16/rex-tillerson-at-the-breaking-point.

Finnegan, Cara A. "Social Engineering, Visual Politics, and the New Deal: FSA Photography in *Survey Graphic.*" *Rhetoric & Public Affairs* 3, no. 3 (2000): 333–62. https://doi.org/10.1353/rap.2010.0029.

Fiske, John, and John Hartley. *Reading Television.* London: Methuen, 1978.

FitzGerald, Frances. *Cities on a Hill: A Journey through Contemporary American Cultures.* New York: Simon & Schuster, 1986.

———. *The Evangelicals: The Struggle to Shape America.* New York: Simon & Schuster, 2017. Kindle.

Fitzgerald, Stephanie. *The Scopes Trial: The Battle over Teaching Evolution.* Minneapolis, MN: Compass Point Books, 2007.

"Florida Alert! Help Stop Gratuitous GUN CONTROL." *NRA-ILA,* February 22, 2018. https://www.nraila.org/articles/20180222/florida-alert-help-stop-gratuitous-gun-control

Foucault, Michel. *Discipline and Punish: The Birth of the Prison.* Translated by Alan Sheridan. London: Tavistock, 1977.

———. "What Is an Author?" In *The Foucault Reader,* edited by Paul Rabinow, 101–20. New York: Pantheon, 1984.

Foust, Christina R., Shannon Bradley, Sophia Ben-Hamoo, and Beri Polonitza. "The Relationship between Political Ideology and Climate Change: An Exploratory Survey and Analysis." Paper presented at the Environmental Communication Interest Group, Western States Communication Association Conference, Albuquerque, NM, February 2012.

Foust, Christina R., and William O'Shannon Murphy. "Revealing and Reframing Apocalyptic Tragedy in Global Warming Discourse." *Environmental Communication* 3, no. 2 (1997): 151–67.

Frank, David A. "Rhetoric's Effects, the *Vita Activa*, and the Rhetorical Turn in Twentieth-Century Thought." In *The Effects of Rhetoric and the Rhetoric of Effects*, edited by Amos Kiewe, and David W. Houck, 101–17. Columbia, SC: University of South Carolina Press, 2015.

Frankel, Joseph. "The Government Won't Fund Research on Gun Violence Because of NRA Lobbying." *Newsweek*, October 2, 2017. http://www.newsweek.com/government-wont-fund-gun-research-stop-violence-because-nra-lobbying-675794.

Fraser, James W. *By the People: A History of the United States*. Boston: Pearson Education, 2015.

Fraser, Nancy. "Rethinking the Public Sphere: A Contribution to the Critique of Actually Existing Democracy." In *Habermas and the Public Sphere*, edited by Craig Calhoun, 109–42. Cambridge, MA: MIT Press, 1992.

Fraser, Steve, and Gary Gerstle, eds. *Ruling America: A History of Wealth and Power in a Democracy*. Cambridge, MA; Harvard University Press, 2005, Kindle.

Friedman, Thomas L. *Thank You for Being Late: An Optimist's Guide to Thriving in the Age of Accelerations*. New York: Farrar, Straus and Giroux, 2016.

Friedrichs, Jorg. *The Future Is Not What It Used to Be: Climate Change and Energy Scarcity*. Cambridge, MA: MIT Press, 2013.

Frykholm, Amy Johnson. *Rapture Culture: Left Behind in Evangelical America*. New York: Oxford University Press, 2004.

Fuchs, Stephen. "What Makes Sciences 'Scientific'?" In *Handbook of Sociological Theory*, edited by Jonathan H. Turner, 21–36. New York, Kluwer, 2002.

Gatchet, Amanda Davis, and Dana L. Cloud. "David, Goliath, and the Black Panthers." *Journal of Communication Inquiry* 37, no. 1 (2013): 5–25.

Giddens, Anthony. *The Politics of Climate Change*. Malden, MA: Polity, 2011.

Giroux, Henry A. *The Terror of Neoliberalism*. Boulder, CO: Paradigm, 2004.

Glazer, Nathan. "Fundamentalism: A Defensive Offensive," In *Piety or Politics: Evangelicals and Fundamentalist Confront the World*, edited by Richard John Neuhaus and Michael Cromartie, 245–58. Washington, DC: Ethics and Public Policy Center, 1987.

"Global Warming: A Scientific and Biblical Expose of Climate Change." Petersburg, KY: Answers in Genesis, 2008.

Global Warming. Produced by Coral Ridge Ministries. Creation Museum, 2008. DVD.

Good, Jennifer Ellen. "The Framing of Climate Change in Canadian, American, and International Newspapers: A Media Propaganda Model Analysis." *Canadian Journal of Communication* 33, no. 2 (2008): 233–55.

Goodnight, G. Thomas. "Gabrielle Giffords: A Study in Civil Courage." *Rhetoric & Public Affairs* 17, no. 4 (2014): 679–709.

———. "The Personal, Technical, and Public Spheres of Argument: A Speculative Inquiry into the Art of Public Deliberation." *Argumentation & Advocacy* 48 (2012): 198–210.

Goodnough, Abby, and Robert Pear. "Trump Administration Sharply Cuts Spending on Health Law Enrollment." *New York Times*, August 31, 2017. https://www.nytimes.com/2017/08/31/health/affordable-care-act-trump-spending.html.

Graham, Billy. *Storm Warning*. Dallas: Word, 1992.

Graham, David A. "Wayne LaPierre's Cynical Exploitation of Outrage." *The Atlantic*, February 22, 2018. https://www.theatlantic.com/politics/archive/2018/02/wayne-lapierres-trumpian-base-strategy/553964/.

Grebstein, Sheldon Norma, ed. *Monkey Trial: The State of Tennessee vs. John Thomas Scopes*. Boston: Houghton Mifflin, 1960.

Green, Joshua. *Devil's Bargain: Steve Bannon, Donald Trump, and the Storming of the Presidency*. New York: Penguin, 2017.

———. "Joshua Green on *Devil's Bargain*." *Washington Journal: C-SPAN*, August 1, 2017. https://www.c-span.org/video/?431977-4/washington-journal-joshua-green-discusses-devils-bargain.

Griffin, Rachel Alicia. "The 'Morning/Mourning' After: When Becoming President Trumps Being a Sexual Predator." *Women's Studies in Communication* 40, no. 2 (2017): 140–44. https://doi.org/10.1080/07491409.2017.1302259.

Gunn, Joshua. "On Political Perversion." *Rhetoric Society Quarterly* 48, no. 2 (2018): 161–86.

Gunn, Joshua, and David E. Beard. "On the Apocalyptic Columbine." *Southern Communication Journal* 68 (2003): 198–216.

Gunn, Joshua, and Dana L. Cloud. "Agentic Orientation as Magical Voluntarism." *Communication Theory* 20, no. 1 (2010): 50–78.

Guth, James L., and Lyman A. Kellstedt. "How Green Is My Pulpit?" *Books and Culture*, May/June 1996, p. 13.

Guyatt, Nicholas. *Have a Nice Doomsday: Why Millions of Americans Are Looking Forward to the End of the World*. New York: HarperCollins, 2007.

Haag, Matthew. "Remington, Centuries-Old Gun Maker, Files for Bankruptcy as Sales Slow." *New York Times*, March 25, 2018. https://www.nytimes.com/2018/03/25/business/remington-bankruptcy-guns.html.

Habermas, Jürgen. *Between Facts and Norms: Contributions to a Discourse Theory of Law and Democracy*. Cambridge, MA: MIT Press, 1996.

———. *On the Pragmatics of Communication*. Edited by Maeve Cooke. Cambridge, MA: MIT Press, 1998.

———. *The Theory of Communicative Action*. Vol. 1, *Reason and Rationalization of Society*. Translated by Thomas McCarthy. Boston: Beacon, 1984.

Hagee, John. *Daniel to Doomsday: The Countdown Has Begun*. Nashville, TN: Thomas Nelson, 2000.

Hague, Canon Dyson. "History of the Higher Criticism." In Vol. 5, *The Fundamentals: A Testimony to Truth*. Chicago, IL: Testimony, 1910–15, 87–122.

Hakkinen, Kirsti, and Nazar Akrami. "Ideology and Climate Change Denial." *Personality and Individual Differences* 70 (2014): 62–65.

Harding, Susan F. *The Book of Jerry Falwell: Fundamentalist Language and Politics*. Princeton, NJ: Princeton University Press, 2000.

Harpine, William D. "The Illusion of Tradition: Spurious Quotations and the Gun Control Debate." *Argumentation & Advocacy* 52, no. 3 (2016): 151–64.

Harris, Gardiner. "Diplomacy? Tillerson Says His Top Priority is Efficiency." *New York Times*, September 14, 2017. https://www.nytimes.com/2017/09/14/us/politics/diplomacy-tillerson-says-his-top-priority-is-efficiency.html.

———. "With Cost-Cutting Zeal, Tillerson Whittles U.N. Delegation, Too." *New York Times,* August 15, 2017. https://www.nytimes.com/2017/09/15/us/politics/tillerson-state-department-united-nations-general-assembly.html.

Hart, Roderick P. *Modern Rhetorical Criticism.* Glenview, IL: Scott, Foresman, 1990.

———. "The Rhetoric of the True Believer." *Speech Monographs* 38, no. 4 (1971): 249–61.

Hauser, Gerard. *Vernacular Voices: The Rhetoric of Publics and Public Spheres.* Columbia: University of South Carolina Press, 1999.

Hayden, Sara. "Family Metaphors and the Nation: Promoting a Politics of Care through the Million Mom March." *Quarterly Journal of Speech* 89 (2003): 196–215.

Hebdige, Dick. *Subculture.* London: Methuen, 1979.

Hepburn, Lisa, and David Hemenway. "Firearm Availability and Homicide: A Review of the Literature." *Aggression and Violent Behavior: A Review Journal* 9 (2004): 417–40.

Hesford, Wendy S., Adela C. Licona, and Christa Teston, eds. *Precarious Rhetorics: New Directions in Rhetoric and Materiality.* Columbus: The Ohio State University Press, 2018.

Hochschild, Arlie Russell. *Strangers in Their Own Land: Anger and Mourning on the American Right.* New York: The New Press, 2016. Kindle.

Hoerl, Kristen. "Monstrous Youth in Suburbia: Disruption and Recovery of the American Dream." *Southern Communication Journal* 67 (2002): 259–75.

Hofstadter, Richard. *The Paranoid Style in American Politics and Other Essays.* New York: Vintage, 1964.

Hogan, J. Michael, and Craig Rood. "Rhetorical Studies and the Gun Debate: A Public Policy Perspective." *Rhetoric & Public Affairs* 18, no. 2 (2015): 359–71.

"Homicide." Harvard Injury Control Research Center. Accessed June 5, 2018. https://www.hsph.harvard.edu/hicrc/firearms-research/guns-and-death/.

Horn, Miriam. *Rancher, Farmer, Fisherman: Conservation Heroes of the American Heartland.* New York: Norton, 2016. Kindle.

"How N.R.A. Fundraising Shapes the Political Landscape." *NPR-The Takeaway,* May 4, 2018. https://www.wnycstudios.org/story/the-takeaway-2018-05-04/.

Hoyningen-Huene, Paul. "Systematicity: The Nature of Science." *Philosophia* 36 (2008): 167–80.

Huertas, Aaron. "Advice for 2020 Candidates: Think Like a Stand-Up." *Medium,* November 11, 2018. https://medium.com/s/story/2020-contenders-who-confront-trump-need-to-think-like-a-standup-c84c0e707a56.

Hulme, Mike. "Climate Change: From Issue to Magnifier." *Open Democracy,* October 19, 2016. Accessed May 1, 2017. https://www.opendemocracy.net/en/climate_change_from_issue_to_magnifier/.

Hunter, James Davidson. *American Evangelicalism: Conservative Religion and the Quandary of Modernity.* New Brunswick, NJ: Rutgers University Press, 1983.

Igielnik, Ruth, and Anna Brown. "Key Takeaways on Americans' Views of Guns and Gun Ownership." *Pew,* June 22, 2017. http://www.pewresearch.org/fact-tank/2017/06/22/key-takeaways-on-americans-views-of-guns-and-gun-ownership/.

Inhofe, James. *The Greatest Hoax: How the Global Warming Conspiracy Threatens Your Future.* Washington, DC: WND Books, 2012.

Ivie, Robert L. "Trump's Unwitting Prophecy." *Rhetoric & Public Affairs* 20, no. 4 (2017): 707–17.

Jameson, Frederick. *The Political Unconscious: Narrative as a Socially Symbolic Act*. Ithaca, NY: Cornell University Press, 1981.

Jamieson, Kathleen Hall. "Antecedent Genre as Rhetorical Constraint." *Quarterly Journal of Speech* 61, no. 4 (December 1975): 412–14.

———. "Generic Constraints and the Rhetorical Situation." *Philosophy & Rhetoric* 6, no. 3 (1973): 162–70.

Jamieson, Kathleen Hall, and Karlyn Kohrs Campbell. "Rhetorical Hybrids: Fusions of Generic Elements." *Quarterly Journal of Speech* 68, no. 2 (1982): 146–57. https://doi.org/10.1080/00335638209383600.

Jamieson, Kathleen Hall, and Joseph N. Cappella. *Echo Chamber: Rush Limbaugh and the Conservative Media Establishment*. Oxford: Oxford University Press, 2008.

Johnson, Anne Janette. *The Scopes "Monkey Trial."* Defining Moments. Detroit, MI: Omnigraphics, 2007.

Johnson, Paul Elliott. "The Art of Masculine Victimhood: Donald Trump's Demagoguery." *Women's Studies in Communication* 40, no. 3 (2017): 229–50. https://doi.org/10.1080/07491409.2017.1346533.

Jones, John M., and Robert C. Rowland. "Redefining the Proper Role of Government: Ultimate Definition in Reagan's First Inaugural." *Rhetoric & Public Affairs* 18, no. 4 (2015): 691–718.

Jones, Robert P. *The End of White Christian America*. New York: Simon & Schuster, 2016. Kindle.

"Jürgen Habermas." *Stanford Encyclopedia of Philosophy*. https://plato.stanford.edu/entries/habermas/#TheComAct.

Jylhä, Kirsti M., and Nazar Akrami. "Social Dominance Orientation and Climate Change Denial: The Role of Dominance and System Justification." *Personality and Individual Differences* 86 (2015): 108–11. https://doi.org/10.1016/j.paid.2015.05.041.

Kahan, Dan M., Ellen Peters, Erica Dawson, and Paul Slovic. "Motivated Numeracy and Enlightened Self-Government." *Behavioural Public Policy* 1: 54–86; Yale Law School, Public Law Working Paper No. 307. https://doi.org/10.2139/ssrn.2319992.

Kaplan, David A. *The Most Dangerous Branch: Inside the Supreme Court's Assault on the Constitution*. New York: Crown, 2018.

Kaplan, Sheila. "Congress Quashed Research into Gun Violence. Since Then, 600,000 People Have Been Shot." *New York Times*, March 12, 2018. https://www.nytimes.com/2018/03/12/health/gun-violence-research-cdc.html.

Kaste, Martin. "Is There a 'War On Police'? The Statistics Say No." *NPR*, September 17, 2015. https://www.npr.org/2015/09/17/441196546/is-there-a-war-on-police-the-statistics-say-no.

Kates, Don B. "Handgun Prohibition and the Original Meaning of the Second Amendment." *Michigan Law Review* 82 (1983): 204–73.

Kellermann, Arthur L., Frederick P. Rivara, Norman B. Rushforth, Joyce G. Banton, Donald T. Reay, Jerry T. Francisco, Ana B. Locci, Janice Prodzinski, Bela B. Hackman, and Grant Somes. "Gun Ownership as a Risk Factor for Homicide in the Home." *New England Journal of Medicine* 329 (1993): 1084–91. https://doi.org/10.1056/NEJM199310073291506.

Kellstedt, Paul, Sammy Zahran, and Arnold Vedlitz. "Personal Efficacy, the Information Environment, and Attitudes toward Global Warming and Climate Change in the United States." *Risk Analysis* 28, no. 1 (2008): 113–26. https://doi.org/10.1111/j.1539-6924.2008.01010.x.

Kertscher, Tom. "Which Is Higher: The Number of People, or the Number of Guns, in America?" *Politifact*, February 20, 2018. http://www.politifact.com/wisconsin/statements/2018/feb/20/kevin-nicholson/which-higher-number-people-or-number-guns-america/.

Kiewe, Amos, and David W. Houck, eds. *The Effects of Rhetoric and the Rhetoric of Effects.* Columbia: University of South Carolina Press, 2015.

———. "Introduction." In Kiewe and Houck, 1–30.

Klein, Naomi. *No Is Not Enough: Resisting Trump's Shock Politics and Winning the World We Need.* Chicago: Haymarket, 2017.

———. *The Shock Doctrine: The Rise of Disaster Capitalism.* New York: Picador, 2007.

———. *This Changes Everything: Capitalism vs. the Climate.* New York: Simon & Schuster, 2014. Kindle.

Klemp, Nathaniel J. *The Morality of Spin: Virtue and Vice in Political Rhetoric and the Christian Right.* Lanham, MD: Rowman & Littlefield, 2012.

Kristof, Nicholas. "How to Reduce Shootings." *New York Times,* November 6, 2017, updated May 18, 2018. https://www.nytimes.com/interactive/2017/11/06/opinion/how-to-reduce-shootings.html.

———. "It's Time to Talk About the NRA." *New York Times,* October 29, 2018. Accessed December 20, 2019. https://www.nytimes.com/interactive/2018/10/29/opinion/nra-mass-shootings-pittsburgh.html.

———. "Overreacting to Terrorism?" *New York Times,* March 24, 2016, accessed May 21, 2017. https://www.nytimes.com/2016/03/24/opinion/terrorists-bathtubs-and-snakes.html.

Krosnick, Jon A., Allyson L. Holbrook, Laura Lowe, and Penny S. Visser. "The Origins and Consequences of Democratic Citizens' Policy Agendas: A Study of Popular Concern about Global Warming." *Climate Change* 77, no. 1–2 (2006): 7–43. https://doi.org/10.1007/s10584-006-9068-8.

Lacombe, Matthew J. "The Political Weaponization of Gun Owners: The NRA's Cultivation, Dissemination, and Use of a Group Social Identity." *The Journal of Politics* 81, no. 4 (2019): 1342–56.

LaHaye, Tim. *Revelation Unveiled.* Grand Rapids, MI: Zondervan, 1999.

Lakoff, George. "Praxis Forum: Why It Matters How We Frame the Environment." *Environmental Communication* 4 (2010): 70–81.

LaPierre, Wayne. "Address to CPAC." *NRA,* March 15, 2013. Accessed September 8, 2015. http://home. nra.org/history/video/cpac-2013-nra-ceo-evp-wayne-lapierre/list/wayne-lapierre-speeches.

———. *The Global War on Your Guns: Inside the U.N. Plan to Destroy the Bill of Rights.* Nashville, TN: Nelson Current, 2006.

———. *Guns, Crime, and Freedom.* Washington, DC: Regnery, 1994.

———. "NRA: Full Statement by Wayne LaPierre in Response to Newtown Shootings." *Guardian,* December 21, 2012. https://www.theguardian.com/world/2012/dec/21/nra-full-statement-lapierre-newtown.

Lears, Jackson. *Something for Nothing: Luck in America.* New York: Viking, 2003.

Lee, Jasmine C., and Kevin Quealy. "The 425 People, Places and Things Donald Trump Has Insulted on Twitter: A Complete List." *New York Times,* January 3, 2018. https://www.nytimes.com/interactive/2016/01/28/upshot/donald-trump-twitter-insults.html.

Lee, Michael J. "Considering Political Identity: Conservatives, Republicans, and Donald Trump." *Rhetoric & Public Affairs* 20, no. 4 (2017): 719–30.

Leiserowitz, Anthony. "Communicating the Risks of Global Warming: American Risk Perceptions, Affective Images, and Interpretive Communities." In *Creating a Climate for Change:*

Communicating Climate Change and Facilitating Social Change, edited by S. C. Moser and L. Dilling, 44–63. Cambridge: Cambridge University Press, 2007.

Leonhardt, David. "Americans Are Again Getting More Worried about the Climate." *New York Times,* June 16, 2015. http://www.nytimes.com/2015/06/17/upshot/americans-are-again-getting-more-worried-about-the-climate.html.

Levitsky, Steven, and Daniel Ziblatt. *How Democracies Die.* New York: Penguin, 2018.

Levitt, Steven D., and Stephen J. Dubner. *Superfreakonomics.* New York: William Morrow, 2009.

Lewandowsky, Stephan, Naomi Oreskes, James S. Risbey, Ben R. Newell, and Michael Smithson. "Seepage: Climate Change Denial and Its Effect on the Scientific Community." *Global Environmental Change* 33 (2015): 1–13. https://doi.org/10.1016/j.gloenvcha.2015.02.013.

Lewis, Michael. *The Fifth Risk.* New York: Norton, 2018.

———. "Inside Trump's Cruel Campaign against the U.S.D.A.'s Scientists." *Vanity Fair,* November 2, 2017. https://www.vanityfair.com/news/2017/11/usda-food-stamps-school-lunch-trump-administration.

"LGBTstats: Quiz: Poverty and the LGBT Community." *Williams Institute, UCLA School of Law,* May 2, 2015. https://williamsinstitute.law.ucla.edu/datablog/quiz-poverty-and-the-lgbt-community/.

Lind, Michael. "Conservative Elites and the Counterrevolution against the New Deal." In *Ruling America: A History of Wealth and Power in a Democracy,* edited by Steve Fraser and Gary Gerstle, chapter 8. Cambridge, MA: Harvard University Press, 2005. Kindle.

Lindsey, Hal. *Apocalypse Code.* Palos Verdes, CA: Western Front, 1997.

Litt, David. "Is Nothing Funny, Mr. President?" *New York Times,* September 16, 2017. https://www.nytimes.com/2017/09/16/opinion/sunday/trump-does-not-laugh.html.

Lopez, German. "More Guns Mean More Gun Murders. Here's How We Know." *Vox,* December 8, 2015. https://www.vox.com/policy-and-politics/2015/12/8/9870240/gun-ownership-deaths-homicides.

Lunceford, Brett. "Armed Victims: The Ego Function of Second Amendment Rhetoric." *Rhetoric & Public Affairs* 18, no. 2 (2015): 333–45.

Machen, J. Gresham. "What Fundamentalism Stands for Now, Defined by a Leading Exponent." *New York Times,* (1923-Current file); June 21, 1925; ProQuest Historical Newspapers: The New York Times with Index pg. XX1

MacLean, Nancy. *Democracy in Chains: The Deep History of the Radical Right's Stealth Plan for America.* New York: Penguin, 2017. Kindle.

Maddux, Kristy. *The Faithful Citizen: Popular Christian Media and Gendered Civic Identities.* Waco, TX: Baylor University Press, 2010.

Marsden, George M. *Fundamentalism and American Culture: The Shaping of Twentieth-Century Evangelicalism, 1870–1925.* New York: Oxford University Press, 1980.

———. *Understanding Fundamentalism and Evangelicalism.* Grand Rapids, MI: William B. Eerdmans, 1991.

Matthews, Dylan. "11 Facts about Gun Violence in the United States." *Vox,* June 13, 2016. https://www.vox.com/2015/10/1/18000422/11-facts-about-gun-violence-in-the-united-states.

Mayer, Jane. *Dark Money: The Hidden History of the Billionaires behind the Rise of the Radical Right.* New York: Doubleday, 2016.

McCann, Bryan J. "On Whose Ground? Racialized Violence and the Prerogative of 'Self-Defense' in the Trayvon Martin Case." *Western Journal of Communication* 78, no. 4 (2014): 480–99.

McDermott, Nathan. "The Myth of Gay Affluence." *The Atlantic*, March 21, 2014. https://www.theatlantic.com/business/archive/2014/03/the-myth-of-gay-affluence/284570/.

McCloskey, Deirdre. "Growth, Not Forced Equality, Saves the Poor." *New York Times*, December 23, 2016. http://www.nytimes.com/2016/12/23/business/growth-not-forced-equality-saves-the-poor.html.

———. *The Rhetoric of Economics*. 2nd ed. Madison: University of Wisconsin Press, 1998.

McCright, Aaron M., and Riley E. Dunlap. "Anti-reflexivity: The American Conservative Movement's Success in Undermining Climate Science and Policy." *Theory, Culture & Society* 27, no. 2–3 (2010): 100–133. https://doi.org/10.1177/0263276409356001.

———. "Cool Dudes: The Denial of Climate Change among Conservative White Males in the United States." *Global Environmental Change* 21 (2011): 1163–72. https://doi.org/10.1016/j.gloenvcha.2011.06.003.

McKerrow, Raymie. "Critical Rhetoric: Theory and Praxis." *Communication Monographs* 56 (1989): 91–111.

McLeod, Paul. "Paul Ryan Defends Trump's Interactions with Comey: 'He's New to This.'" *BuzzFeed News*, June 8, 2017. https://www.buzzfeednews.com/article/paulmcleod/paul-ryan-defends-trumps-interactions-with-comey-hes-new-to.

McLoughlin, William G. *Billy Graham: Revivalist in a Secular Age*. New York: Ronald Press, 1960.

———. *Modern Revivalism: Charles Grandison Finney to Billy Graham*. New York: Ronald Press, 1959.

Medlock, Scott. "NRA = No Rational Argument? How the National Rifle Association Exploits Public Irrationality." *Texas Journal on Civil Liberties & Civil Rights* 11 (2005): 39–63.

Merica, Dan. "Trump Argues He Won New Hampshire Because It Is a 'Drug-Infested Den.'" *CNN*, August 3, 2017. http://www.cnn.com/2017/08/03/politics/trump-new-hampshire-drugs/index.html.

Miller, Carolyn R. "Should We Name the Tools? Concealing and Revealing the Art of Rhetoric." In *The Public Work of Rhetoric: Citizen-Scholars and Civic Engagement*, edited by John M. Ackerman and David J. Coogan, 19–38. Columbia: University of South Carolina Press, 2010.

Miller, Matthew, Deborah Azrael, and David Hemenway. "Firearms and Violent Death in the United States." In *Reducing Gun Violence in America*, edited by Daniel W. Webster and Jon S. Vernick, 3–20. Baltimore, MD: Johns Hopkins University Press, 2013.

———. "Household Firearm Ownership Levels and Homicide Rates across U.S. Regions and States, 1988–1997." *American Journal of Public Health* 92 (2002): 1988–93.

———. "State-Level Homicide Victimization Rates in the U.S. in Relation to Survey Measures of Household Firearm Ownership, 2001–2003." *Social Science and Medicine* 64 (2007): 656–64.

Minnery, Tom. "Our Father Knows Best: Those Who Advocate for Traditional Values Are Accused of Trying to Take Us Back to the 1950s. Is That So Bad?" *Focus on the Family*. http://www.focusonthefamily.com/focusmagazine/publicpolicy/A000000189.cfm.

Mirowski, Philip, and Dieter Plehwe, eds. *The Road from Mont Pèlerin: The Making of the Neoliberal Thought Collective*. Cambridge, MA: Harvard University Press, 2009.

Montgomery, Scott L., and Daniel Chirot. *The Shape of the New: Four Big Ideas and How They Made the Modern World*. Princeton, NJ: Princeton University Press, 2015.

Mooallem, Jon. "Enrico L. Quarantelli: He Proved That Disasters Bring Out the Best in Us." *New York Times Magazine*, December 31, 2017.

———. "Our Climate Future Is Actually Our Climate Present." *New York Times Magazine*, April 23, 2017. https://www.nytimes.com/2017/04/19/magazine/our-climate-future-is-actually-our-climate-present.html.

Moody, Dwight Lyman. "Heaven and How to Get There." In *Short Talks*. Chicago: Bible Institute Colportage Association, 1900, p. 94.

———. *The New Sermons of Dwight Lyman Moody*. New York: Goodspeed, 1880.

Moran, Jeffrey P. *The Scopes Monkey Trial: A Brief History with Documents*. New York: Palgrave, 2002.

Morello-Frosch, Rachel, Manuel Pastor, James Sadd, and Seth B. Shonkoff. "The Climate Gap: Inequalities in How Climate Change Hurts Americans & How to Close the Gap." https://dornsife.usc.edu/assets/sites/242/docs/The_Climate_Gap_Full_Report_FINAL.pdf.

Moser, Susanne C., and Lisa Dilling. "Communicating Climate Change: Closing the Science-Action Gap." In *The Oxford Handbook of Climate Change and Society*, edited by John S. Dryzek, Richard B. Norgaard, and David Schlosberg, 161–74. Oxford: Oxford University Press, 2011.

Mouffe, Chantal. *The Democratic Paradox*. London: Verso, 2000.

———. *The Return of the Political*. London: Verso, 1993.

Mueller, J. *Retreat from Doomsday: The Obsolescence of Major War*. New York: Basic Books, 1989.

"Mulvaney Says Climate Change Research Is 'a Waste of Your Money.'" *Washington Post*, March 16, 2017. Accessed May 20, 2017. https://www.washingtonpost.com/video/national/mulvaney-says-climate-change-research-is-a-waste-of-your-money/2017/03/16/7e67c20c-0a85-11e7-bd19-fd3afa0f7e2a_video.html.

Naylor, Bryan. "Trump Administration Has More Than 250 Unfilled Jobs." *NPR*, November 22, 2017. https://www.npr.org/2017/11/22/566098660/trump-administration-has-more-than-250-unfilled-jobs.

Nerlich, Brigitte, Nelya Koteyko, and Brian Brown. "Theory and Language of Climate Change Communication." *WIREs Climate Change* 1, no. 1 (2010): 97–110. https://doi.org/10.1002/wcc.2.

Newport, Frank. "Little Increase in Americans' Global Warming Worries." *Gallup*, April 21, 2008. http://news.gallup.com/poll/106660/little-increase-americans-global-warming-worries.aspx.

———. "One-Third of Americans Believe the Bible Is Literally True." *Gallup*, May 25, 2007. https://news.gallup.com/poll/27682/onethird-americans-believe-bible-literally-true.aspx.

Nimmo, Dan, and James Combs. *Mediated Political Realities*. New York: Longman, 1983.

Norgaard, Kari Marie. *Living in Denial: Climate Change, Emotions, and Everyday Life*. Cambridge, MA: MIT Press, 2011.

O'Connor, Brendan. "How Fossil Fuel Money Made Climate Change Denial the Word of God." *Splinter*. Accessed December 19, 2019. http://splinternews.com/how-fossil-fuel-money-made-climate-denial-the-word-of-g-1797466298.

Ockwell, David L., Lorraine Whitmarsh, and Saffron O'Neill. "Reorienting Climate Change Communication for Effective Mitigation Forcing People to Be Green or Fostering Grass-Roots Engagement?" *Science Communication* 30 (2009): 305–27. https://doi.org/10.1177/1075547008328969.

Ogden, Charles K., and Ivor A. Richards. *The Meaning of Meaning*. New York: Harcourt, Brace, 1923.

Oliver, J. Eric, and Thomas Wood. "Conspiracy Theories of the Paranoid Styles(s) of Mass Opinion." *American Journal of Political Science* 58, no. 4 (2014): 952–66.

Olson, Christa J. "Performing Embodiable Topoi: Strategic Indigeneity and the Incorporation of Ecuadorian National Identity." *Quarterly Journal of Speech* 96, no. 3 (2010): 300–23.

Olson, Kathryn M. "The Comic Strategy of 'Deferral to Study': Creating Space in Divisive Religious Disputes to Value Both Community and Convictions." *Journal of Communication & Religion* 30, no. 2 (2007): 266–307.

———. "Detecting a Common Interpretive Framework for Impersonal Violence: The Homology in Participants' Rhetoric on Sport Hunting, 'Hate Crimes,' and Stranger Rape." *Southern Communication Journal* 67 (2002): 215–44.

Oshatz, Molly. *Slavery and Sin: The Fight against Slavery and the Rise of Liberal Protestantism.* New York: Oxford University Press, 2012.

Ott, Brian L., Eric Aoki, and Greg Dickinson. "Ways of (Not) Seeing Guns: Presence and Absence at the Cody Firearms Museum." *Communication and Critical/Cultural Studies* 8, no. 3 (2011): 215–39.

Packer, George. *The Unwinding: An Inner History of the New America.* New York: Farrar, Straus and Giroux, 2013.

Palczewski, Catherine Helen. "Cyber-movements, New Social Movements, and Counterpublics." In *Counterpublics and the State,* edited by Robert Asen and Daniel C. Brouwer, 161–86. Albany: State University of New York Press, 2001.

Parker, James. "Live-Streaming the Apocalypse: The Paranoid Style of NRATV." *The Atlantic,* June 2018, p. 30.

Pason, Amy, Christina R. Foust, and Kate Zittlow Rogness. "Introduction: Rhetoric and the Study of Social Change." In *What Democracy Looks Like: The Rhetoric of Social Movements and Counterpublics,* edited by Christina R. Foust, Amy Pason, and Kate Zittlow Rogness, 1–26. Rhetoric, Culture, and Social Critique. Tuscaloosa: University of Alabama Press, 2017.

Pearson, Rachel. *No Apparent Distress: A Doctor's Coming-of-Age on the Front Lines of American Medicine.* New York: Norton, 2017.

Peeples, Jennifer, Pete Bsumek, Steve Schwarze, and Jen Schneider. "Industrial Apocalyptic: Neoliberalism, Coal, and the Burlesque Frame." *Rhetoric & Public Affairs* 17, no. 2 (2014): 227–53.

Perelman, Chaim, and Lucie Olbrechts-Tyteca. *The New Rhetoric.* Translated by John Wilkinson and Purcell Weaver. South Bend, IN: Notre Dame Press, 1969.

Perez-Pena, Richard. "Contrary to Trump's Claims, Immigrants Are Less Likely to Commit Crimes." *New York Times,* January 26, 2017. https://www.nytimes.com/2017/01/26/us/trump-illegal-immigrants-crime.html.

Perkowitz, Robert M. "Praxis Forum: Climate Communications: Conflicts and Opportunities." *Environmental Communication* 4 (2010): 66–69.

Peters, Jeremy W., and Michael M. Grynbaum. "Steve Bannon, Back in the Outside, Prepares His Enemies List." *New York Times,* August 18, 2017. https://www.nytimes.com/2017/08/18/business/media/bannon-said-to-be-planning-his-return-to-breitbart-news.html.

Pew Research Center for the People and the Press. "Increasing Partisan Divide on Energy Policies: Little Change in Opinions about Global Warming." October 27, 2010. Accessed May 1, 2017. http://people-press.org/report/669/.

Pezzullo, Phaedra C. "Resisting 'National Breast Cancer Awareness Month': The Rhetoric of Counterpublics and Their Cultural Performances." *Quarterly Journal of Speech* 89 (2003): 345–65. https://doi.org/10.1080/0033563032000160981.

Pfau, Michael William. "Bright Lines or Blurred Lines? Universal Background Checks and the NRA Slippery Slope Argument." *Argumentation & Advocacy* 53, no. 4 (2017): 253–70.

Phillips, Kristine. "Confronted with the Bloody Behavior of Autocrats, Trump, Instead, Blames the World." *Washington Post*, November 22, 2018. https://www.washingtonpost.com/politics/2018/11/22/confronted-with-bloody-behavior-autocrats-trump-instead-blames-world/.

Phillips-Fein, Kim. *Invisible Hands: The Businessmen's Crusade Against the New Deal*. New York: Norton, 2010. Kindle.

Pigliucci, Massimo. "The Demarcation Problem: A (Belated) Response to Laudan." In *Philosophy of Pseudoscience: Reconsidering the Demarcation Problem*, edited by Massimo Pigliucci and Maarten Boudry, 9–28. Chicago: University of Chicago Press, 2013.

Pilkington, Ed. "Obama Angers Midwest Voters with Guns and Religion Remark." *The Guardian*, April 14, 2008. https://www.theguardian.com/world/2008/apr/14/barackobama.uselections2008.

Pinker, Steven. *The Better Angels of Our Nature: Why Violence Has Declined*. New York: Penguin, 2011. Kindle.

———. *Enlightenment Now: The Case for Reason, Science, Humanism, and Progress*. New York: Viking, 2018.

Platt, Carrie Anne. "Focus on the Past: Nostalgia in the Same-Sex Marriage Debate." *Conference Papers—National Communication Association*, January 2008, 1.

———. "Focusing the Family: The Argumentative Evolution of 'Family Values' in the Same-Sex Marriage Debate." *Conference Proceedings—National Communication Association/American Forensic Association (Alta Conference on Argumentation)*, January 2007, 599–608.

Popp, Richard K. "Visual Culture, Public Space, and Piety in Focus on the Family's *Citizen Magazine*." *Critical Studies in Media Communication* 27, no. 5 (2010): 498–518. https://doi.org/10.1080/15295030903583622.

Quarantelli, Enrico, and R. R. Dynes. "Community Conflict: Its Absence and Its Presence in Natural Disasters." *Mass Emergencies* 1 (1976): 139–56.

Rehg, William. "Evaluating Complex Collaborative Expertise: The Case of Climate Change." *Argumentation* 25, no. 3 (2011): 385–400, 467–468, 471.

———. "Rhetoric, Cogency, and the Radically Social Character of Persuasion: Habermas's Argumentation Theory Revisited." *Philosophy & Rhetoric* 46, no. 4 (2013): 465–92.

Reid, Roddy. *Families in Jeopardy: Regulating the Social Body in France, 1750–1910*. Stanford, CA: Stanford University Press, 1993.

Reid, Thomas. *The Works of Thomas Reid; with an Account of His Life and Writings*. Vol. 2, edited by Dugald Stewart. New York: Duyckinck, Collins, Hannay, and Bartow, 1822.

"Resisting the Green Dragon: A Biblical Response to One of the Greatest Deceptions of Our Day." Accessed July 1, 2017. http://www.resistingthegreendragon.com/.

Richards, Ivor A. *The Philosophy of Rhetoric*. London: Oxford University Press, 1936/1965.

"RNC August 6 Debate." *Washington Post*, August 6, 2015. https://www.washingtonpost.com/news/post-politics/wp/2015/08/06/annotated-transcript-the-aug-6-gop-debate/.

Robelia, Beth, and Tony Murphy. "What Do People Know about Key Environmental Issues? A Review of Environmental Knowledge Surveys." *Environmental Education Research* 18 (2012): 299–321.

Rogers, Katie, and Jeffery C. Mays. "Trump Calls for Unity After Synagogue Shooting, Then Swiftly Denounces Democrats." *New York Times.* October 27, 2018. https://www.nytimes.com/2018/10/27/us/politics/trump-pittsburgh-synagogue-shooting.html.

Romm, Joe. "Front Group for Polluting Billionaires Wastes $140K on World's Dumbest Global Warming Denier Ads." *Think Progress,* February 17, 2009. https://thinkprogress.org/front-group-for-polluting-billionaires-wastes-140k-on-worlds-dumbest-global-warming-denier-ads-adbfc6160566/.

Rood, Craig. "'Our Tears Are Not Enough': The Warrant of the Dead in the Rhetoric of Gun Control." *Quarterly Journal of Speech* 104, no. 1 (2018): 47–70.

Rossing, Barbara R. *The Rapture Exposed: The Message of Hope in the Book of Revelation.* Cambridge, MA: Westview, 2004.

Rossing, Jonathan P. "No Joke: Silent Jesters and Comedic Refusals." *Rhetoric & Public Affairs* 20, no. 3 (2017): 545–55.

Rothwell, Jonathan. "Myth of the 1 Percent: What Puts Some People at the Top." *New York Times,* November 24, 2017, p. B2. https://www.nytimes.com/2017/11/17/upshot/income-inequality-united-states.html.

Rowland, Robert. "Purpose, Evidence, and Pedagogy in Rhetorical Criticism." In Kiewe and Houck, 59–81.

Rozsa, Matthew. "Donald Trump's Argument for America." *Salon,* November 7, 2016. https://www.salon.com/2016/11/07/watch-donald-trumps-last-campaign-ad-is-a-fitting-end-to-an-anti-semitic-campaign/.

Rubin, Jennifer. "Here's Proof That Trump Is Ignorant and Deluded about Crime." *Washington Post,* April 18, 2017. https://www.washingtonpost.com/blogs/right-turn/wp/2017/04/18/heres-proof-that-trump-is-ignorant-and-deluded-about-crime/.

Rueckert, William H. *Encounters with Kenneth Burke.* Urbana: University of Illinois Press, 1994.

Russill, Chris. "Tipping Point Forewarnings in Climate Change Communication: Some Implications of an Emerging Trend." *Environmental Communication* 2 (2008): 133–53.

Saad, Lydia. "Americans as Concerned as Ever about Global Warming." *Gallup,* March 25, 2019. https://news.gallup.com/poll/248027/americans-concerned-ever-global-warming.aspx.

Safire, William. *Safire's Political Dictionary.* Oxford: Oxford University Press, 2008.

Sapolsky, Robert. *Behave: The Biology of Humans at Our Best and Worst.* New York: Penguin, 2017.

Savage, Charlie. "Poor Vetting Sinks Trump's Nominees for Federal Judge." *New York Times,* December 18, 2017. https://www.nytimes.com/2017/12/18/us/politics/matthew-petersen-judge-nominee-withdraws-trump.html.

Schaeffer, Francis A. *The Complete Works of Francis Schaeffer: A Christian World View.* Vol. 5, *A Christian View of the West.* Wheaton, IL: Crossway Books, 1982.

Schaffner, Brian F., Matthew MacWilliams, and Tatishe Nteta. "Explaining White Polarization in the 2016 Vote for President: The Sobering Role of Racism and Sexism." Paper prepared for presentation at the Conference on the U.S. Elections of 2016: Domestic and International Aspects. January 8–9, 2017, IDC Herzliya Campus. https://people.umass.edu/schaffne/schaffner_et_al_IDC_conference.pdf.

Schwarze, Steven. "Environmental Melodrama." *Quarterly Journal of Speech* 92, no. 3 (2006): 239–61.

Scott, Dylan. "We Aren't Having an Evidence-Based Debate About Guns." *Vox*, March 12, 2018. https://www.vox.com/policy-and-politics/2018/2/28/17058236/gun-control-research-parkland-shooting.

Scott, Robert L. "Justifying Violence: The Rhetoric of Militant Black Power." *Communication Studies* 19 (1968): 96–104. https://doi.org/10.1080=10510976809362912.

Smith, Barbara Herrnstein. *Belief and Resistance: Dynamics of Contemporary Intellectual Controversy*. Cambridge, MA: Harvard University Press, 1997.

Smith, Christian. *American Evangelicalism: Embattled and Thriving*. Chicago: Chicago University Press, 1998.

Smith, Craig R. "Ronald Reagan's Rhetorical Re-Invention of Conservatism." *Quarterly Journal of Speech* 103, no. 1–2 (2017): 33–65. https://doi.org/10.1080/00335630.2016.1231415.

Smith, Francesca M., and Thomas A. Hollihan. "'Out of Chaos Breathes Creation': Human Agency, Mental Illness, and Conservative Arguments Locating Responsibility for the Tucson Massacre." *Rhetoric & Public Affairs* 17 (2014): 585–618.

Smith, Sonia. "Unfriendly Climate." *Texas Monthly*, May 2016. http://www.texasmonthly.com/articles/katharine-hayhoe-lubbock-climate-change-evangelist/.

Spadaro, Antonio, and Marcelo Figueroa. "Evangelical Fundamentalism and Catholic Integralism: A Surprising Ecumenism." *La Civiltà Cattolica*, July 13, 2017. Accessed August 1, 2017. http://www.laciviltacattolica.it/articolo/evangelical-fundamentalism-and-catholic-integralism-in-the-usa-a-surprising-ecumenism/.

Spitzer, Robert J. *The Politics of Gun Control*. 3rd ed. Washington, DC: CQ Press, 2004.

Standaert, Michael. *Skipping Towards Armageddon: The Politics and Propaganda of the Left Behind Novels and the LaHaye Empire*. Brooklyn, NY: Soft Skull Press, 2006.

Stanley, Jason. *How Fascism Works: The Politics of Us and Them*. New York: Random House, 2018.

Stanton, G. T. "Are Same-Sex Families Good for Children? What the Social Sciences Say (and Don't Say) about Family Experimentation." *Family Policy Alliance*. Accessed February 1, 2019. http://www.citizenlink.org/pdfs/fosi/marriage/Citizen_ Health_of_SSF.pdf.

"Statement by President Trump on the Paris Climate Accord." *The White House*, June 1, 2017. https://www.whitehouse.gov/briefings-statements/statement-president-trump-paris-climate-accord/.

Steidley, Trent, and Martin T. Kosla. "Toward a Status Anxiety Theory of Macro-level Firearm Demand." *Social Currents* 5, no. 1 (2018): 86–103. https://doi.org/10.1177/2329496517725332.

Stewart, Charles J., Craig Allen Smith, and Robert E. Denton. *Persuasion and Social Movements*. 6th ed. Long Grove, IL: Waveland Press, 2014.

Stewart, Matthew. "The Birth of a New American Aristocracy." *The Atlantic*, June 2018. https://www.theatlantic.com/magazine/archive/2018/06/the-birth-of-a-new-american-aristocracy/559130/.

Strozier, Charles. *Apocalypse: On the Psychology of Fundamentalism in America*. Boston: Beacon, 1994.

Stuckey, Mary, E. "American Elections and the Rhetoric of Political Change: Hyperbole, Anger, and Hope in U.S. Politics." *Rhetoric & Public Affairs* 20, no. 4 (2017): 667–94.

Suderman, Peter. "The G.O.P. Is a Mess. It's Not All Trump's Fault." *New York Times*, October 13, 2017. https://www.nytimes.com/2017/10/13/opinion/trump-republican-party-mess.html.

Sullivan, Eileen. "House Intel Chair: Media Take Trump Tweets Too Literally." *U.S. News & World Report,* March 7, 2017. https://www.usnews.com/news/politics/articles/2017-03-07/house-intel-to-hold-first-russia-hearing-later-this-month.

Sullivan, Peter, and Rachel Roubein. "Critics See Trump Sabotage on ObamaCare." *The Hill,* October 7, 2017. http://thehill.com/policy/healthcare/354308-trump-sabotage-seen-on-obamacare.

Swedler, David I., Molly M. Simmons, Francesca Dominici, and David Hemenway. "Firearm Prevalence and Homicides of Law Enforcement Officers in the United States." *American Journal of Public Health* 105 (2015): 2042–48.

Taylor, Adam. "Trump's Comments about Gun Laws in Britain and France Prompt Anger and Rebukes." *Washington Post,* May 5, 2018. https://www.washingtonpost.com/news/worldviews/wp/2018/05/05/trump-brings-british-knife-attacks-into-u-s-gunfight-and-upsets-londoners-again/.

Terrill, Robert E. "The Post-Racial and Post-Ethical Discourse of Donald J. Trump." *Rhetoric & Public Affairs* 20, no. 3 (2017): 493–510.

"The Inaugural Address." *The White House,* January 20, 2017. https://www.whitehouse.gov/briefings-statements/the-inaugural-address/.

Thief in the Night. Directed by Donald W. Thompson. Russ Doughten Films, 1972.

Thomas, W. H. Griffith. "Old Testament Criticism and New Testament Christianity." In Vol. 8, *The Fundamentals: A Testimony to Truth.* Chicago, IL: Testimony, 1910–15, pp. 47–58.

Thompson, Mark. *Enough Said: What's Gone Wrong with the Language of Politics?* New York: St. Martin's Press, 2016.

Tonn, Mari B., Valerie A. Endress, and John N. Diamond. "Hunting and Heritage on Trial: A Dramatistic Debate over Tragedy, Tradition, and Territory." *Quarterly Journal of Speech,* 79 (1993): 165–81.

Torrey, Reuben. "The Certainty and Importance of the Bodily Resurrection of Jesus Christ from the Dead." In Vol. 5, *The Fundamentals: A Testimony to Truth.* Chicago, IL: Testimony, 1910–15, ch. 32.

Trump, Donald J. (@realDonaldTrump). "The concept of global warming was created by and for the Chinese in order to make U.S. manufacturing non-competitive." *Twitter,* November 6, 2012. https://twitter.com/realdonaldtrump/status/265895292191248385?lang=en.

Tyson, Alec, and Shiva Maniam. "Behind Trump's Victory: Divisions by Race, Gender, Education." *Pew Research Center,* November 9, 2016. http://www.pewresearch.org/fact-tank/2016/11/09/behind-trumps-victory-divisions-by-race-gender-education/.

Vox, Lisa. *Existential Threats: American Apocalyptic Beliefs in the Technological Era.* Philadelphia, PA: University of Pennsylvania Press, 2017.

Waldman, Michael. *The Second Amendment: A Biography.* New York: Simon and Schuster, 2014.

Walker, Lauren. "Why the U.S. Lacks Gun Violence Research." *Newsweek,* December 3, 2015. http://www.newsweek.com/why-there-lack-gun-violence-research-unites-states-400912.

Wall text, *What do we teach?* Creation Museum, Petersburg, Kentucky.

Wall text, *The Lake of Fire,* Creation Museum, Petersburg, Kentucky.

Wall text. "7 C's in God's Eternal Plan." Creation Museum, Petersburg, Kentucky.

Wander, Philip. "The Third Persona: An Ideological Turn in Rhetorical Theory." *Communication Studies* 35 (1984): 197–216.

Wanliss, James. *Resisting the Green Dragon: Dominion, Not Death*. Burke, VA: Cornwall Alliance, 2013.

Warner, Michael. *Publics and Counterpublics*. Brooklyn, NY: Zone Books, 2002.

———. "Publics and Counterpublics." *Quarterly Journal of Speech* 88, no 4. (2002): 49–90.

"We Get It." http://www.we-get-it.org/ (accessed July 1, 2017).

Where the Grass Is Greener: Biblical Stewardship vs. Climate Alarmism. Cornwall Alliance. DVD. http://wherethegrassisgreenerthemovie.com/.

Wilkens, Steve, and Don Thorsen. *Everything You Know About Evangelicals Is Wrong: Well, Almost Everything*. Grand Rapids, MI: Baker, 2010.

Willingham, A. J. "The NRA's Message for Students Walking Out Today: 'I'll Control My Own Guns, Thank You.'" *CNN*, March 14, 2018. https://www.cnn.com/2018/03/14/us/nra-tweet-response-stoneman-douglas-shooting-walkout-trnd/index.html.

Willis, Paul. *Profane Culture*. London: Routledge, 1978.

Wills, Garry. "Our Moloch." *New York Review of Books*, December 15, 2012. Accessed February 18, 2014. http://www.nybooks.com/blogs/nyrblog/2012/dec/15/our-moloch/.

Wilson, Harry L. *Guns, Gun Control, and Elections*. Lanham, MD: Rowman & Littlefield, 2007.

Wilz, Kelly. "Bernie Bros and Woman Cards: Rhetorics of Sexism, Misogyny, and Constructed Masculinity in the 2016 Election." *Women's Studies in Communication* 39, no. 4 (2016): 357–60. https://doi.org/10.1080/07491409.2016.1227178.

Winkler, Adam. *Gunfight: The Battle over the Right to Bear Arms in America*. New York: Norton, 2011. Kindle.

———. "MLK and His Guns." *HuffPost*, January 17, 2011. https://www.huffingtonpost.com/adam-winkler/mlk-and-his-guns_b_810132.html.

Winslow, Luke. "Colonizing Caster Semenya: Gender Transformation and the Makeover Genre." *Western Journal of Communication* 76, no. 3 (2012): 298–313.

———. *Economic Injustice and the Rhetoric of the American Dream*. Lanham, MD: Lexington, 2017.

———. "Promise Keepers and the Rhetoric of the Stylized Other." *Journal of Communication & Religion* 35 (2012): 73–89.

———. "Rhetorical Homology and the Caveman Mythos: An(Other) Way to Ridicule the Aggrieved." *Communication Studies* 61 (2010): 257–71.

———. "Rhetorical Matriphagy and the Online Commodification of Higher Education." *Western Journal of Communication* 81, no. 5 (2017): 582–600.

———. "Rich, Blessed, and Tenured: A Homological Exploration of Grant Writing, Prosperity Theology, and Neoliberalism." *Western Journal of Communication* 79, no. 3 (2015): 257–82.

———. "The Undeserving Professor: Neoliberalism and the Reinvention of Higher Education." *Rhetoric & Public Affairs* 18, no. 2 (2015): 201–45.

Witte, Kim, and Mike A. Allen. "Meta-analysis of Fear Appeals: Implications for Effective Public Health Campaigns." *Health Education and Behaviour* 27 (2000): 591–605.

Woodward, Bob. *Fear: Trump in the White House*. New York: Simon & Schuster, 2018.

"Word of the Year 2016 Is . . ." *Oxford Dictionaries*. Accessed June 5, 2018. https://en.oxforddictionaries.com/word-of-the-year/word-of-the-year-2016.

The World Bank. *Acting on Climate Change and Disaster Risk for the Pacific.* 2013. Accessed July 1, 2017. http://documents.worldbank.org/curated/en/354821468098054153/pdf/808690Revise d000Box379874B00PUBLIC0.pdf.

Worthen, Molly. *Apostles of Reason: The Crisis of Authority in American Evangelicalism.* Oxford: Oxford University Press, 2013.

Wright, David. "Donald Trump: Our Country Needs a Good 'Shutdown,' Suggests Senate Rule Change." *CNN,* May 2, 2017. https://www.cnn.com/2017/05/02/politics/donald-trump-shutdown-tweet/index.html.

Wuertenberg, Nathan. "Gun Rights Are About Keeping White Men on Top." *Washington Post,* March 9, 2018. https://www.washingtonpost.com/news/made-by-history/wp/2018/03/09/gun-rights-are-about-keeping-white-men-on-top/.

Zengerle, Jason. "Rex Tillerson and the Unraveling of the State Department." *New York Times Magazine,* October 17, 2017. https://www.nytimes.com/2017/10/17/magazine/rex-tillerson-and-the-unraveling-of-the-state-department.html.

Zinn, Howard. *A People's History of the United States: 1492–Present.* New York: Harper Collins, 2003.

Zirin, Dave. "The Fragile, Toxic Masculinity of Donald Trump." *The Nation,* September 24, 2017. https://www.thenation.com/article/the-fragile-toxic-masculinity-of-donald-trump/.

INDEX

Abebe, Nitsuh, 117, 118, 189
Abel, Daniel, 97
Acheson, Dean, 120, 121
Ackerman, John, 9, 189
ACLU, 54
Affordable Care Act. *See* Obamacare
agonistic, 141. *See also* agonism, 157
Al Qaeda, 30
Alexander, Scott, 187n29, 189
American Rifleman, 93, 96, 108
anti-environmentalism, 63; and aesthetics, 72; and the Bible, 68, 70, 80, 81; and climate change denial, 68; and dominion, 80–81; and energy industries, 74; and fear appeals, 84; Green Dragon, 75, 81; and the market, 71, 77; and militant individualism, 75, 77, 78; *Resisting the Green Dragon*, 67, 80, 176n21, 204; and perceived marginalization, 68, 69, 70, 71; and prophetic perversion, 69, 71, 73, 74, 75; and political impact, 152, 155; and poverty, 71; and science, 67, 82, 83; systematic hermeneutic, 71, 72, 74, 75; and telic temporality, 79, 80, 161
apocalypse, ix, 15, 16, 25, 52, 61, 107, 155
Armageddon, 24, 25, 52. *See also* Second Coming; rapture
Asen, Robert, 10, 157, 170n38, 189

Bachman, Michele, 126
Ball, Timothy, 67, 68, 76, 77
Ballew, Ken, 96
Balmer, Randall, 174, 174n163, 190
Balog, James, 161
Bannon, Steve, 16, 91, 124–25, 126, 134, 140, 141–42, 144, 160, 184n79
Beard, David, 111
Beginning of the End, The (LaHaye), 52
Beisner, Calvin, 67, 69, 71–72, 73, 75, 76, 77, 78, 79, 156, 158, 159, 160, 190
Bible, the, 11–12, 19, 35, 37, 38, 41
Bill of Rights, 11
Biola University, 37
birtherism, 126
Black, Jason Edward, 8, 190
Blankfein, Lloyd, 131
Bob Jones University, 53. *See also* Bob Jones
Boehner, John, 124
Bostdorff, Denise, 9–10, 23, 190
Breitbart, 6, 125, 126
Breitbart, Andrew, 124
Brown, Peter, 97, 190
Brummett, Barry, 4, 7–8, 16, 190–91
Bruner, Kurt, 32

Bryan, William Jennings, 42, 43, 51

Buckley, William F., 125

Burger, Warren, 97

Burke, Edmund, 16

Burke, Kenneth, 5, 138, 158, 159, 191

Bush, George, H. W., 156

Bush, George, W., 59, 123, 124, 124, 147–48

Campbell, Karlyn Kohrs, 8

Capone, Al, 115

Carlson, Jennifer, 93, 98, 105, 191

Carlson, Tucker, 72

Carter, Harlon, 90

Carter, Jimmy, 6

Carter, Robert, 76

catastrophe: alternatives to, 159, 161, 163, 187n29; definition, 4, 167n13; and image, 161; and institutional trust, 1, 9–10, 13, 15, 120–21, 122; and liberalism, 1; and rhetoric, ix, 3, 8–11

catastrophic homology, 5, 16

Ceccarelli, Leah, 74, 83, 191–92

Charland, Maurice, 4

Chasing Ice, 161, 192

Chavez, Karma, 56, 192

Children at Risk (Dobson), 49, 193

Chilton, Ken, 68

Christian fundamentalism: and abortion, 33, 48, 49, 54, 56, 57, 60; and the American Revolution, 49; and biblical inerrancy, 21, 24, 25, 33, 34, 35, 36, 39, 40, 42, 44, 45, 46, 47, 60, 131, 155, 156, 169n7; and Catholics, 23, 24, 25, 27, 28, 35, 169n7; and climate change, 32, 33, 51, 61, 69, 75, 85; and communism, 31; and counterpublics, 170n38; and darwinism, 21, 24, 30, 33; and feminism, 32, 48; and gay rights, 53, 54, 57, 174; and hell, 34, 35; and higher education, 24, 34, 39, 41, 47–48, 58; and gender, 48, 56; and immigration, 53; and Jesus Christ, 17, 35, 37, 47, 49, 52; and mainline Protestants, 20, 24, 25, 27, 28, 39, 40, 42; and media bias, 32, 48; and militant individualism, 20, 27, 48, 49, 50; and modernism, 21, 22–24, 26, 28, 32, 33, 34, 35–36, 38, 40, 42, 43, 47, 49; and perceived marginalization, 20, 22, 25, 27, 28, 29, 30, 31, 36, 48, 50, 51; and prophetic perversion, 20, 22, 40, 41; and Puritan Calvinism, 35–36; and racism, 58, 59, 60; and rationality, 17, 19, 45, 47, 58. *See also* rational argumentation; and the Republican Party, 29, 58; Satan, 31, 53, 50, 55; and science, 19, 21, 24, 26, 28, 36, 37, 38, 51; and school segregation, 59, 60; and subjectivity, 4; and systematicity, 20, 26, 36, 39, 46, 51; and telic temporality, 20, 44, 50, 51, 52, 53, 54, 55, 56, 57, 153, 174n163; and violence, 53, 153

Christie, Chris, 141

Christy, John, 68

Citizen-Protectors: The Everyday Politics of Guns in an Age of Decline (Carlson), 93

civil rights movement, 39, 50, 51, 54, 92

Civil War, 23, 24, 90

climate change: and denial, 64; and homology, 63; and the market, 64; and media, 75. *See also* anti-environmentalism

climate gap, 186n5

Clinton, Bill, 68, 94, 108, 136

Clinton, Hillary, 30, 61, 94, 108, 110, 112, 118, 130, 131–32, 133, 134, 136, 138, 139, 144, 159 182n11

Cogan, David, 9

Cohn, Gary, 140, 184n68, 184n79

Collins, Laura, 94, 192

Columbine high school, 103, 104, 162

Comey, James, 132, 139

comic corrective, 158–59

Condit, Celeste Michelle, 158–59, 192

Confucius, 14

conservativism, 14–16

conspiracy theory, 9, 28, 31, 33, 48, 61, 69, 79

Contract With America, 123

convenient cynicism, 152

Cornwall Alliance, 67, 75, 176n21

Coulter, Ann, 85, 134

counterpublic speech, 20, 28, 29, 30, 31, 32, 33, 34, 50, 55, 56, 170n38, 207

INDEX • 213

Cox, Chris, 88, 94, 104, 105, 106, 114, 192
Creation Museum (Petersburg, KY), 41, 53, 70, 72, 79, 80, 160, 176n21, 195
creationism, 11–12, 41, 43, 45, 46, 80
crisis, 9, 14, 15
Crowley, Sharon, 40, 156, 192
Cruz, Ted, 139
Cunningham, Walter, 69

Daniel to Doomsday: The Countdown has Begun (Hagee), 52
Darby, John Nelson, 24, 79, 173n153
Dare to Discipline (Dobson), 32
Darrow, Clarence, 42, 43
Darsey, James, 12, 41, 185n86, 192
Davidson, Osha Gray, 98, 102, 112, 192
democratic deliberation, 2–3
Department of Energy, 146, 147
Devil's Bargain (Greene), 118, 196
DeVos, Betsy, 145, 148, 149
Dilling, Lisa, 66, 85
Dionne, E. J., 117, 118, 193
Dobson, James, 16, 20, 30, 32, 33, 48, 49, 50, 54, 55, 56, 59, 60, 158, 160, 174, 193
Doxtader, Erik, 43
Driessen, Paul, 76
Drollinger, Ralph, 80
Duerringer, Christopher, 109, 193

Eckstein, Justin, 103, 193
Economic Injustice and the Rhetoric of the American Dream (Winslow), 121
Edelman, Murray, 9, 23, 194
Edwards, Jonathan J., 30, 32, 35, 41, 43, 56, 58, 194
Einstein's Opponents: The Public Controversy about the Theory of Relativity (Wazeck), 74
Eisenhower, Dwight, 16, 100
Emperor with No Clothes, The, 12–13, 38, 46–47

Engels, Jeremy, 103, 194
Equal Rights Amendment, 20

fake news, 44
Falwell, Jerry, 16, 17, 20, 25, 27, 30, 36, 48, 49, 50, 52, 54, 59, 60, 106, 121, 152, 153, 158, 159, 160, 173n153, 173n162, 194
Fifth Risk, The (Lewis), 13, 174, 200
FitzGerald, Francis, 20, 38, 49, 50, 59, 194
Focus on the Family, 28, 32, 51, 56–57, 59
Foucault, Michel, 88, 132, 194
Foust, Christina, 14, 66, 194, 195
Frank, David, 159, 195
Franklin, Benjamin, 1
French Revolution, 16
fundamentalism. *See* Christian fundamentalism
Fundamentals, The: A Testimony to the Truth, 26, 28, 30, 37, 38, 42

Gallup, George, 60
German biblical criticism, 23, 24, 25, 26, 28–29, 30, 33, 34, 37
Germany, 24
Giffords, Gabriel, 103
Gingrich, Newt, 122, 126, 156
Giroux, Henry, 152, 157, 195
Glazer, Nathan, 127, 195
Global Warming (documentary), 70, 72, 195
Goldwater, Barry, 32
Goodnight, Thomas, 5, 195
Gorsuch, Neil, 58
Graham, Billy, 30, 31, 55, 69, 195
Great Britain, 24, 87
Great Depression, the, 174
Great Society, the, 16
Greatest Hoax, The: How the Global Warming Conspiracy Threatens Your Future (Inhofe), 79, 176n21, 197
Green, Joshua, 118, 120, 125, 196
Griffith Thomas, W. H., 37, 207

gun-rights discourse: and the 1934 Federal Firearms Act, 115; and the 1994 Federal Assault Weapons Ban, 113; and alternatives, 161; and the Black Panthers, 91, 92, 93, 98, 99, 100; and the Bureau of Alcohol, Tobacco, and Firearms, 112–13; and catastrophe, 61; and Catholics, 90, 98; and crime, 91, 93, 98; and the Dickey Amendment, 113; *District of Columbia v. Heller*, 97; and elitism, 88; and gender, 93, 181n106; and the Gun Control Act of 1968, 94; and gun violence research, 113; individual-rights interpretation, 97–98, 99–100; and the inevitability of evil, 108, 112; and institutional trust, 105, 112, 113; and mass shootings, 102–3, 104, 109, 112. *See also* Sandy Hook; Marjory Stoneman Douglas; and Marjory Stoneman Douglas High School (Parkland, FL), 104, 108, 109, 162; and mental health, 103; and militant individualism, 101–2, 103, 104, 105, 106, 107, 110; and perceived marginalization, 91, 92, 93, 94, 95, 99; and prophetic perversion, 99, 106, 108; and race, 90, 93, 106; and the Republican Party, 100, 101, 112; and the Saint Valentine's Day Massacre, 115; and Sandy Hook (Newtown, CN), 103, 105, 108–9, 110, 162; and the Second Amendment, 94, 95, 97, 98, 99, 101, 156; and the Supreme Court, 97, 99; and systematicity, 96, 97, 99, 101; and telic temporality, 107, 109, 111, 112, 113, 114, 153; and violence, 87, 88, 102, 105, 106, 107, 112, 113, 114, 115, 131, 153, 162, 181n106

Gunn, Joshua, 1–2, 6, 10, 111, 196

Guth, James, 85

Habermas, Jürgen, 2–3, 11, 196, 198

Hagee, John, 52, 196

Hague, Canon Dyson, 26

half-wish, 54, 55, 85, 107

Hammer, Marion, 102, 109–10

Hampton, Fred, 99

Hannity, Sean, 124

Harvard, 35, 48

Harding, Susan, 45, 46, 59, 60, 196

Harris, Eric, 103

Harris, Gardiner, 147, 196

Hart, Roderick, 33, 53, 157, 197

Heartland Institute, 67–68, 73, 75, 176n21

Hefner, Hugh, 119

Hesford, Wendy, 15, 197

Heston, Charlton, 88, 96, 98, 99, 101, 104, 105, 106, 108, 109, 112, 114

Hochschild, Arlie, 118, 197

Hodge, Charles, 36, 37

Hoerl, Kristen, 103, 197

Hogan, Michael, 103, 104, 105, 197

Holland, Francois, 125

Hollihan, Thomas, 103

homology. *See* rhetorical homology

How Democracies Die (Levistky and Ziblatt), 11

Huertas, Aaron, 163, 197

humor, 7, 34, 104, 157–58

impossible majority, 30, 32, 56

Industrial Revolution, 23

information deficit assumption, 83, 84, 161

Ingraham, Laura, 141

Inhofe, James (Jim), 16, 71, 73, 74, 79, 176n21, 197

Institute for Legislative Action, the, 90, 94, 114

ISIS, 30, 55

Ivie, Robert, 141, 197

James, Nancy, 20, 54, 99

Jamieson, Kathleen Hall, 6, 8, 198

John Birch Society, the, 31, 76

Johnson, Anne Janette, 44, 198

Johnson, Paul, 131, 198

Jones, Bob, 53, 55. *See also* Bob Jones University

Justus, Z. S., 109, 193

Kates, Don, 97

Kavanaugh, Brett, 58

Kayfabe, 13
Kellstedt, Lyman, 85
Kellstedt, Paul, 66, 198
Kid Rock, 124
King, Stephen, 87
Klebold, Dylan, 103
Klein, Naomi, 117, 118, 199
Knobloch, Kevin, 146
Knox, Neal, 90
Kolbert, Elizabeth, 68
Kosla, Martin, 110, 206
Kristof, Nicholas, 113–14, 180n63, 199
Kuhn, Thomas, 82
Kushner, Jared, 140

Lacombe, Matt, 110, 199
LaHaye, Tim, 52, 173n153, 199
Lalonde, Patti, 77
Land, Richard, 68, 80
Lanza, Adam, 103, 108, 112
LaPierre, Wayne, 16, 88, 94, 96, 98, 99, 101, 102, 103, 105, 106, 108, 114, 154, 158, 159, 160, 199
Laws, Curtis Lee, 26, 30
League of Nations, 30
Lefevre, Sarah, 103, 193
Left Behind (LaHaye and Jenkins), ix, 41, 54
Levitsky, Steven, 11, 200
Lewandowsky, Stephan, 74, 200
Lewis, Michael, 13, 145, 160, 174, 200
LGBTQ discourse, 29–30, 32, 200. *See also* same-sex marriage
Liberty University, 127, 128
Licona, Adela, 15, 197
Limbaugh, Rush, 134
Lincoln, Abe, 119
Lind, Michael, 142, 200
Lindsey, Hal, 68, 200
Lisle, Jason, 80

Listen! America (Falwell), 36, 194
Litt, David, 158
Living in Denial: Climate Change, Emotions, and Everyday Life (Norgaard), 83
Loughner, Jared, 103
Lunceford, Brett, 95, 200

Machen, J. Gresham, 36, 38, 39, 42, 200
Make America Great Again, 128, 143
Malinowski, Tom, 147
Mann, Michael, 78
Mann, Thomas, 117, 193
manufactured scientific controversy, 74, 75
Marsden, George, 26, 42, 43, 44, 200
Marxism, 12, 40
Mather, Increase, 173n153
McCann, Bryan, 92, 200
McConnell, Mitch, 140
McManus, John F., 76
McMaster, H. R., 184n79
McQueen, Ackerman 114–15
Mencken, H. L., 44
Merkel, Angela, 125
Meyers, Seth, 128
militant individualism, 13–14
mind furnishing, 38, 39, 41, 42
Mississippi, 143
Mnuchin, Steven, 184n68, 184n79
Monckton, Christopher Lord, 74, 76
Moody Bible Institute, 47
Moody, Dwight L., 22, 24, 25, 27, 28, 30, 31, 32, 33, 36, 47, 59, 202
Moore, Roy, 33, 51
Morano, Marc, 73, 74, 76, 77
Moser, Susanne, 66, 85, 200
Mouffe, Chantal, 22, 55, 157, 200
MTV, 55
Mulvaney, Mick, 66, 200
Murphy, William, 14, 66, 195

National Rifle Association (NRA), 87, 88, 89, 90, 93, 96, 97, 98, 101, 102, 106, 109, 110, 112, 113, 114–15, 156

Nauert, Heather, 146

Navarro, Peter, 184n79

Negroponte, John, 147–48

New Deal, the, 16, 39, 115, 142

New Hampshire, 118

New York Times, the, 43, 44, 46, 113

Newport, Frank, 65, 200

Newton, Huey, 92

Newton, Isaac, 14

Nixon, Richard, 97, 137

Norgaard, Kari Marie, 83, 200

Nunes, Devin, 139

Oard, Michael, 72

Obama, Barack, 31, 76, 94, 108, 123, 124, 125, 128, 129, 135, 139

Obamacare, 146

Ogden, C. K. 5, 200

Olson, Christa, 21, 200

Olson, Kathryn, 8, 200

One Nation After Trump (Dionne, Ornstein, and Mann), 117, 193

Onion, the, 104

originalism, constitutional, 40

Ornstein, Norman, 117, 193

Orwellian, 139

Othering, 8

Outgunned (Brown and Abel), 97

Palczewski, Catherine Helen, 170n38, 203

Palin, Sarah, 88, 103, 124, 126

Paris climate accord, 78, 128

Parks, Rosa, 51

Pelosi, Nancy, 112, 138, 156

perceived marginalization, 9–10

Perry, Rick, 145

Peterson, Jordan, 72

Petraeus, David, 132

Pinker, Steven, 160, 204

Platt, Carrie Anne, 57, 204

Popp, Richard, 57, 204

post-truth, 1–3, 6, 9, 13, 17, 134, 163, 208

postmillennialism, 25, 170n23

poverty, 2, 25, 53

Powell, Dina, 140

precarity, 15, 30, 197

premillennial dispensationalism, 16, 24, 25, 52, 61, 79, 85, 154, 155, 156, 170n23, 173n153

Priebus, Reince, 184n68

Princeton Theological Seminary, 24, 36–37, 42

procrastination penalty, 78

prophetic perversion: definition of, 10–11, 16; and republican perspicacity, 10, 37, 41

Pruitt, Scott, 145, 148, 149

public sphere, 11

Public Work of Rhetoric, The (Ackerman and Coogan), 9, 189

Putin, Vladimir, 153

Quarantelli, Enrico, 155, 204

rapture, the, 53, 61

rational argumentation, ix, x, 1–3, 11, 33, 35, 64, 66, 73, 81, 106, 151, 159, 160, 162, 163

Rayburn, Sam, 149

Reagan, Ronald, 13, 32, 59, 92, 100, 101, 103, 122, 137

Reeve, J. J. 38

Rehg, William, 3, 204

Rehnquist, William, 29

Reid, Thomas, 38, 204

Remington, 106, 110, 111, 114

rhetorical homology, 4, 6–8, 15, 60, 63; and awareness, 16; and form, 4–8, 9, 15, 60, 61, 157, 174n172; and higher education, 8; and neoliberalism, 8; and prosperity theology, 8 rhetorical methods, x, 3–4, 40, 169n68, 174n172; and audience, 3, 5–7, 16, 151, 155; constitutive rhetoric, x, 3, 59, 107; doxa, 28, 85; dynamic oscillation, 60, 101, 126, 155; fetishizing the rhetor, 106–7; and genre, 6, 8, 15, 16; predictive potential, 33; referential audience, 50, 60, 63, 98, 100, 119; rhetorical invention, 20, 21, 35–36, 39, 40, 42, 46, 54, 101, 107, 115, 138, 155; rhetorical criticism, 6–8, 53, 151, 159; rhetorical theory, x, 55; and warrant, 2, 64, 66, 82, 86, 89, 106, 148

Richards, I. A., 5, 200

Riley, William Bell, 26, 30, 33, 34, 36, 106, 152, 158

Roberts, Oral, 31

Robertson, Pat, 20, 30, 31, 48, 49, 50, 54, 55, 121, 160, 174, 174n163

Romney, Mitt, 124, 125

Rood, Craig, 103, 104, 105, 197, 205

Roosevelt, Eleanor, 30

Rove, Karl, 59

Ryan, Paul, 124, 139, 140

same-sex marriage, 30, 39

Santorum, Rick, 144

Scalia, Antonin, 29–30

Schaeffer, Francis, 49, 59, 205

Schlafly, Phyllis, 32

Schmul, H. E. 174

Schultz, Ed, 112

Schultz, Howard, 94–95

Schwarze, Stephen, 159, 160, 205

Scofield, Cyrus, 37

Scopes, John T., 42

Scopes Monkey Trial, 30, 42, 50, 51, 59

Scott, Dylan, 113, 205

Scott, Robert, 92, 205

Scripture. *See* Bible, the

Second Coming, the, 24, 52, 54, 58

September 11, 2001 attacks (9/11), 54, 111, 123, 125

Sessions, Jeff, 145

Shah, Tarak, 147

Simpsons, The, 7, 151

Sixth Extinction, The (Kolbert)

Smith, Francesca Marie, 103, 206

social gospel, 25

Soros, George, 131

Sound of Music, The, 158

Southern Baptist Convention, 68

Spencer, Roy, 68

Spitzer, Robert, 90, 96, 97, 98, 109, 206

Sputnik, 31, 33, 61. *See also* USSR

Stalin, 31, 54–55. *See also* USSR

Steidley, Trent, 110, 206

stewardship, 77–78, 81, 146, 147, 148

Stewart, Lyman and Milton, 26, 30

Storm Warning (Graham), 69, 195

Strength for the Journey (Falwell), 19, 194

Strozier, Charles, 54, 85, 107, 206

suffrage, 25, 53

Systematic Theology (Hodge), 37

systematicity, hermeneutic of, 11–13

Taylor, James M., 67

Tea Party, the, 123–24, 125, 126

telic temporality, 14–15

temperance, 25, 53

terrorism. *See* September 11, 2001 attacks

Teston, Christa, 15, 197

Thief in the Night, A 52, 207

Thomas, Clarence, 29

Tiberi, Pat, 161

Tillerson, Rex, 135, 145–46, 147, 148, 184n79

time. *See* telic temporality

Tonkowich, James, 79

Torrey, Rueben, 36, 37, 47, 207

Truman, Harry, 30

Trump, Donald, x, 1–2, 4, 6, 12, 16, 58, 118, 119, 158, 159, 160, 193, 207; and American carnage, 128–29, 138; and catastrophe, 121; and climate change, 65, 66, 78, 141; and conspiracy theory, 124, 126, 132, 133–34, 136, 147, 184n60, 184n68; cultural marginalization, 130; and economic populism, 117; and Fox News, 141; and gun-rights, 88, 91, 108, 109; and health care, 147; and immigration, 129, 130, 136, 141, 174; and institutional trust, 125, 133, 136, 143, 144, 147, 149; and militant individualism, 136, 137–38, 139, 140, 141–42; and Never Trumpers, 140; and perceived marginalization, 126–27, 128–29, 130, 133, 182n15, 183n57; prophetic perversion, 127, 132, 133, 134, 138, 139, 152, 185n86; and rational argumentation, 117, 119, 122, 131, 134, 136, 148, 184n79; and the Republican Party, 140, 142, 143, 156; systematic hermeneutic, 131, 132, 135; and trade, 141, 144; and telic temporality, 126, 143, 144, 145, 146, 149, 153; and Trump University, 134–35. *See also* Make America Great Again

Trump, Donald, Jr., 180n63

Trump, Ivanka, 140

United Nations, 14, 53, 58, 68, 76, 77, 78, 94, 125, 147, 148, 186n4

US Constitution, 11, 144

USDA, 145

USSR (Soviet Union), 30, 31, 61. *See also* Sputnik; Stalin, Joseph

Vedlitz, Arnold, 66, 198

Vox, Lisa, 68, 75–76, 156, 207

Waiting for Godot, 6

Wander, Philip, 153, 207

Wanliss, James, 80, 207

Washington, George, 5–6

Wazeck, Milena, 74

We Get It (website), 70, 72, 77, 79, 81, 176n21, 207

What the Bible Teaches (Torrey), 37

Wheaton College, 29–30

Where the Grass is Greener, 69, 72, 73, 76, 77, 79, 156, 176n21, 208

White House Correspondents' dinner, 128

Wile, Jay, 72

Wilson, E. O., 68

Winkler, Adam, 89, 90, 100–101, 115, 208

Woodward, Bob, 184n79, 208

World War I, 24, 39

World War II, 120, 121

Yellen, Janet, 131

Zahran, Sammy, 66, 198

Zengerle, Jason, 135, 140, 209

Ziblatt, Daniel, 11, 200

www.ingramcontent.com/pod-product-compliance
Lightning Source LLC
Chambersburg PA
CBHW020652230426
43665CB00008B/406